W9-CMU-236

FIFTY YEARS LATER

ADAM P. KNAVE &
SEAN E. WILLIAMS writers

ANDREW LOSQ artist

FRANK CVETKOVIC letterer
Artful Daggers logo designed by **B.J. WITTS**

Artful Daggers created by
Adam P. Knave, Sean E. Williams,
& Andrew Losq

Apologies & Thanks to Mark Twain

Bloomington Public Library
205 E. Olive 5-14
Bloomington, IL, 61701

www.artfuldaggers.com

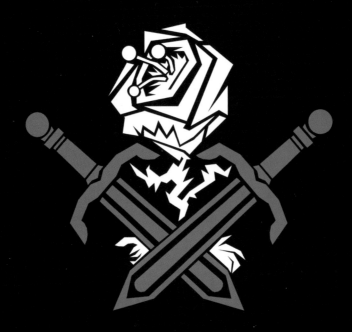

SPECIAL THANKS TO

Allison Baker, Allison Dressler, D.J. Kirkbride,
Nick Losq, David & Julia Petersen, Kevin & Jody Rapp,
Chris Roberson, Sheilah Villari, & Lindsey Duoos Williams

ISBN: 978-1-61377-885-2

17 16 15 14   1 2 3 4

IDW

www.IDWPUBLISHING.com
IDW founded by Ted Adams, Alex Garner, Kris Oprisko, and Robbie Robbins

Ted Adams, CEO & Publisher
Greg Goldstein, President & COO
Robbie Robbins, EVP/Sr. Graphic Artist
Chris Ryall, Chief Creative Officer/Editor-in-Chief
Matthew Ruzicka, CPA, Chief Financial Officer
Alan Payne, VP of Sales
Dirk Wood, VP of Marketing
Lorelei Bunjes, VP of Digital Services
Jeff Webber, VP of Digital Publishing & Business Development

Facebook: **facebook.com/idwpublishing**
Twitter: **@idwpublishing**
YouTube: **youtube.com/idwpublishing**
Instagram: **instagram.com/idwpublishing**
deviantART: **idwpublishing.deviantart.com**
Pinterest: **pinterest.com/idwpublishing/idw-staff-faves**

ARTFUL DAGGERS: FIFTY YEARS LATER. MARCH 2014. FIRST PRINTING. © 2014 Adam P. Knave, Sean E. Williams, and Andrew Losq. All Rights Reserved. © 2014 Idea and Design Works, LLC. The IDW logo is registered in the U.S. Patent and Trademark Office. IDW Publishing, a division of Idea and Design Works, LLC. Editorial offices: 5080 Santa Fe St., San Diego, CA 92109. Any similarities to persons living or dead are purely coincidental. With the exception of artwork used for review purposes, none of the contents of this publication may be reprinted without the permission of Idea and Design Works, LLC. IDW Publishing does not read or accept unsolicited submissions of ideas, stories or artwork. Printed in Korea.

Originally published digitally by Monkeybrain Comics as ARTFUL DAGGERS issues #1–9.

Well, my book is written—let it go. But if it were only to write over again there wouldn't be so many things left out. They burn in me; and they keep multiplying; but now they can't ever be said. And besides, they would require a library—and a pen warmed up in hell.
- **Mark Twain** in a letter to William Dean Howells, September 22, 1889

Before the dawn of the 20th century, Samuel Clemens, better known by his pen name Mark Twain, created what would become one of the first novels to use time travel as a plot device. Although debatably one of the earliest examples of science fiction, A CONNECTICUT YANKEE IN KING ARTHUR'S COURT finds Hank Morgan, an employee of Hartford's Colt Firearms factory, knocked on the head and magically transported to King Arthur's Camelot in the 6th century.

Beginning as a satire on chivalry and knights errant, the story takes on a progressively darker tone as Morgan introduces 19th century technology to a world ill-prepared to accept such advances. Bicycles, guns, fireworks, explosives and telephones soon take their place alongside horses, swords, armor and jousting. Twain uses the Connecticut Yankee's interactions with the Round Table to expose the exploitation of the working class, the hypocrisy of organized religion, and the shamelessly fraudulent behavior of the ruling elite. The action of the novel culminates with an apocalyptic confrontation where Morgan's Steampunked Camelot is blown to smithereens and corpses of knights litter the once-idyllic countryside. It's hard to read the above quote from Twain, written after the novel was submitted for publication, and wonder what he could have possibly left out of this subversive book.

ARTFUL DAGGERS picks up 50 years after the conclusion of Hank Morgan's climactic and destructive war. The weaponry introduced in CONNECTICUT YANKEE's alternate history has now become a part of the fabric of society and the pitch-black atmosphere of the novel's finale persists. Although the title is cribbed from Charles Dickens' OLIVER TWIST, ARTFUL DAGGERS is an action-packed homage to Twain's dark vision of courtly duplicity and violence.

Clearly working with a "pen warmed up in hell," writers **Adam P. Knave** and **Sean E. Williams** create less of a straight-out sequel and more of a continuation of the themes in A CONNECTICUT YANKEE IN KING ARTHUR'S COURT. Twain's full-length works tended to be published with copious illustrations. **Andrew Losq's** arresting visuals could not be further in tone from CONNECTICUT YANKEE's original humorous drawings by Daniel Carter Beard. Losq's propulsive illustrations ensure that readers know that this is not your daddy's Twain.

Do you need to read A CONNECTICUT YANKEE IN KING ARTHUR'S COURT to appreciate ARTFUL DAGGERS on its own terms? Not at all. It's a kick-ass yarn all its own. Do I hope ARTFUL DAGGERS will inspire the unfamiliar to sit down and read Twain's explosively funny and vicious masterwork? I sure as hell do.

INTRODUCTION

I love alternate worlds. The whole "What if" factor is a great way to begin any story and trigger the imagination. Talk to any kid long enough and he or she will start going on about "What if." "What if that train went so fast it flew off the track and kept going into space?" Then you'd get the classic anime *GALAXY EXPRESS 999*. "What if monkeys took over the zoo and put us in it?" Well kid, you'd get *PLANET OF THE APES*. "What if a modern day Yankee ended up in King Arthur's court?" Well, Mark Twain, you'd eventually get *ARTFUL DAGGERS*!

I love the set up in this book. Check out the opening page: such a simple, perfect and clear set up. It is what every fantasy writer strives for. It's just a design and a few words that capture the mood of Twain's tale so that, even if you are like me and you only know that story by proxy, it still sets the table nicely for the story you are about to read.

After reading the first issue, it reminds me a bit of Ralph Bakshi's *WIZARDS*, a world where fantasy and science fiction play hand-in-hand. Wizards, robots, lasers, swords, fairies and old horny men abound. Here we are following Thieves-for-Hire Piper and Arden as they steal in the Middle Ages. But the story then shifts for breakthroughs in optics and more science, and you are in for a sweet blend of "What-If Dinner."

Writers **Adam P. Knave** and **Sean E. Williams** put together the perfect world for **Andrew Losq** to draw with such a young, exciting style mixed with a simple stylistic choice in coloring that further adds a sense of place to the story.

This is what storytelling is about. This is what comics are about, especially creator-owned comics. Creative minds making up "what if" stories filtered through the imagination we forged as children and brought to life through adult and learned eyes. Strap on your cloak, your flashlights, and optic sensors and get ready for a journey only *ARTFUL DAGGERS* can bring you.

Michael Avon Oeming

Co-creator of *POWERS*
and *THE VICTORIES*
Portland, 2013

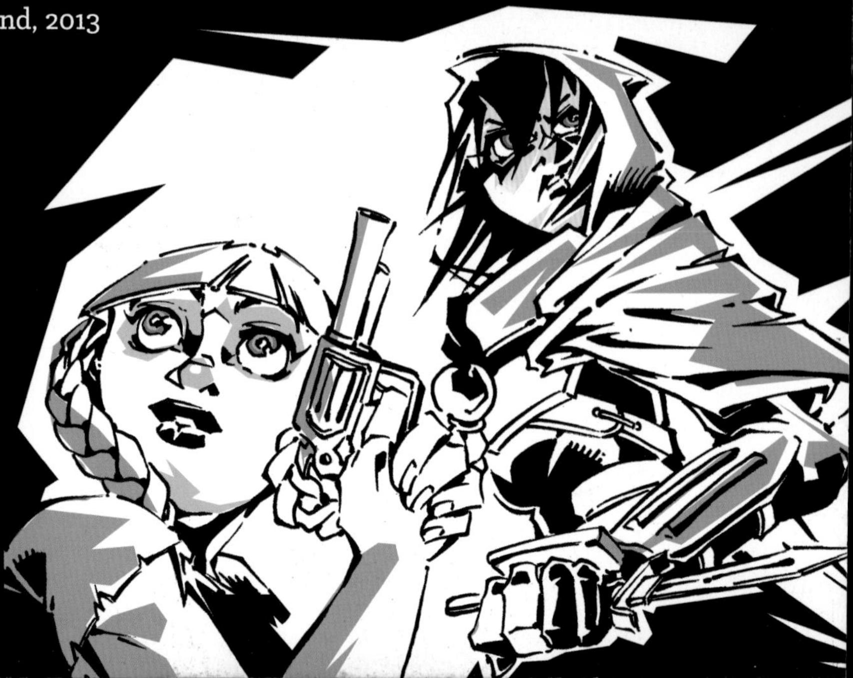

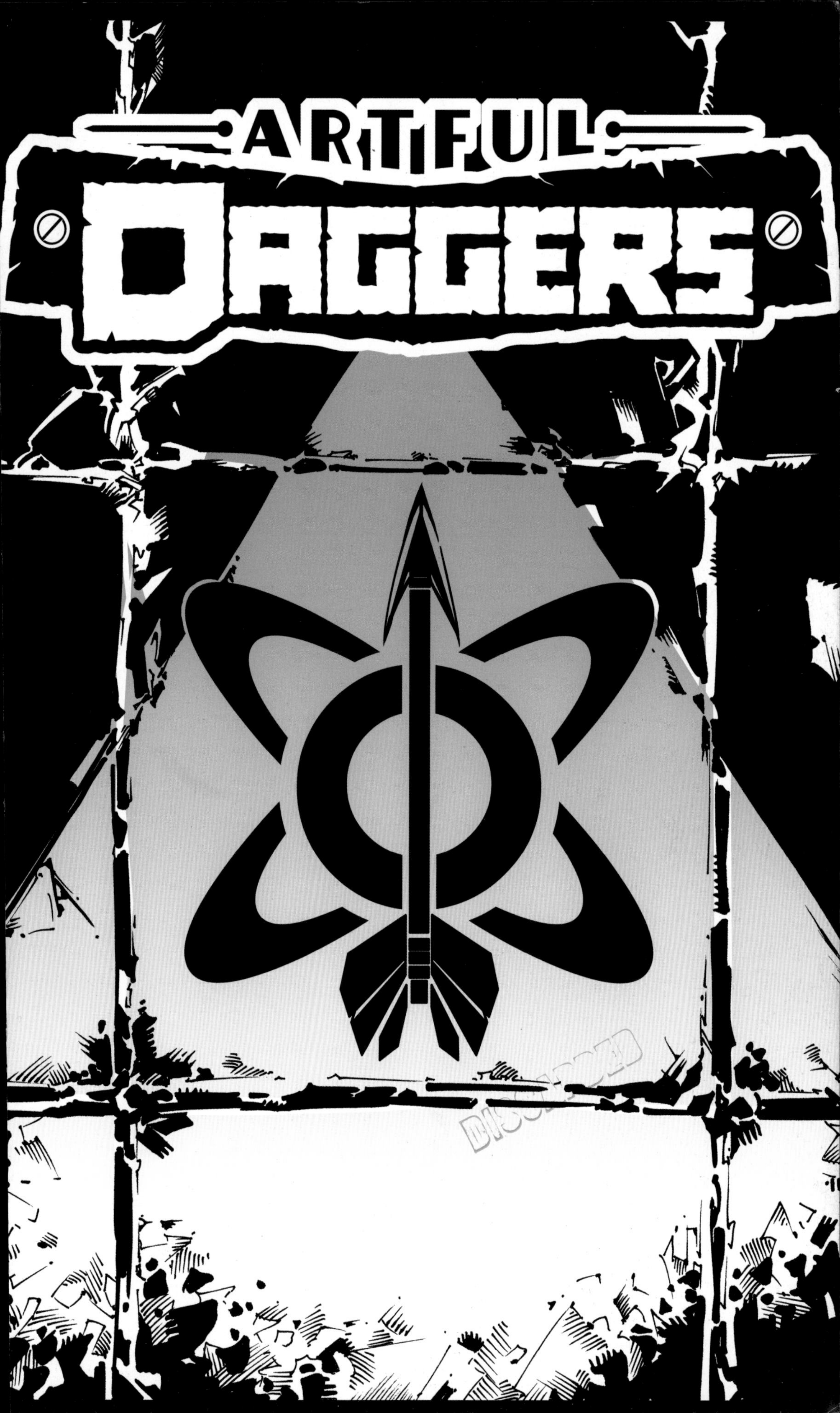
ARTFUL
DAGGERS

PREVIOUSLY...

A CONNECTICUT YANKEE SHOWED
UP IN KING ARTHUR'S COURT.

SEVEN YEARS PASSED AND HE
DISAPPEARED, BUT NOT BEFORE
CHANGING THE WORLD AS WE
KNEW IT.

OUR STORY PICKS UP...

FIFTY YEARS LATER

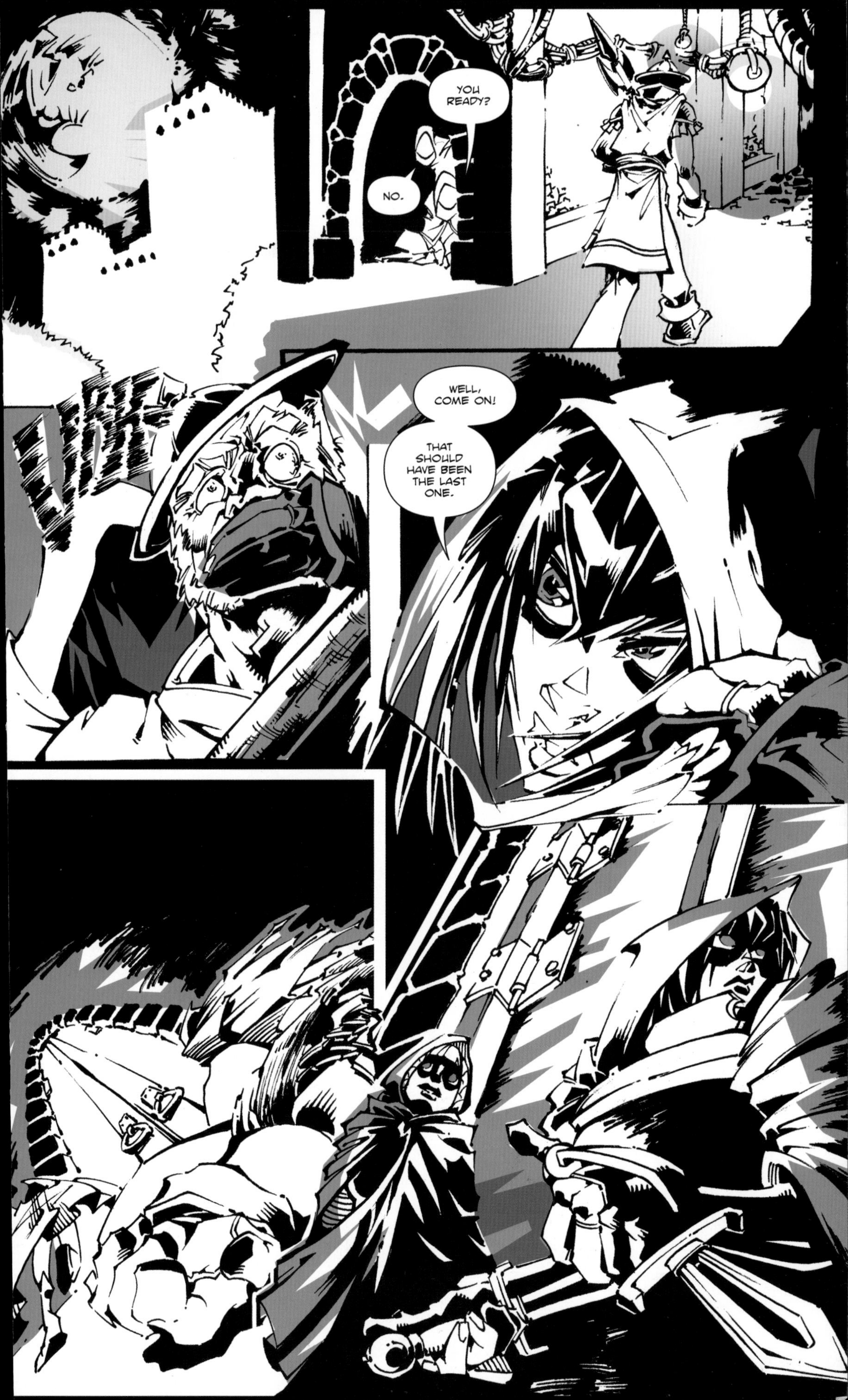
YOU READY?
NO.
WELL, COME ON!
THAT SHOULD HAVE BEEN THE LAST ONE.

DID YOU FIND IT?

YES.

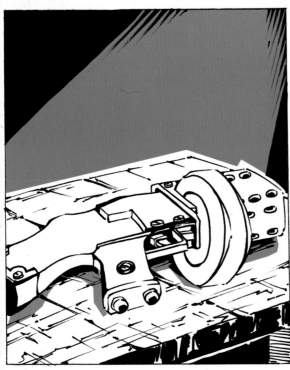

AND... AND WE JUST *TAKE* IT?

THAT'S THE JOB.

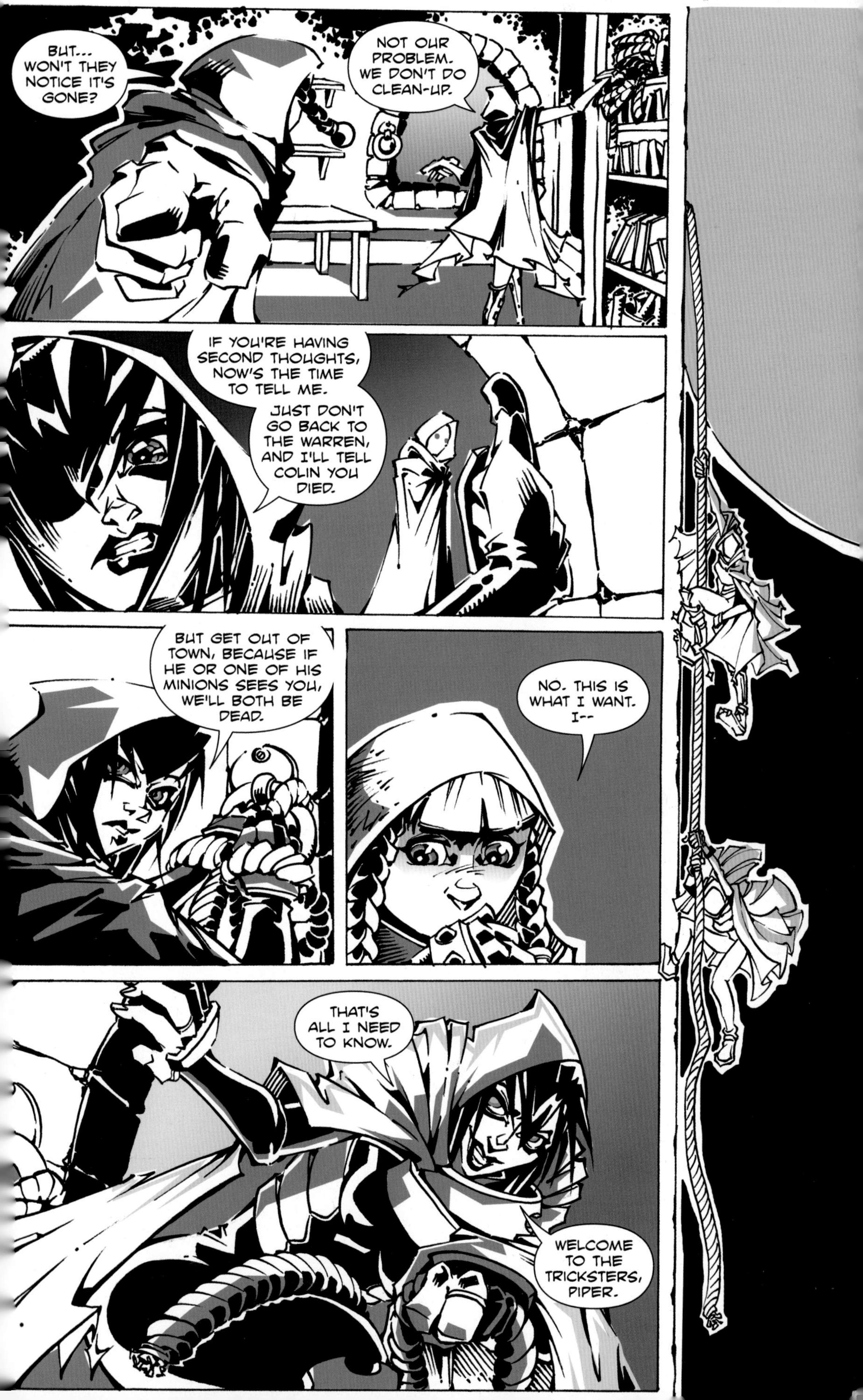
BUT... WON'T THEY NOTICE IT'S GONE?
NOT OUR PROBLEM. WE DON'T DO CLEAN-UP.
IF YOU'RE HAVING SECOND THOUGHTS, NOW'S THE TIME TO TELL ME.
JUST DON'T GO BACK TO THE WARREN, AND I'LL TELL COLIN YOU DIED.
BUT GET OUT OF TOWN, BECAUSE IF HE OR ONE OF HIS MINIONS SEES YOU, WE'LL BOTH BE DEAD.
NO. THIS IS WHAT I WANT. I--
THAT'S ALL I NEED TO KNOW.
WELCOME TO THE TRICKSTERS, PIPER.

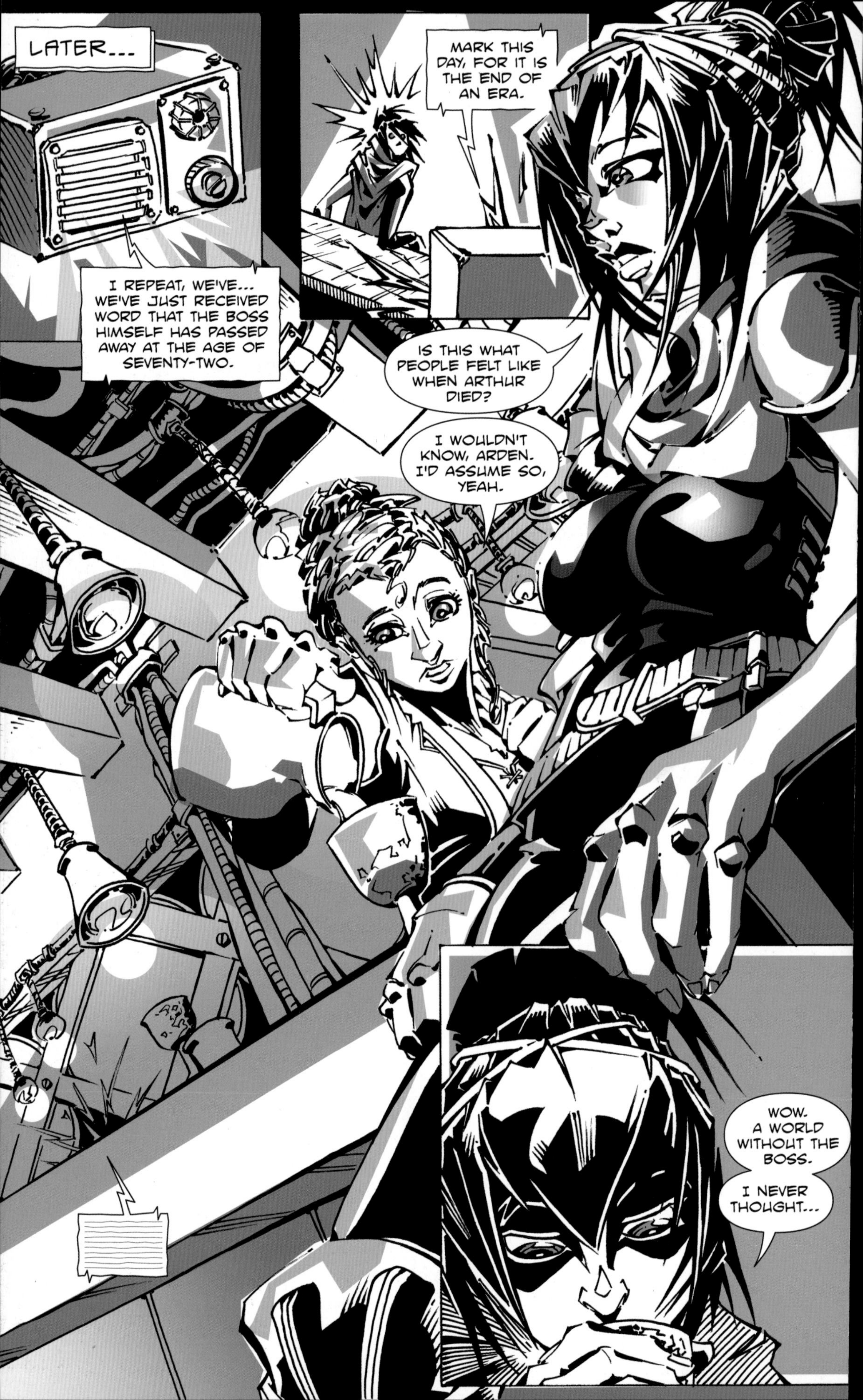

LATER...
I REPEAT, WE'VE... WE'VE JUST RECEIVED WORD THAT THE BOSS HIMSELF HAS PASSED AWAY AT THE AGE OF SEVENTY-TWO.
MARK THIS DAY, FOR IT IS THE END OF AN ERA.
IS THIS WHAT PEOPLE FELT LIKE WHEN ARTHUR DIED?
I WOULDN'T KNOW, ARDEN. I'D ASSUME SO, YEAH.
WOW. A WORLD WITHOUT THE BOSS.
I NEVER THOUGHT...

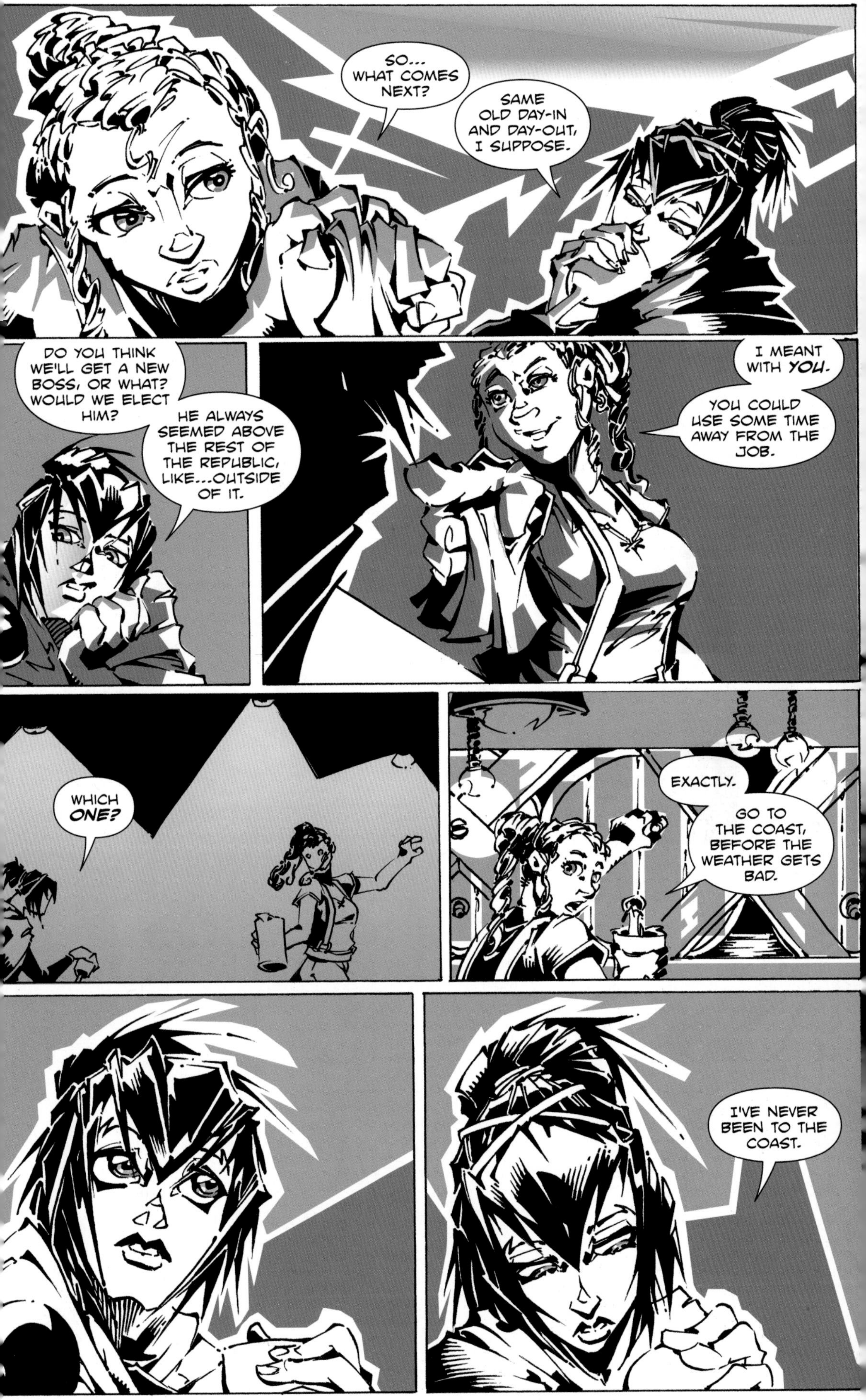
SO... WHAT COMES NEXT?
SAME OLD DAY-IN AND DAY-OUT, I SUPPOSE.
DO YOU THINK WE'LL GET A NEW BOSS, OR WHAT? WOULD WE ELECT HIM?
HE ALWAYS SEEMED ABOVE THE REST OF THE REPUBLIC, LIKE...OUTSIDE OF IT.
I MEANT WITH YOU.
YOU COULD USE SOME TIME AWAY FROM THE JOB.
WHICH ONE?
EXACTLY.
GO TO THE COAST, BEFORE THE WEATHER GETS BAD.
I'VE NEVER BEEN TO THE COAST.

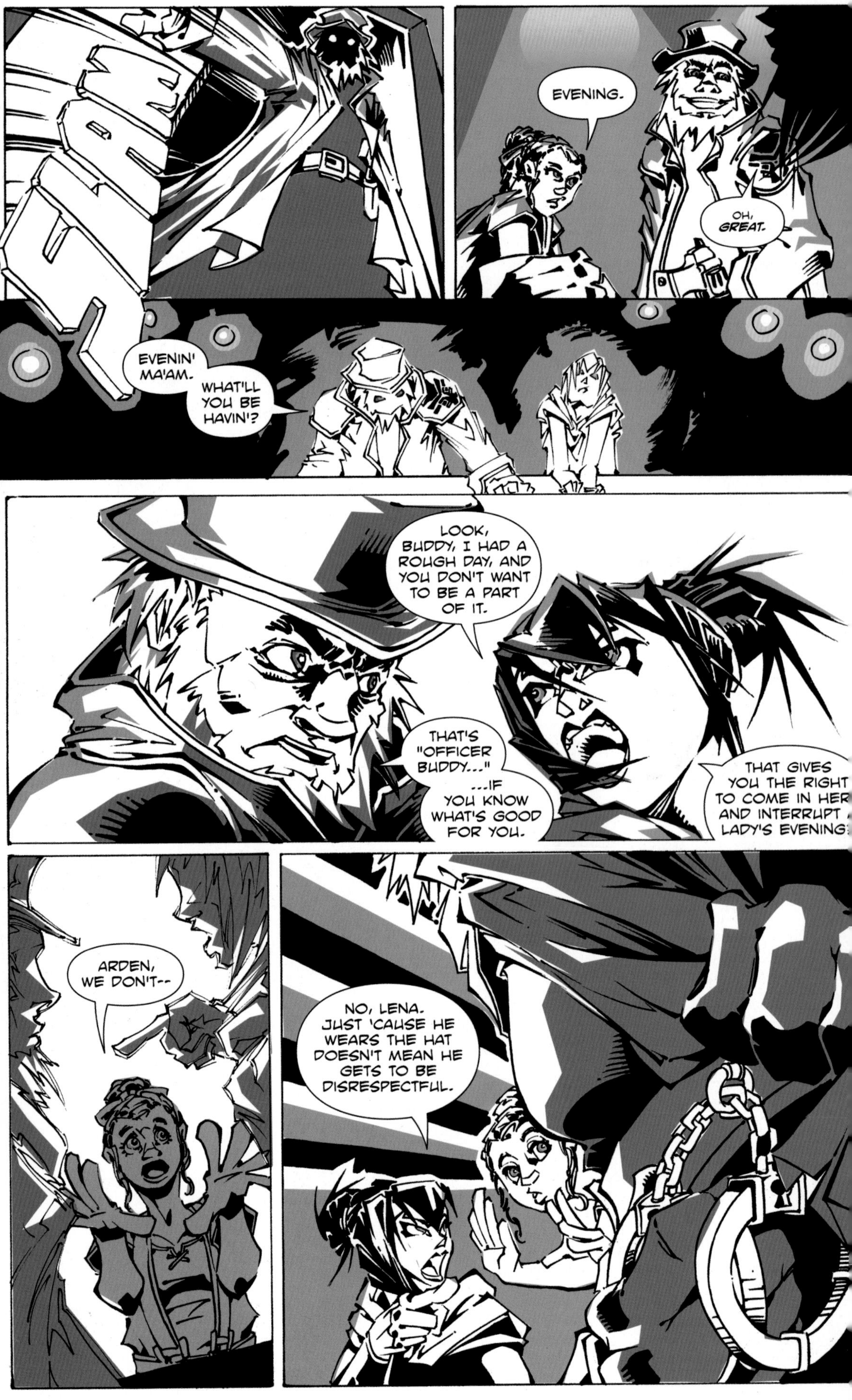
EVENING.
OH, GREAT.
EVENIN' MA'AM.
WHAT'LL YOU BE HAVIN'?
LOOK, BUDDY, I HAD A ROUGH DAY, AND YOU DON'T WANT TO BE A PART OF IT.
THAT'S "OFFICER BUDDY..."
...IF YOU KNOW WHAT'S GOOD FOR YOU.
THAT GIVES YOU THE RIGHT TO COME IN HER AND INTERRUPT LADY'S EVENING
ARDEN, WE DON'T--
NO, LENA. JUST 'CAUSE HE WEARS THE HAT DOESN'T MEAN HE GETS TO BE DISRESPECTFUL.

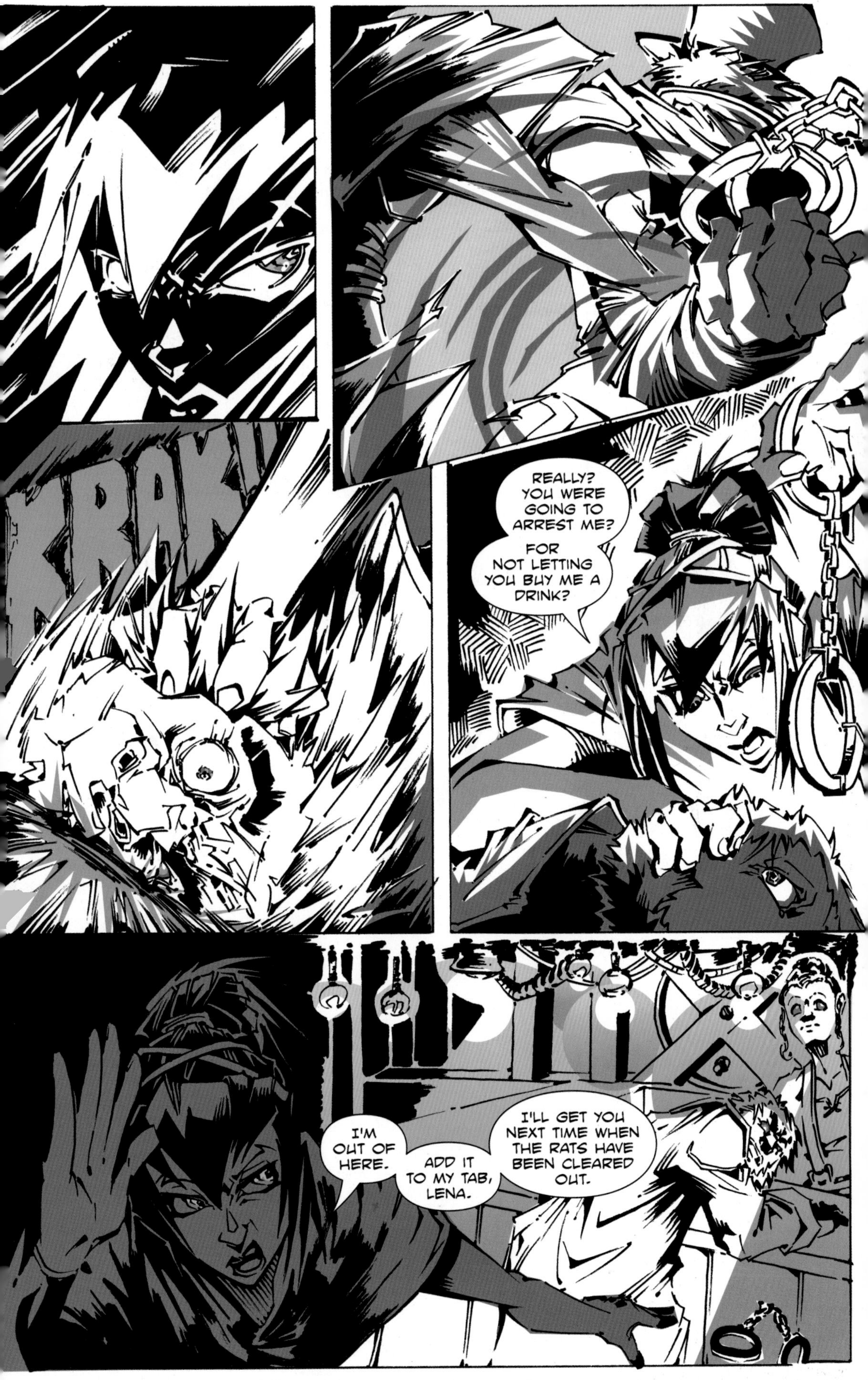
REALLY? YOU WERE GOING TO ARREST ME?
FOR NOT LETTING YOU BUY ME A DRINK?
I'M OUT OF HERE.
ADD IT TO MY TAB, LENA.
I'LL GET YOU NEXT TIME WHEN THE RATS HAVE BEEN CLEARED OUT.

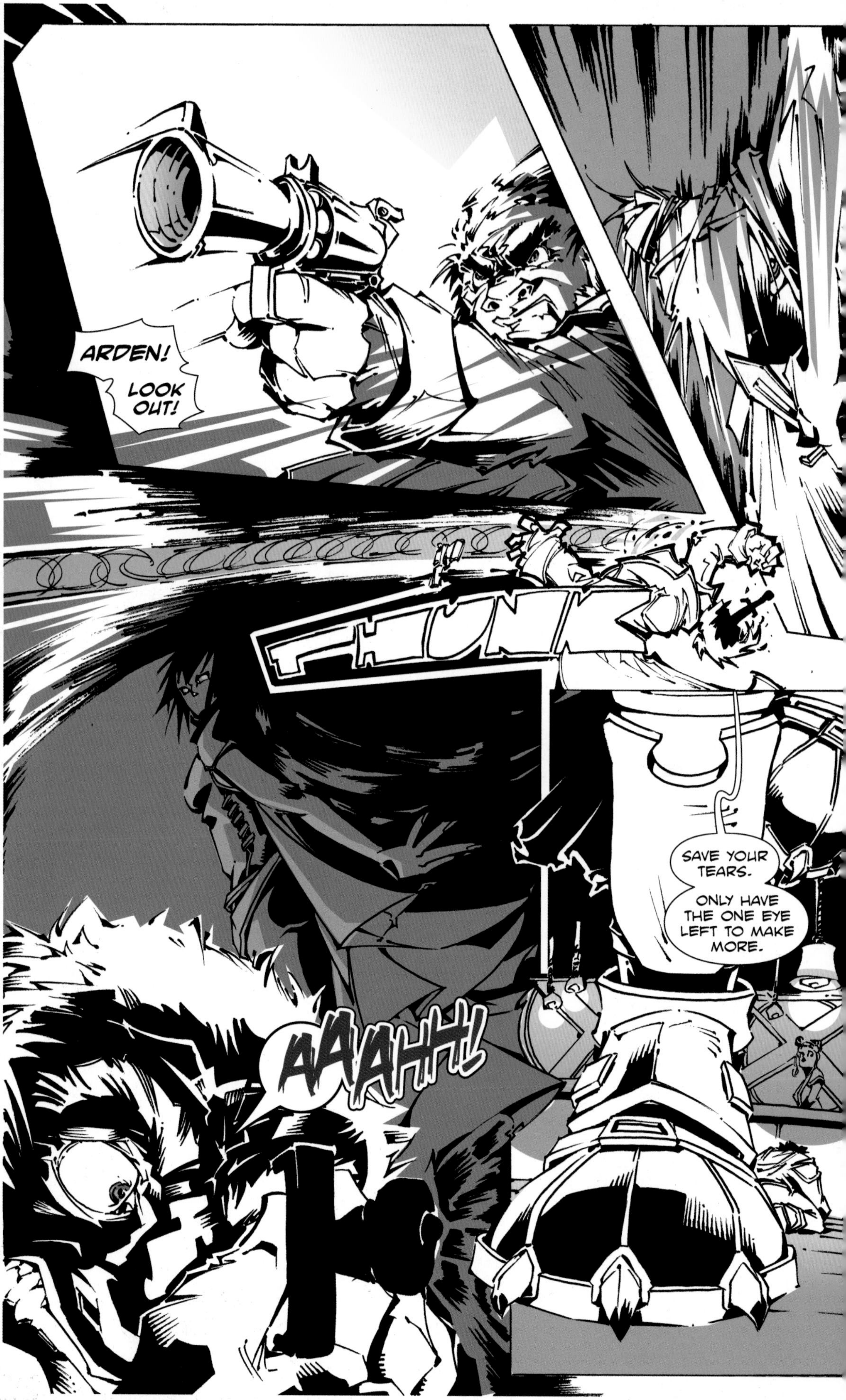
ARDEN!
LOOK OUT!
THUNK
SAVE YOUR TEARS.
ONLY HAVE THE ONE EYE LEFT TO MAKE MORE.
AAAHH!

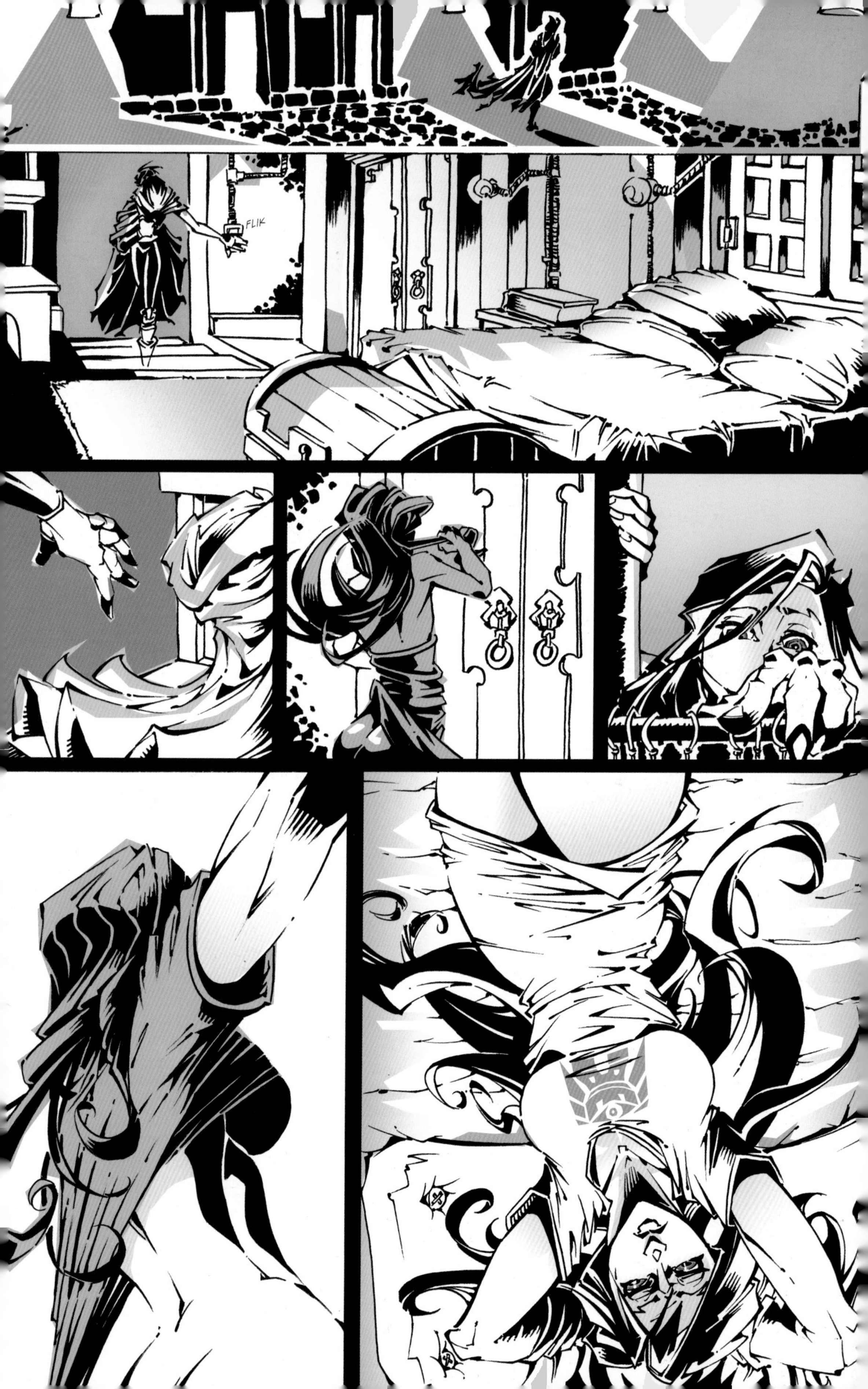
FLIK

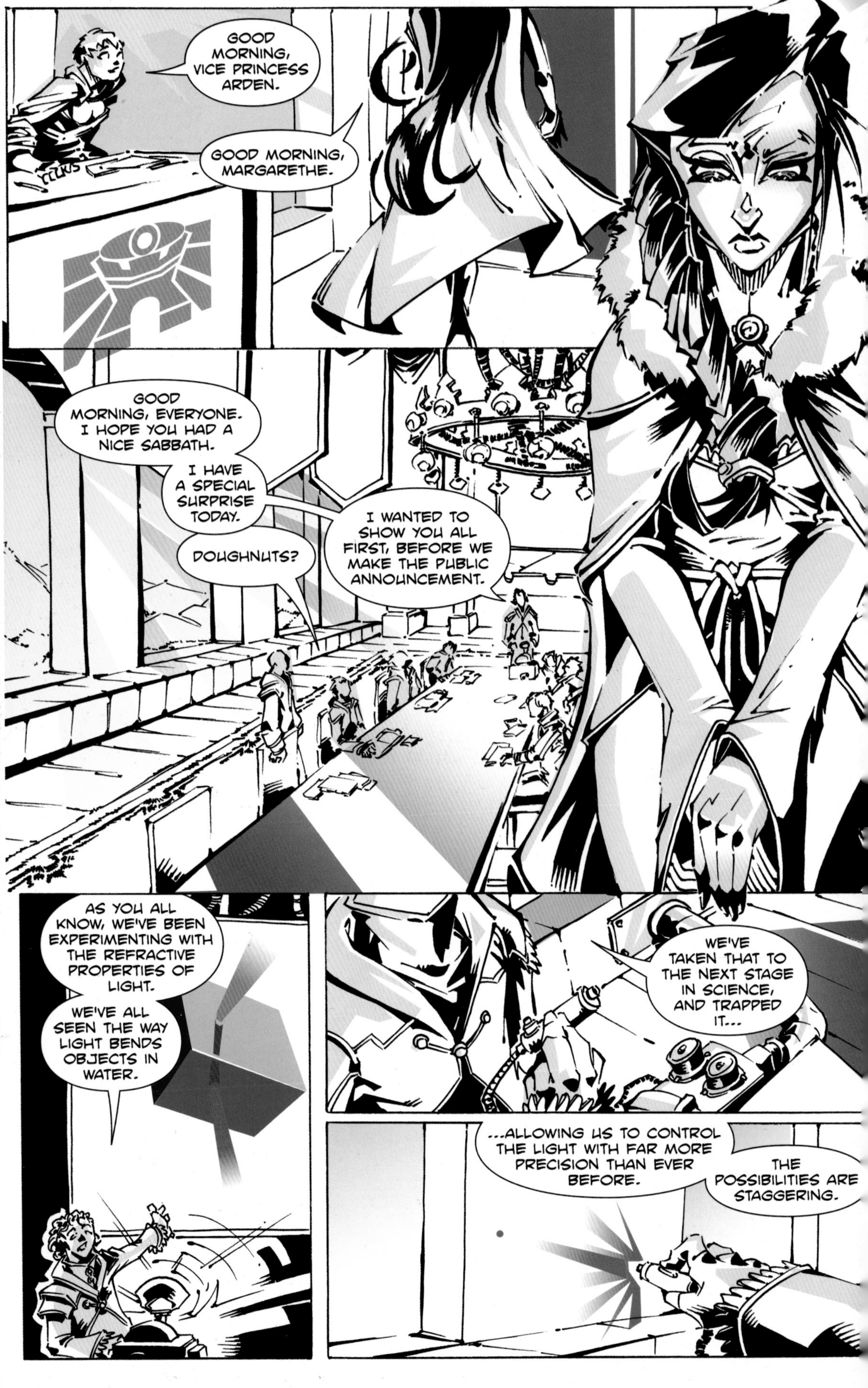

GOOD MORNING, VICE PRINCESS ARDEN.
GOOD MORNING, MARGARETHE.
GOOD MORNING, EVERYONE. I HOPE YOU HAD A NICE SABBATH.
I HAVE A SPECIAL SURPRISE TODAY.
DOUGHNUTS?
I WANTED TO SHOW YOU ALL FIRST, BEFORE WE MAKE THE PUBLIC ANNOUNCEMENT.
AS YOU ALL KNOW, WE'VE BEEN EXPERIMENTING WITH THE REFRACTIVE PROPERTIES OF LIGHT.
WE'VE ALL SEEN THE WAY LIGHT BENDS OBJECTS IN WATER.
WE'VE TAKEN THAT TO THE NEXT STAGE IN SCIENCE, AND TRAPPED IT...
...ALLOWING US TO CONTROL THE LIGHT WITH FAR MORE PRECISION THAN EVER BEFORE.
THE POSSIBILITIES ARE STAGGERING.

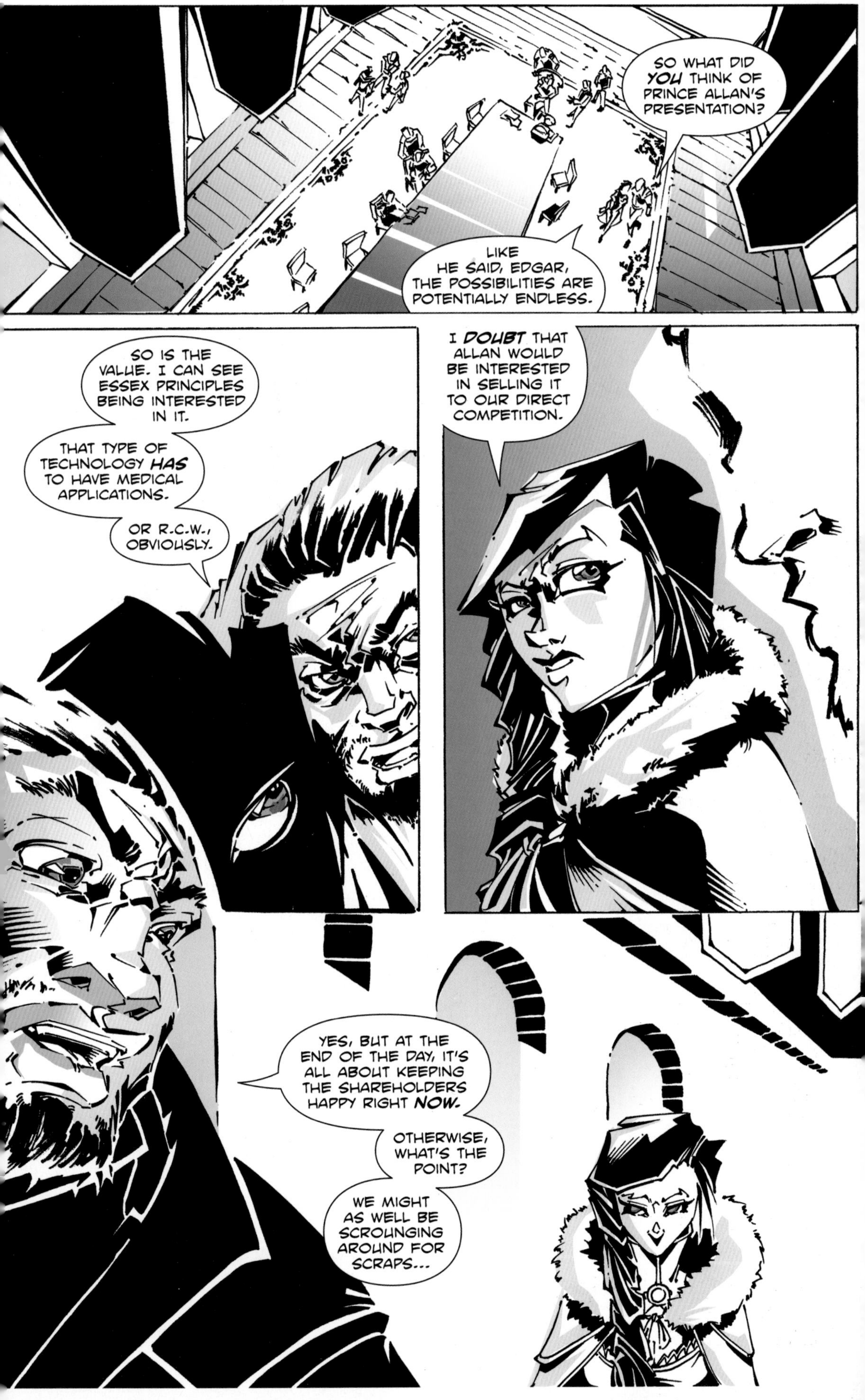
SO WHAT DID YOU THINK OF PRINCE ALLAN'S PRESENTATION?
LIKE HE SAID, EDGAR, THE POSSIBILITIES ARE POTENTIALLY ENDLESS.
SO IS THE VALUE. I CAN SEE ESSEX PRINCIPLES BEING INTERESTED IN IT.
THAT TYPE OF TECHNOLOGY HAS TO HAVE MEDICAL APPLICATIONS.
OR R.C.W., OBVIOUSLY.
I DOUBT THAT ALLAN WOULD BE INTERESTED IN SELLING IT TO OUR DIRECT COMPETITION.
YES, BUT AT THE END OF THE DAY, IT'S ALL ABOUT KEEPING THE SHAREHOLDERS HAPPY RIGHT NOW.
OTHERWISE, WHAT'S THE POINT?
WE MIGHT AS WELL BE SCROUNGING AROUND FOR SCRAPS...

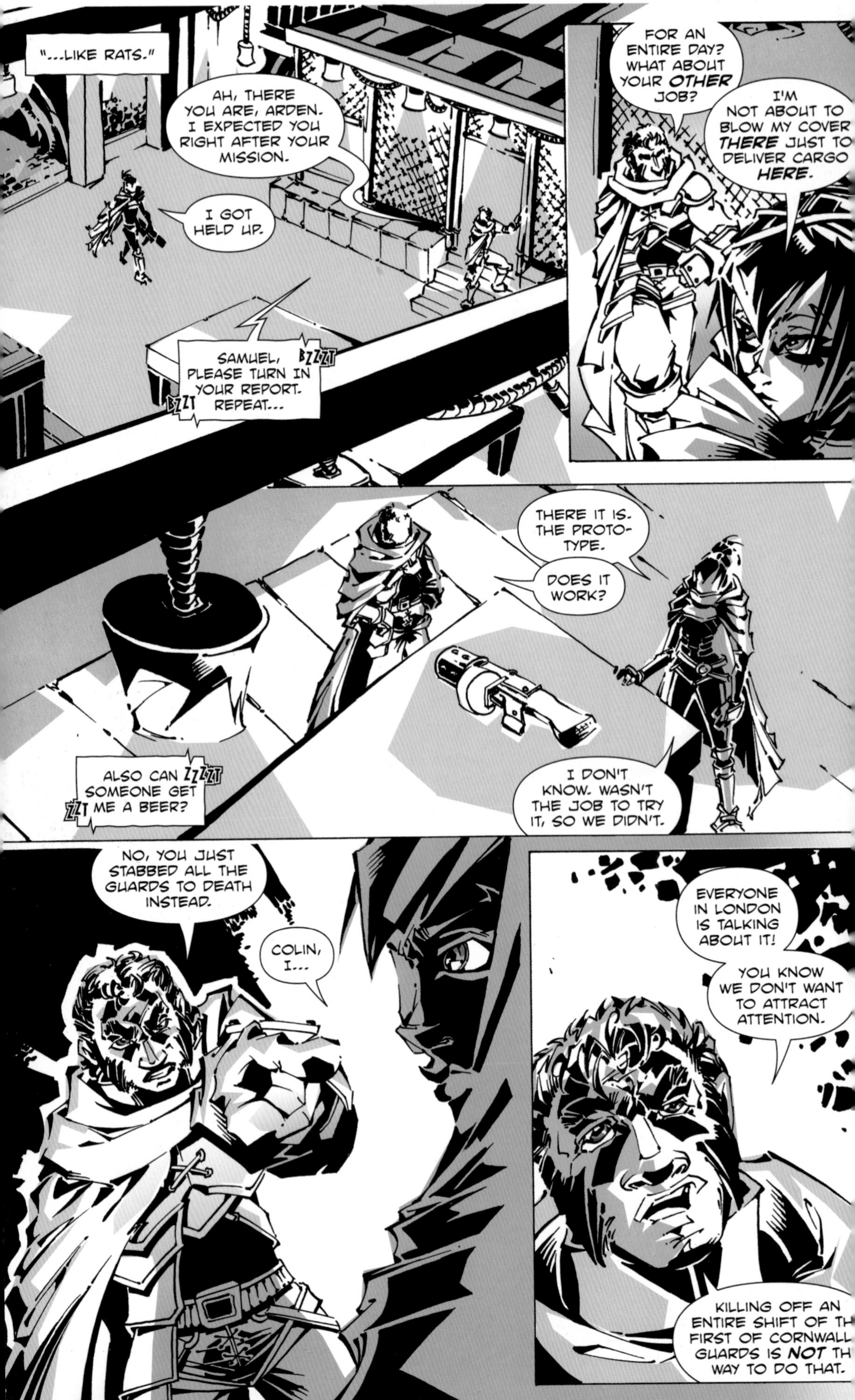
"...LIKE RATS."
AH, THERE YOU ARE, ARDEN. I EXPECTED YOU RIGHT AFTER YOUR MISSION.
I GOT HELD UP.
FOR AN ENTIRE DAY? WHAT ABOUT YOUR OTHER JOB?
I'M NOT ABOUT TO BLOW MY COVER THERE JUST TO DELIVER CARGO HERE.
SAMUEL, BZZZT PLEASE TURN IN YOUR REPORT. BZZT REPEAT...
THERE IT IS. THE PROTO-TYPE.
DOES IT WORK?
ALSO CAN ZZZZT SOMEONE GET ZZT ME A BEER?
I DON'T KNOW. WASN'T THE JOB TO TRY IT, SO WE DIDN'T.
NO, YOU JUST STABBED ALL THE GUARDS TO DEATH INSTEAD.
COLIN, I...
EVERYONE IN LONDON IS TALKING ABOUT IT!
YOU KNOW WE DON'T WANT TO ATTRACT ATTENTION.
KILLING OFF AN ENTIRE SHIFT OF TH FIRST OF CORNWALL GUARDS IS NOT TH WAY TO DO THAT.

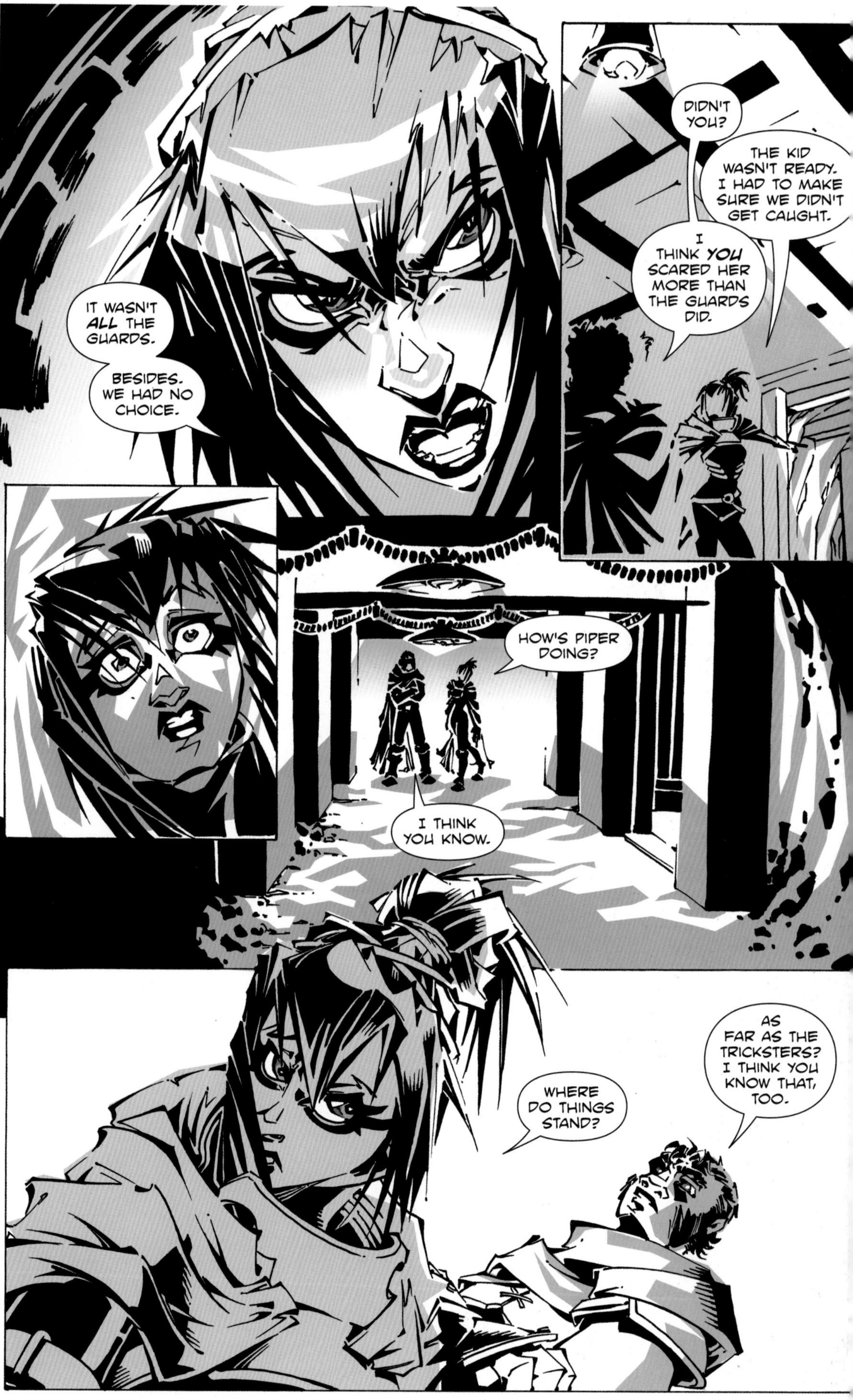
IT WASN'T ALL THE GUARDS.
BESIDES. WE HAD NO CHOICE.
DIDN'T YOU?
THE KID WASN'T READY. I HAD TO MAKE SURE WE DIDN'T GET CAUGHT.
I THINK YOU SCARED HER MORE THAN THE GUARDS DID.
HOW'S PIPER DOING?
I THINK YOU KNOW.
WHERE DO THINGS STAND?
AS FAR AS THE TRICKSTERS? I THINK YOU KNOW THAT, TOO.

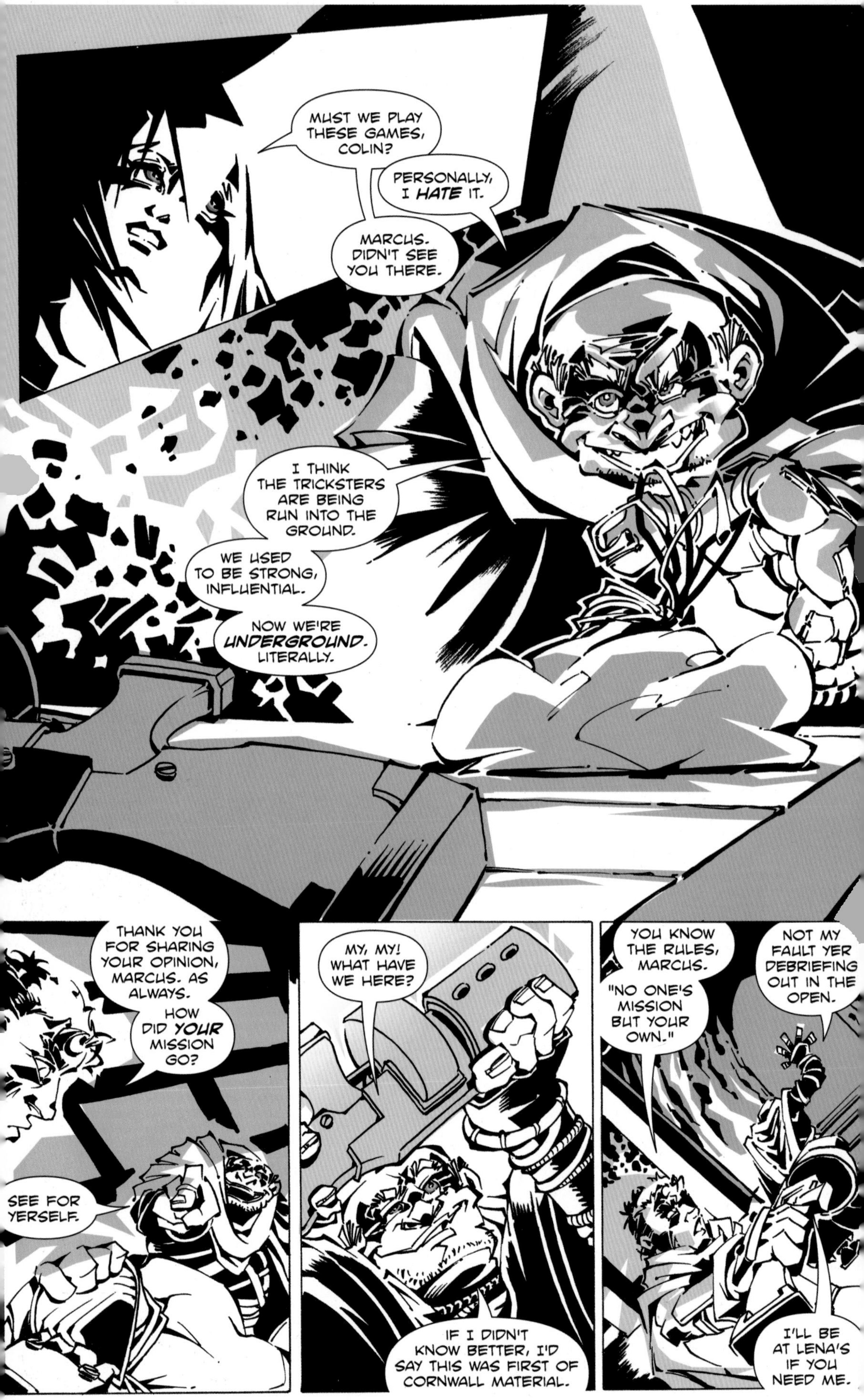
MUST WE PLAY THESE GAMES, COLIN?
PERSONALLY, I *HATE* IT.
MARCUS. DIDN'T SEE YOU THERE.
I THINK THE TRICKSTERS ARE BEING RUN INTO THE GROUND.
WE USED TO BE STRONG, INFLUENTIAL.
NOW WE'RE *UNDERGROUND*. LITERALLY.
THANK YOU FOR SHARING YOUR OPINION, MARCUS. AS ALWAYS.
HOW DID *YOUR* MISSION GO?
SEE FOR YERSELF.
MY, MY! WHAT HAVE WE HERE?
IF I DIDN'T KNOW BETTER, I'D SAY THIS WAS FIRST OF CORNWALL MATERIAL.
YOU KNOW THE RULES, MARCUS.
"NO ONE'S MISSION BUT YOUR OWN."
NOT MY FAULT YER DEBRIEFING OUT IN THE OPEN.
I'LL BE AT LENA'S IF YOU NEED ME.

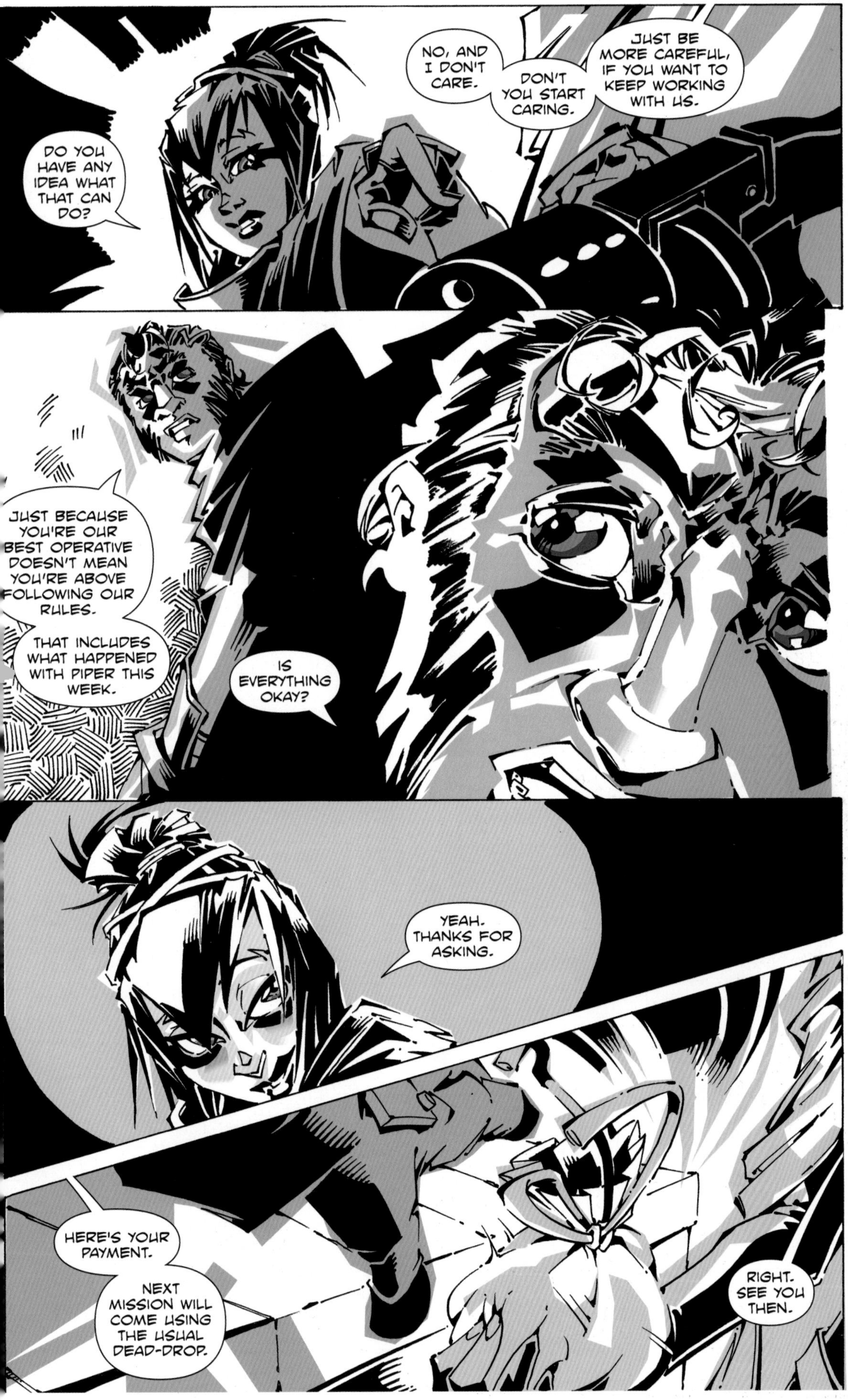
DO YOU HAVE ANY IDEA WHAT THAT CAN DO?
NO, AND I DON'T CARE.
DON'T YOU START CARING.
JUST BE MORE CAREFUL, IF YOU WANT TO KEEP WORKING WITH US.
JUST BECAUSE YOU'RE OUR BEST OPERATIVE DOESN'T MEAN YOU'RE ABOVE FOLLOWING OUR RULES.
THAT INCLUDES WHAT HAPPENED WITH PIPER THIS WEEK.
IS EVERYTHING OKAY?
YEAH. THANKS FOR ASKING.
HERE'S YOUR PAYMENT.
NEXT MISSION WILL COME USING THE USUAL DEAD-DROP.
RIGHT. SEE YOU THEN.

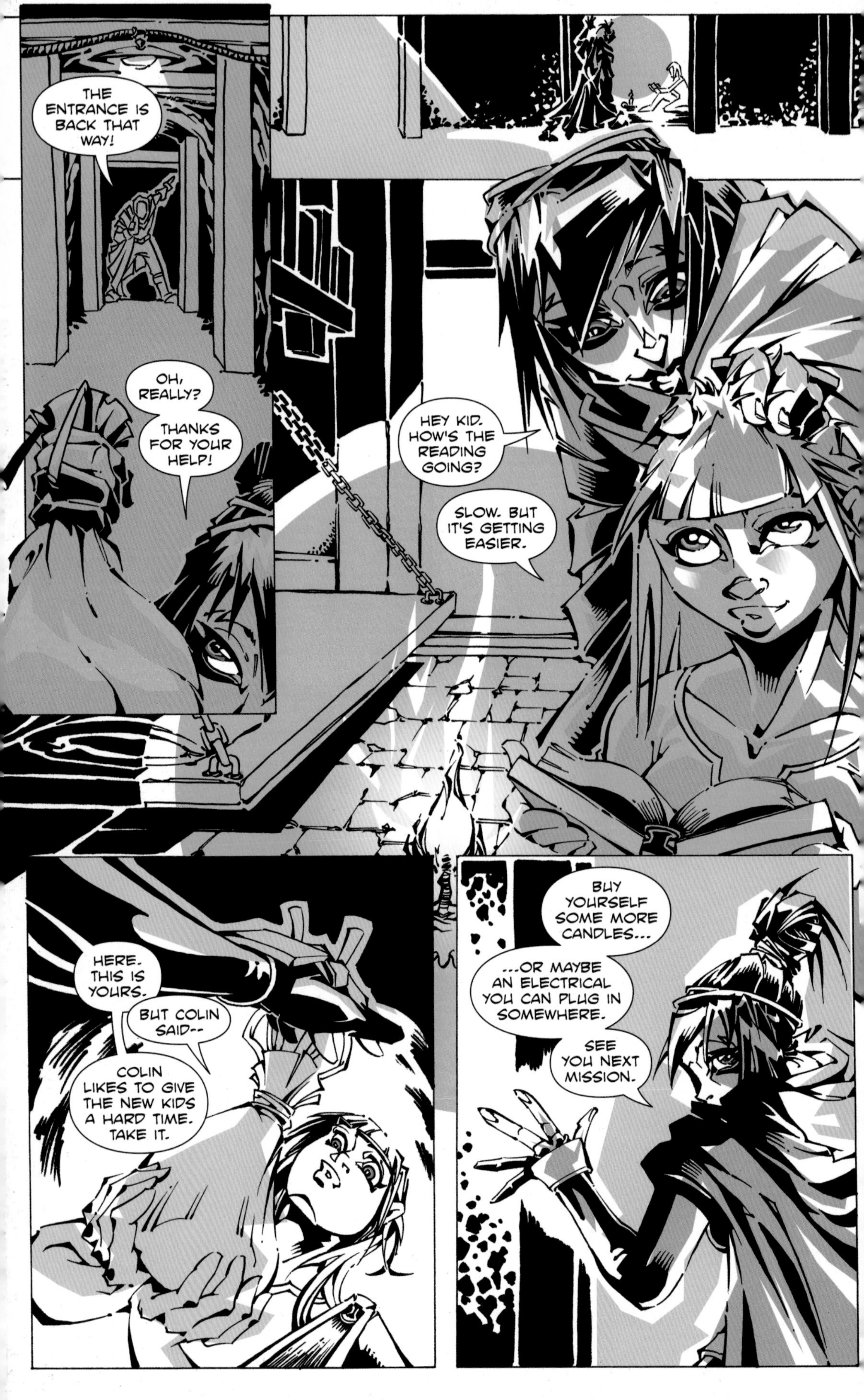
THE ENTRANCE IS BACK THAT WAY!
OH, REALLY?
THANKS FOR YOUR HELP!
HEY KID. HOW'S THE READING GOING?
SLOW. BUT IT'S GETTING EASIER.
HERE. THIS IS YOURS.
BUT COLIN SAID--
COLIN LIKES TO GIVE THE NEW KIDS A HARD TIME. TAKE IT.
BUY YOURSELF SOME MORE CANDLES...
...OR MAYBE AN ELECTRICAL YOU CAN PLUG IN SOMEWHERE.
SEE YOU NEXT MISSION.

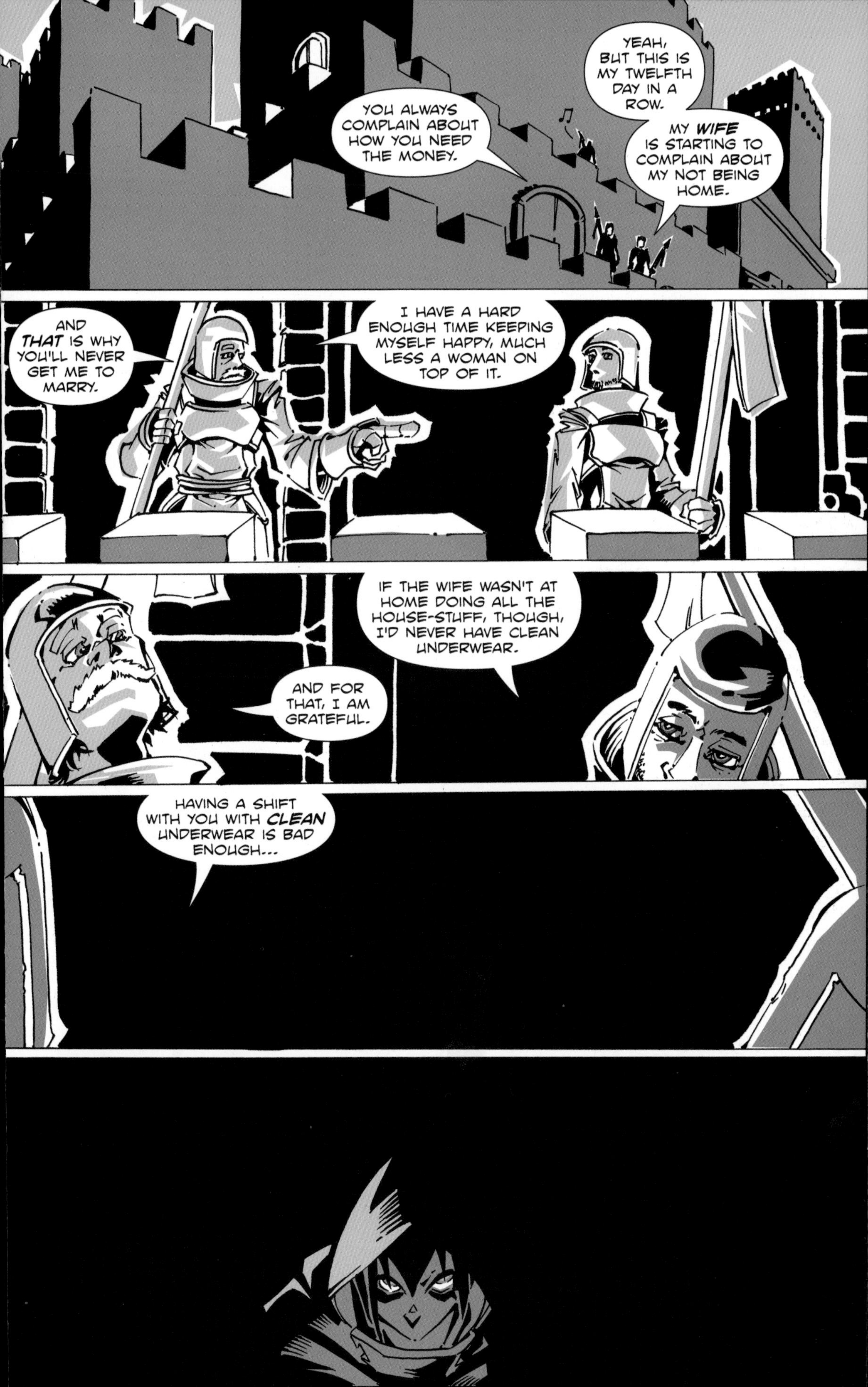
YOU ALWAYS COMPLAIN ABOUT HOW YOU NEED THE MONEY.
YEAH, BUT THIS IS MY TWELFTH DAY IN A ROW.
MY WIFE IS STARTING TO COMPLAIN ABOUT MY NOT BEING HOME.
AND THAT IS WHY YOU'LL NEVER GET ME TO MARRY.
I HAVE A HARD ENOUGH TIME KEEPING MYSELF HAPPY, MUCH LESS A WOMAN ON TOP OF IT.
IF THE WIFE WASN'T AT HOME DOING ALL THE HOUSE-STUFF, THOUGH, I'D NEVER HAVE CLEAN UNDERWEAR.
AND FOR THAT, I AM GRATEFUL.
HAVING A SHIFT WITH YOU WITH CLEAN UNDERWEAR IS BAD ENOUGH...

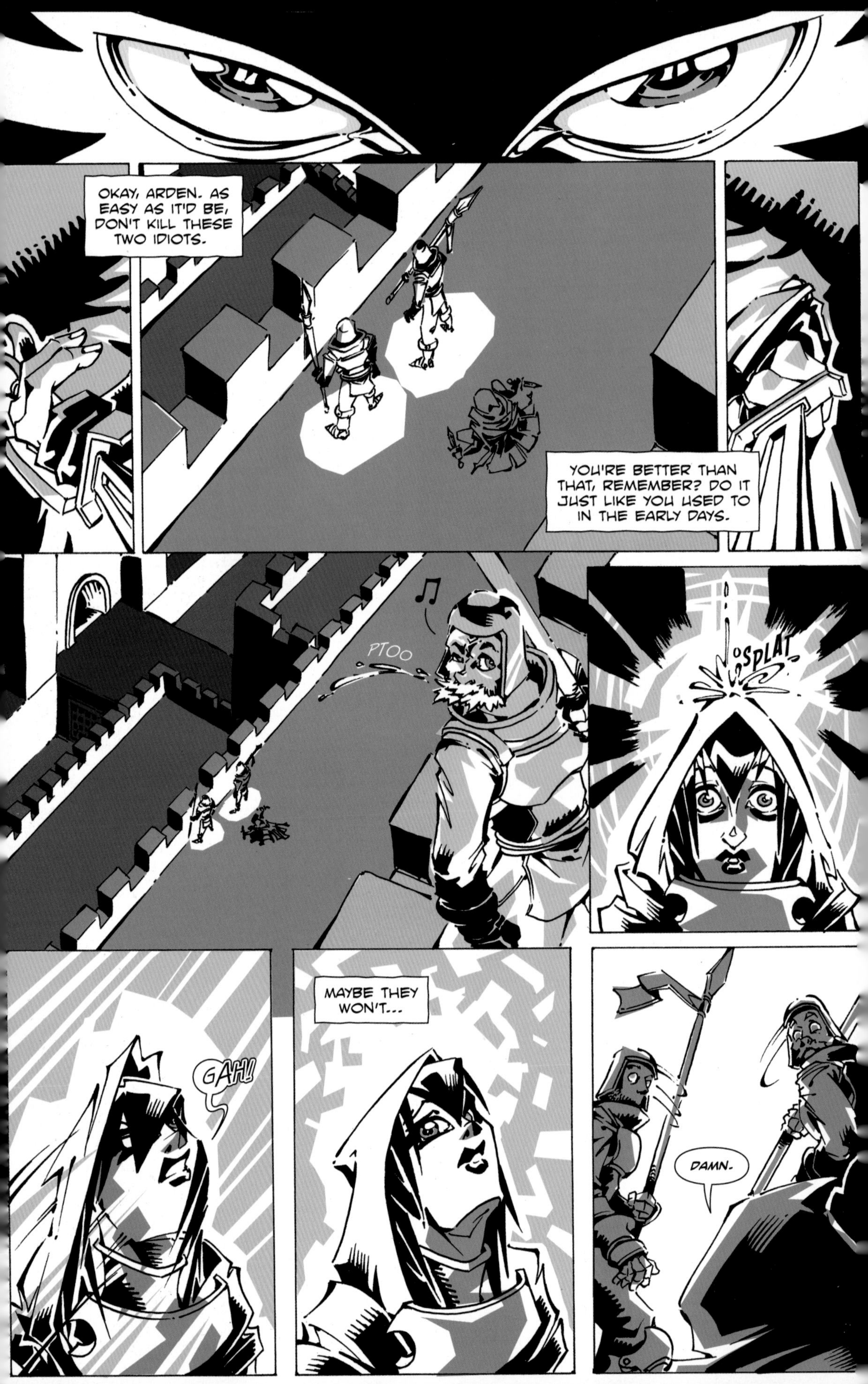
OKAY, ARDEN. AS EASY AS IT'D BE, DON'T KILL THESE TWO IDIOTS.
YOU'RE BETTER THAN THAT, REMEMBER? DO IT JUST LIKE YOU USED TO IN THE EARLY DAYS.
♪
PTOO
SPLAT
GAH!
MAYBE THEY WON'T...
DAMN.

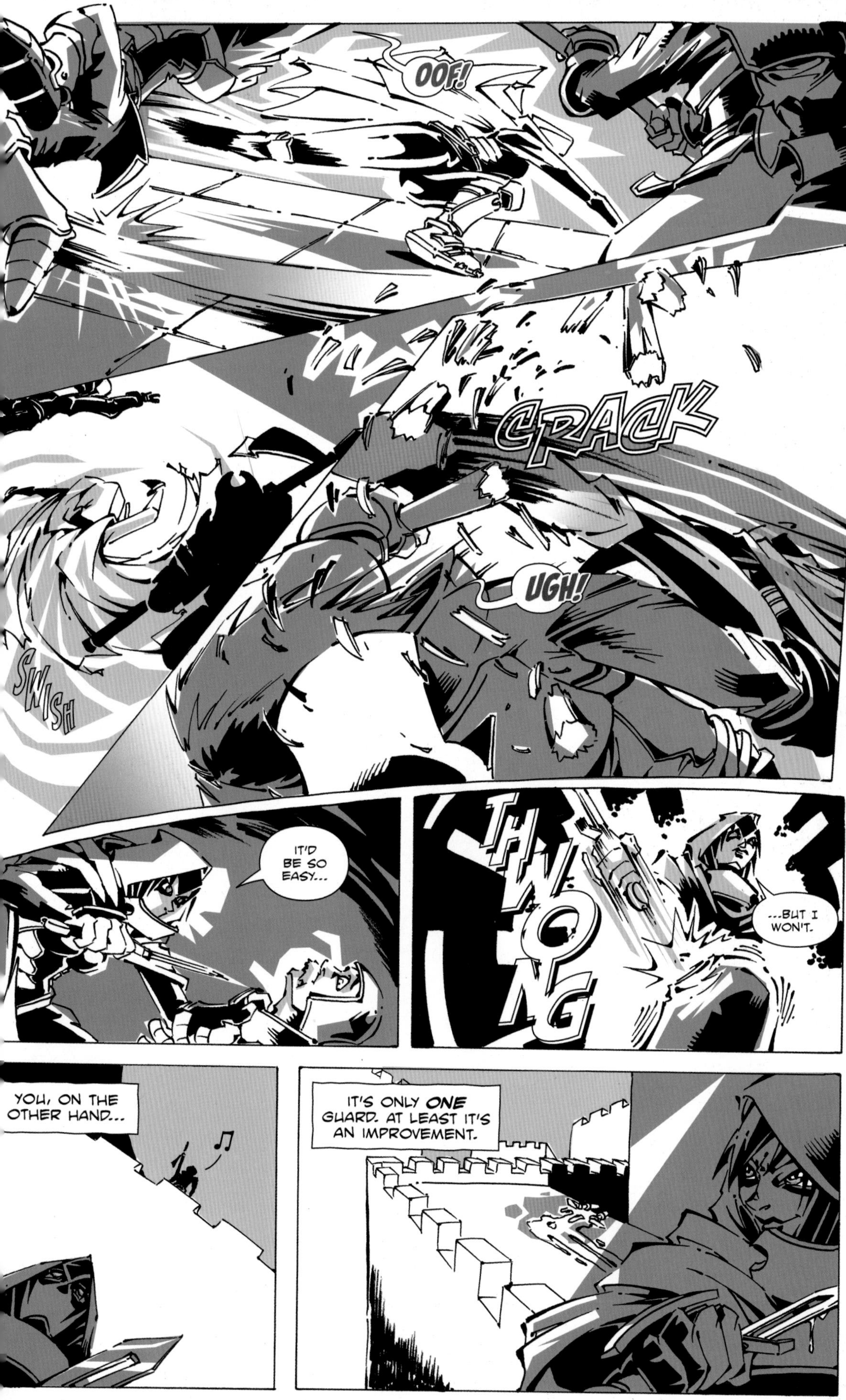
OOF!
CRACK
SWISH
UGH!
IT'D BE SO EASY...
THWONG
...BUT I WON'T.
YOU, ON THE OTHER HAND...
IT'S ONLY ONE GUARD. AT LEAST IT'S AN IMPROVEMENT.

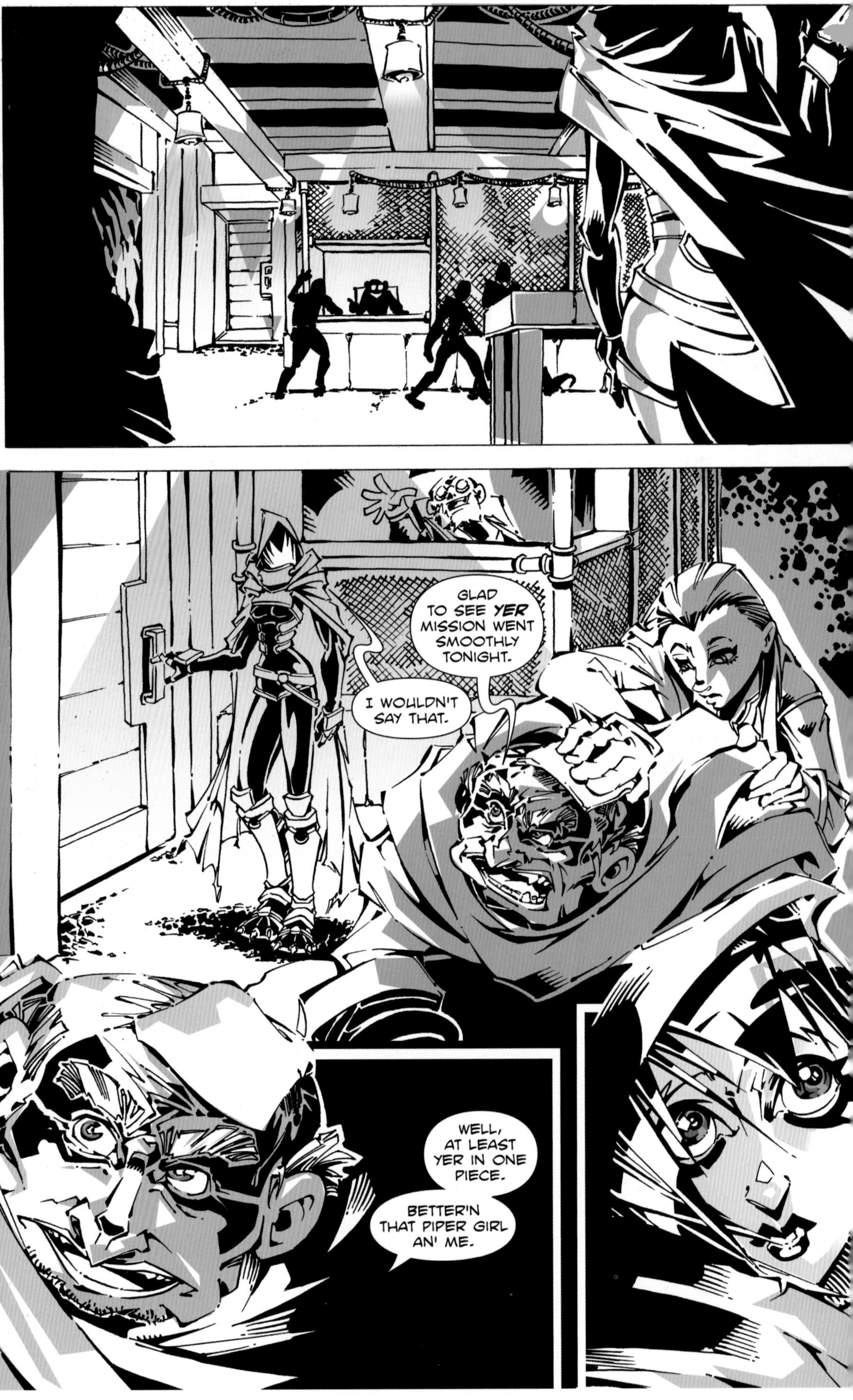

GLAD TO SEE *YER* MISSION WENT SMOOTHLY TONIGHT.
I WOULDN'T SAY THAT.
WELL, AT LEAST YER IN ONE PIECE.
BETTER'N THAT PIPER GIRL AN' ME.

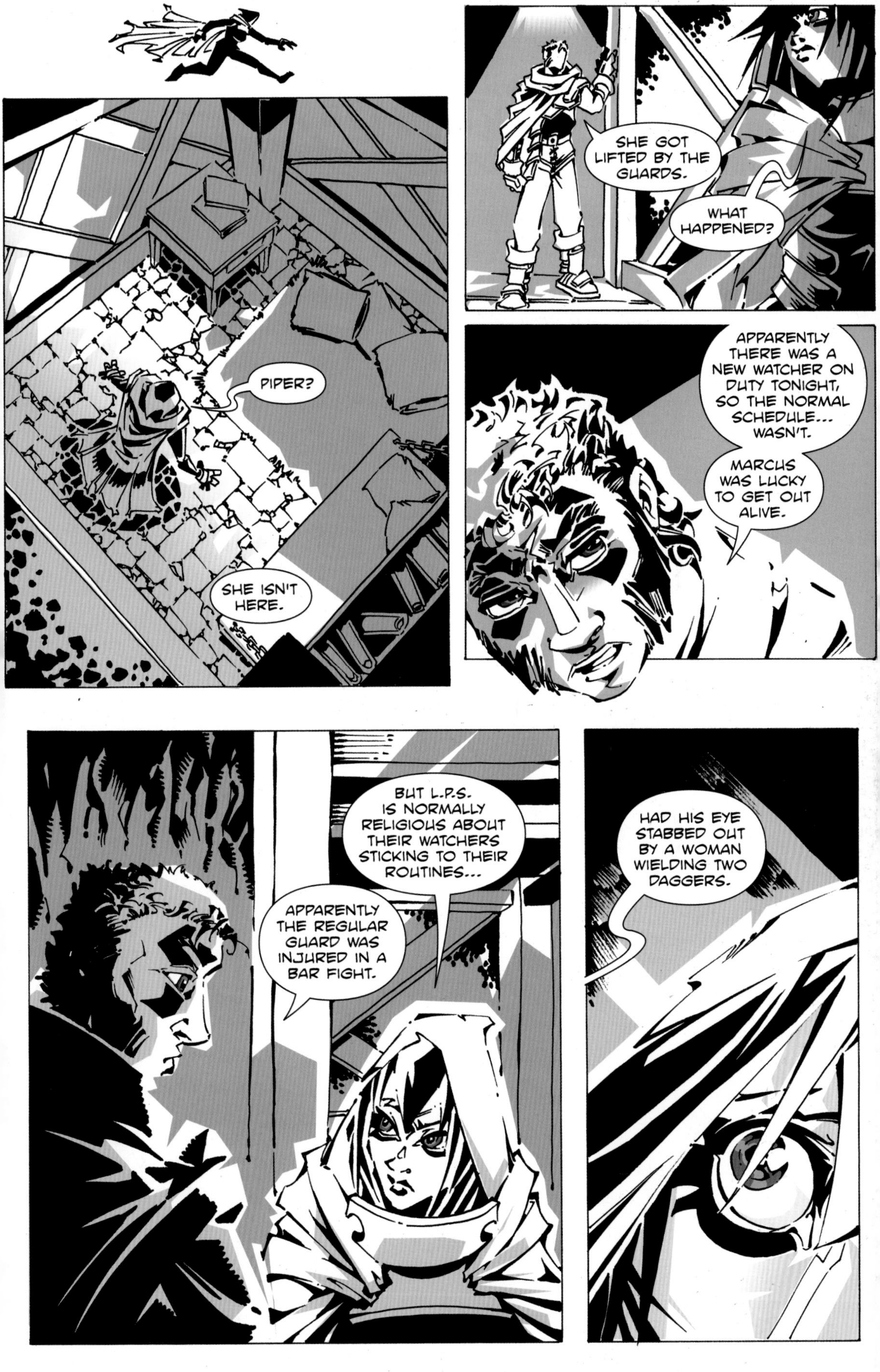
PIPER?
SHE ISN'T HERE.
WHAT HAPPENED?
SHE GOT LIFTED BY THE GUARDS.
APPARENTLY THERE WAS A NEW WATCHER ON DUTY TONIGHT, SO THE NORMAL SCHEDULE... WASN'T.
MARCUS WAS LUCKY TO GET OUT ALIVE.
BUT L.P.S. IS NORMALLY RELIGIOUS ABOUT THEIR WATCHERS STICKING TO THEIR ROUTINES...
APPARENTLY THE REGULAR GUARD WAS INJURED IN A BAR FIGHT.
HAD HIS EYE STABBED OUT BY A WOMAN WIELDING TWO DAGGERS.

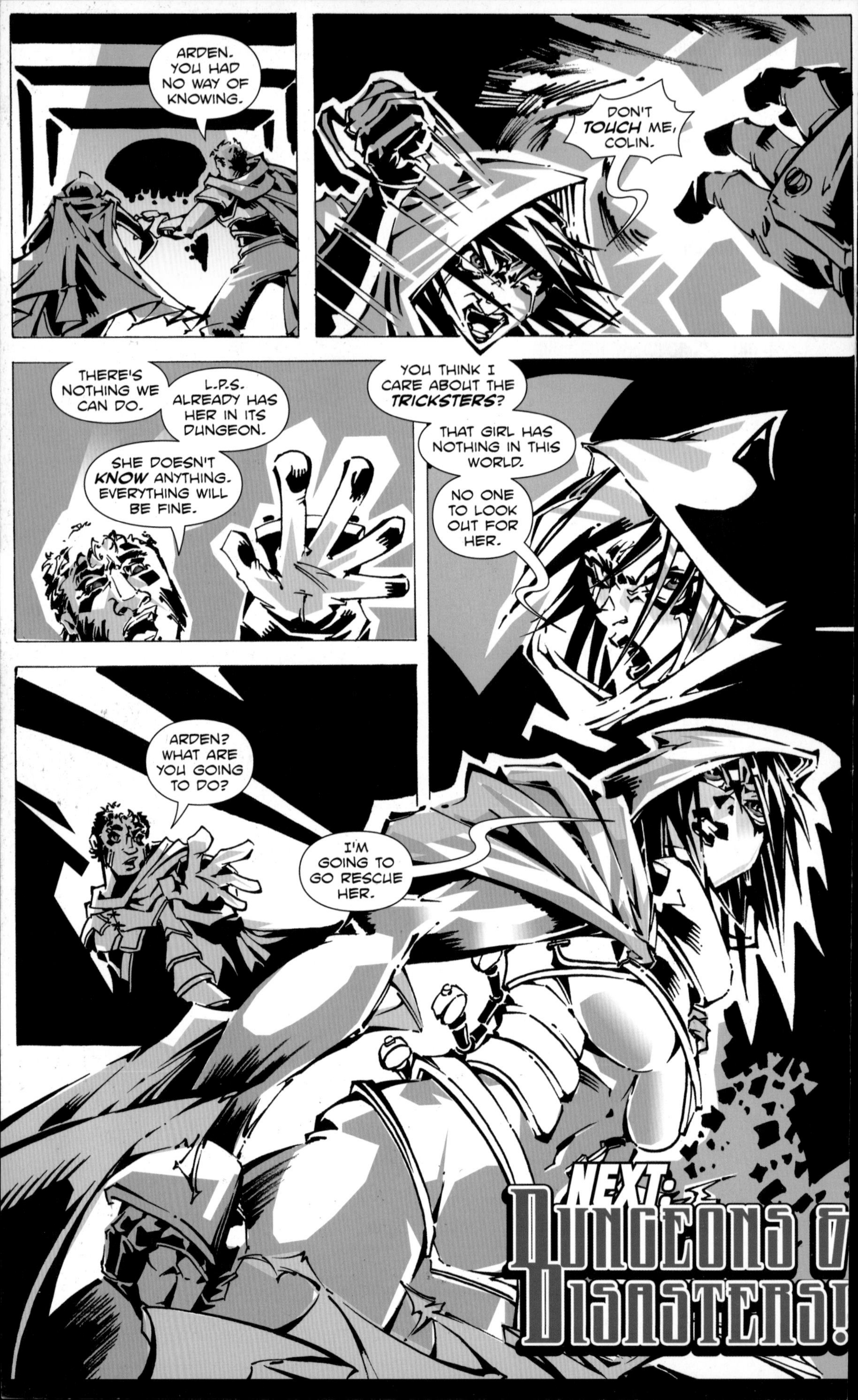
ARDEN. YOU HAD NO WAY OF KNOWING.
DON'T TOUCH ME, COLIN.
THERE'S NOTHING WE CAN DO.
L.P.S. ALREADY HAS HER IN ITS DUNGEON.
SHE DOESN'T KNOW ANYTHING. EVERYTHING WILL BE FINE.
YOU THINK I CARE ABOUT THE TRICKSTERS?
THAT GIRL HAS NOTHING IN THIS WORLD.
NO ONE TO LOOK OUT FOR HER.
ARDEN? WHAT ARE YOU GOING TO DO?
I'M GOING TO GO RESCUE HER.
NEXT:
DUNGEONS &
DISASTERS!

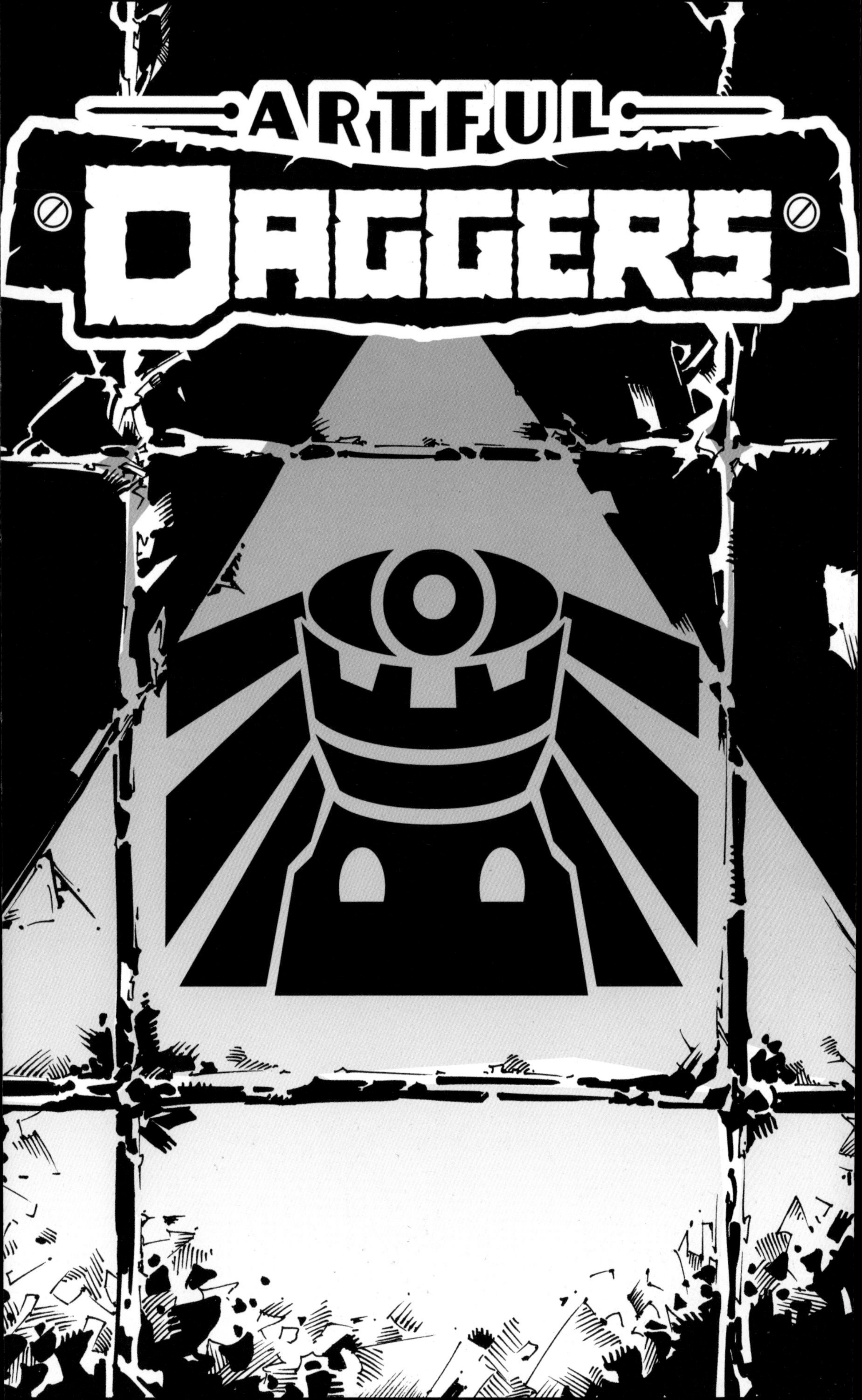
ARTFUL
DAGGERS

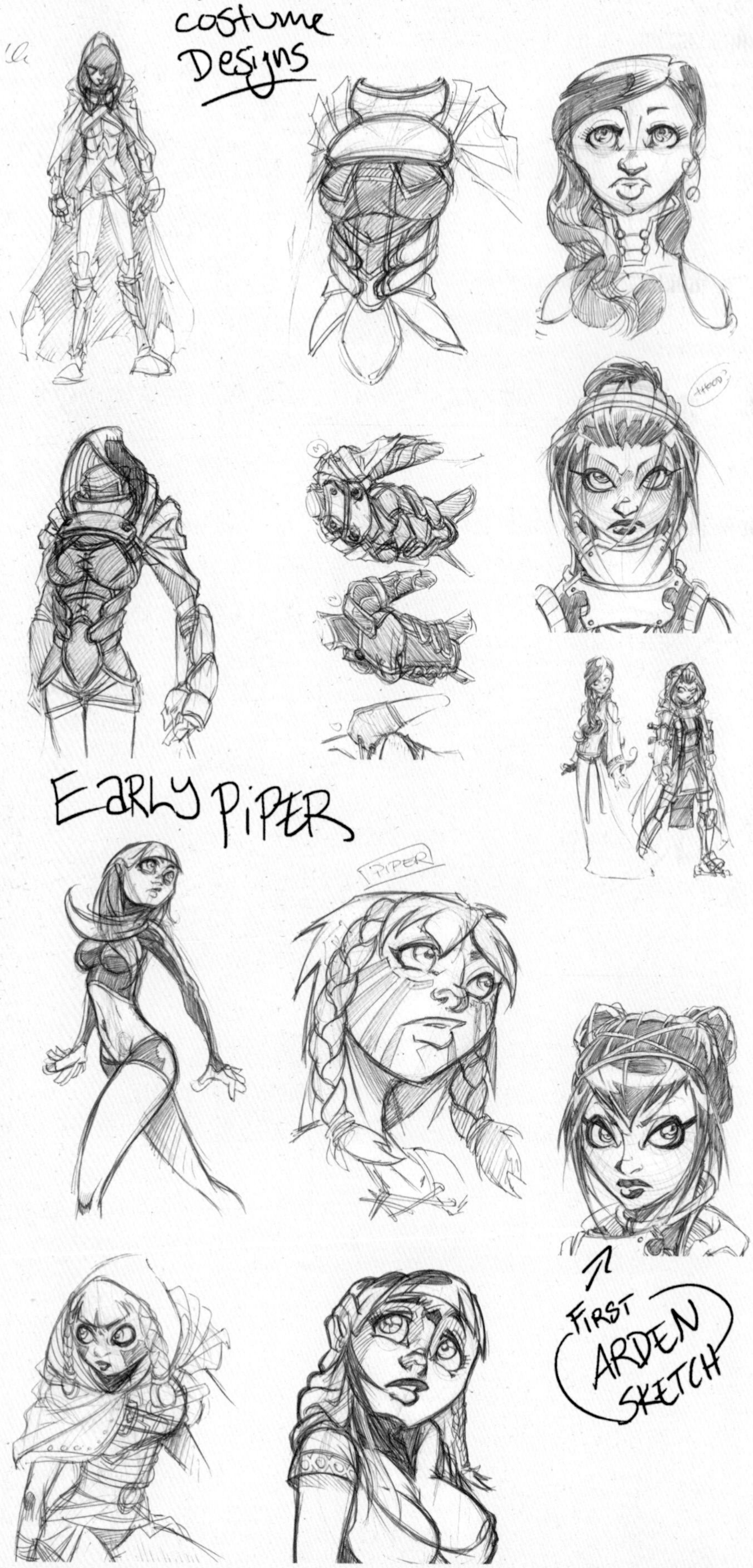
costume Designs
HOOD
EARLY PIPER
PIPER
FIRST ARDEN SKETCH

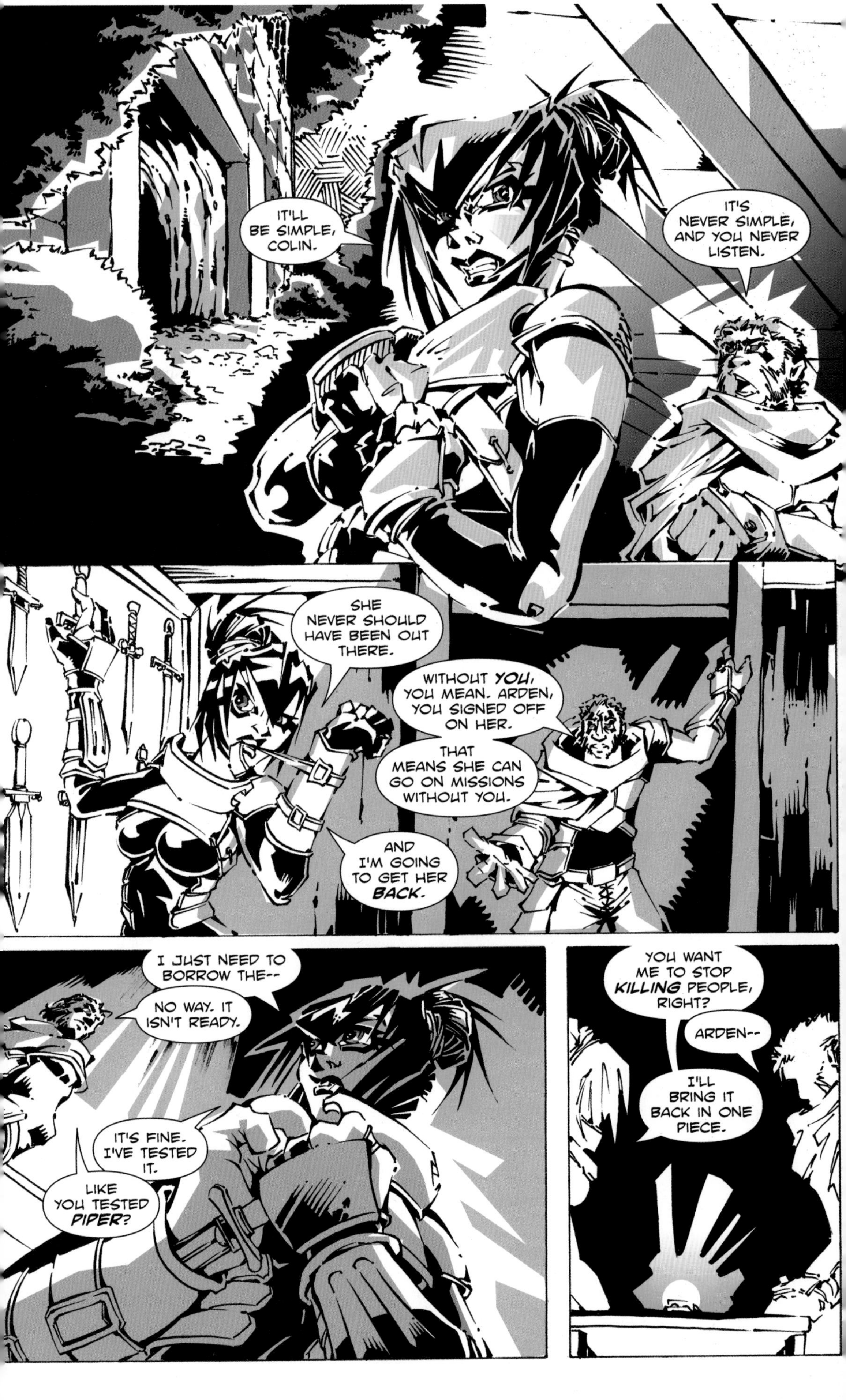
IT'LL BE SIMPLE, COLIN.
IT'S NEVER SIMPLE, AND YOU NEVER LISTEN.
SHE NEVER SHOULD HAVE BEEN OUT THERE.
WITHOUT *YOU*, YOU MEAN. ARDEN, YOU SIGNED OFF ON HER.
THAT MEANS SHE CAN GO ON MISSIONS WITHOUT YOU.
AND I'M GOING TO GET HER *BACK*.
I JUST NEED TO BORROW THE--
NO WAY. IT ISN'T READY.
IT'S FINE. I'VE TESTED IT.
LIKE YOU TESTED *PIPER*?
YOU WANT ME TO STOP *KILLING* PEOPLE, RIGHT?
ARDEN--
I'LL BRING IT BACK IN ONE PIECE.

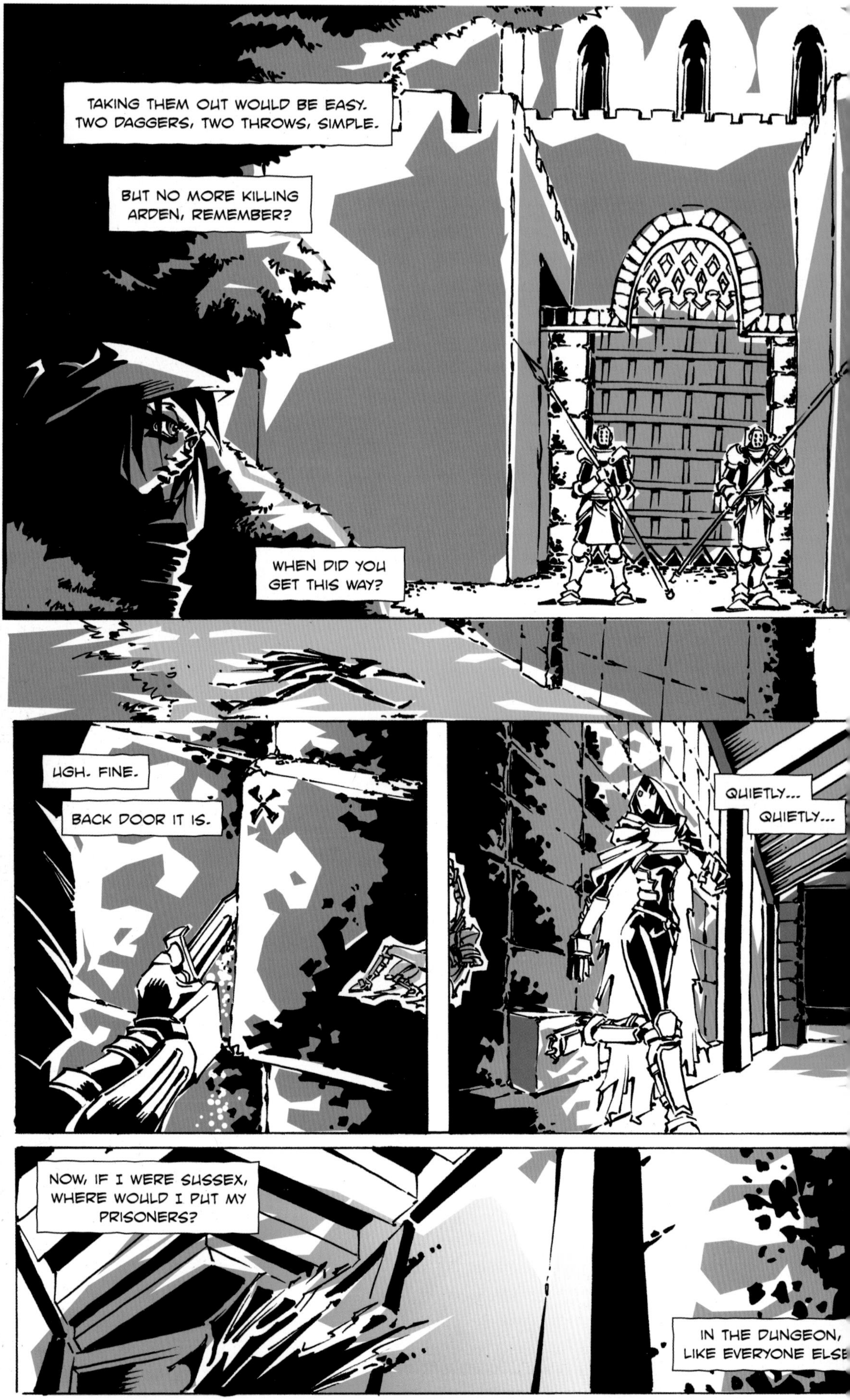
TAKING THEM OUT WOULD BE EASY. TWO DAGGERS, TWO THROWS, SIMPLE.
BUT NO MORE KILLING ARDEN, REMEMBER?
WHEN DID YOU GET THIS WAY?
UGH. FINE.
BACK DOOR IT IS.
QUIETLY...
QUIETLY...
NOW, IF I WERE SUSSEX, WHERE WOULD I PUT MY PRISONERS?
IN THE DUNGEON, LIKE EVERYONE ELSE

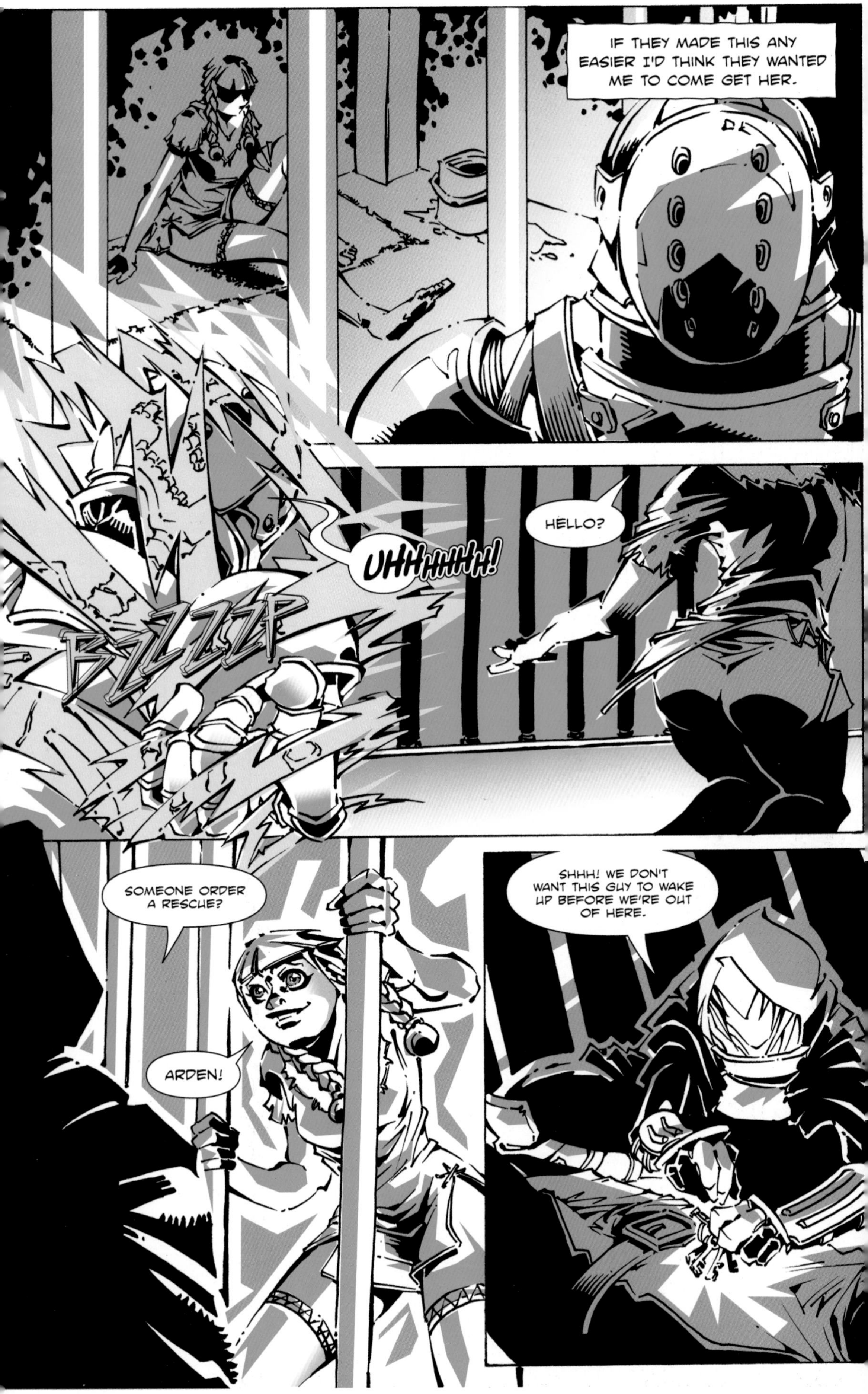
IF THEY MADE THIS ANY EASIER I'D THINK THEY WANTED ME TO COME GET HER.
HELLO?
UHHHHHH!
BZZZZP
SOMEONE ORDER A RESCUE?
ARDEN!
SHHH! WE DON'T WANT THIS GUY TO WAKE UP BEFORE WE'RE OUT OF HERE.

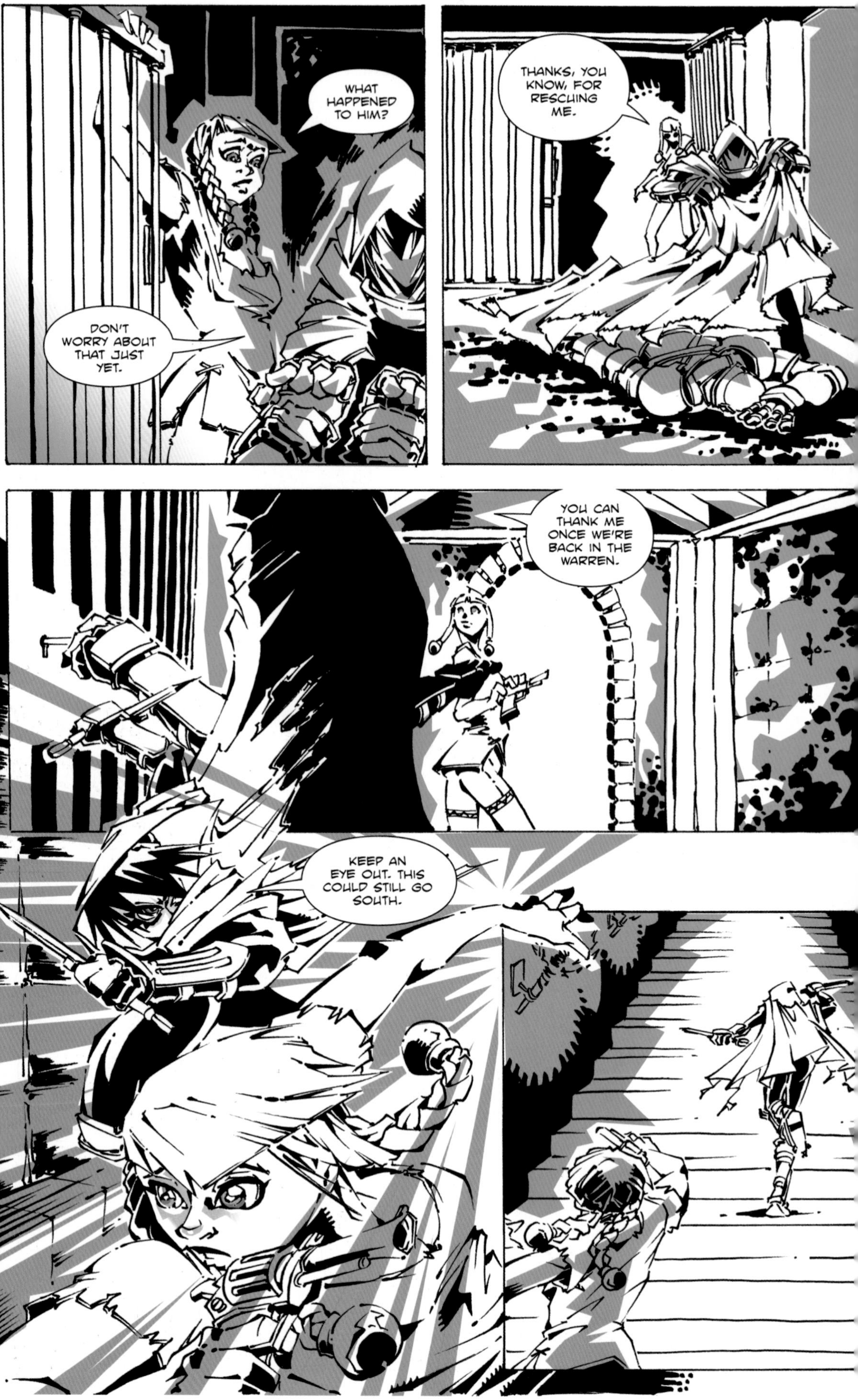
WHAT HAPPENED TO HIM?
DON'T WORRY ABOUT THAT JUST YET.
THANKS, YOU KNOW, FOR RESCUING ME.
YOU CAN THANK ME ONCE WE'RE BACK IN THE WARREN.
KEEP AN EYE OUT. THIS COULD STILL GO SOUTH.

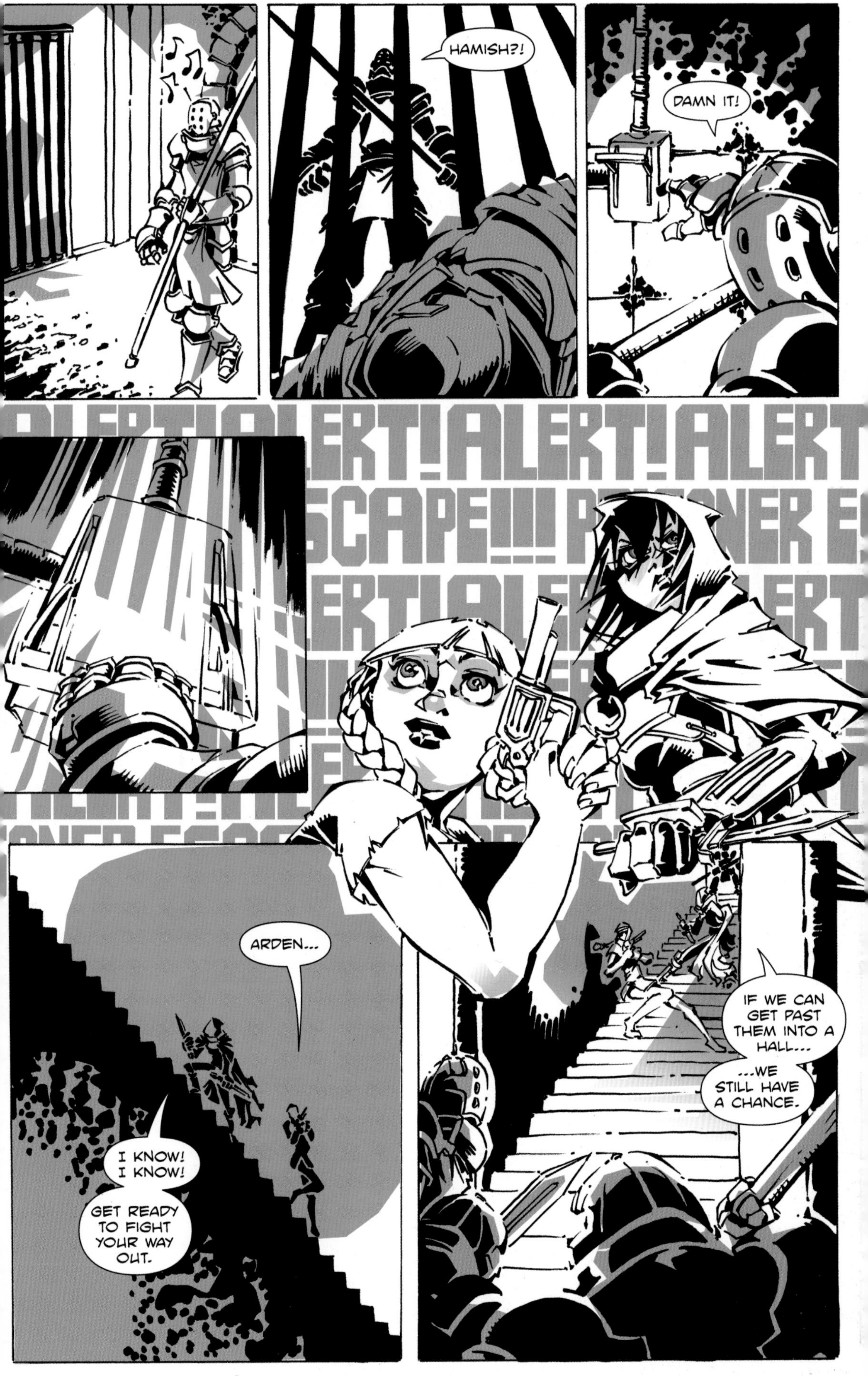
HAMISH?!
DAMN IT!
ALERT! ALERT! ALERT
PRISONER ESCAPE!!!
ARDEN...
I KNOW! I KNOW!
GET READY TO FIGHT YOUR WAY OUT.
IF WE CAN GET PAST THEM INTO A HALL...
...WE STILL HAVE A CHANCE.

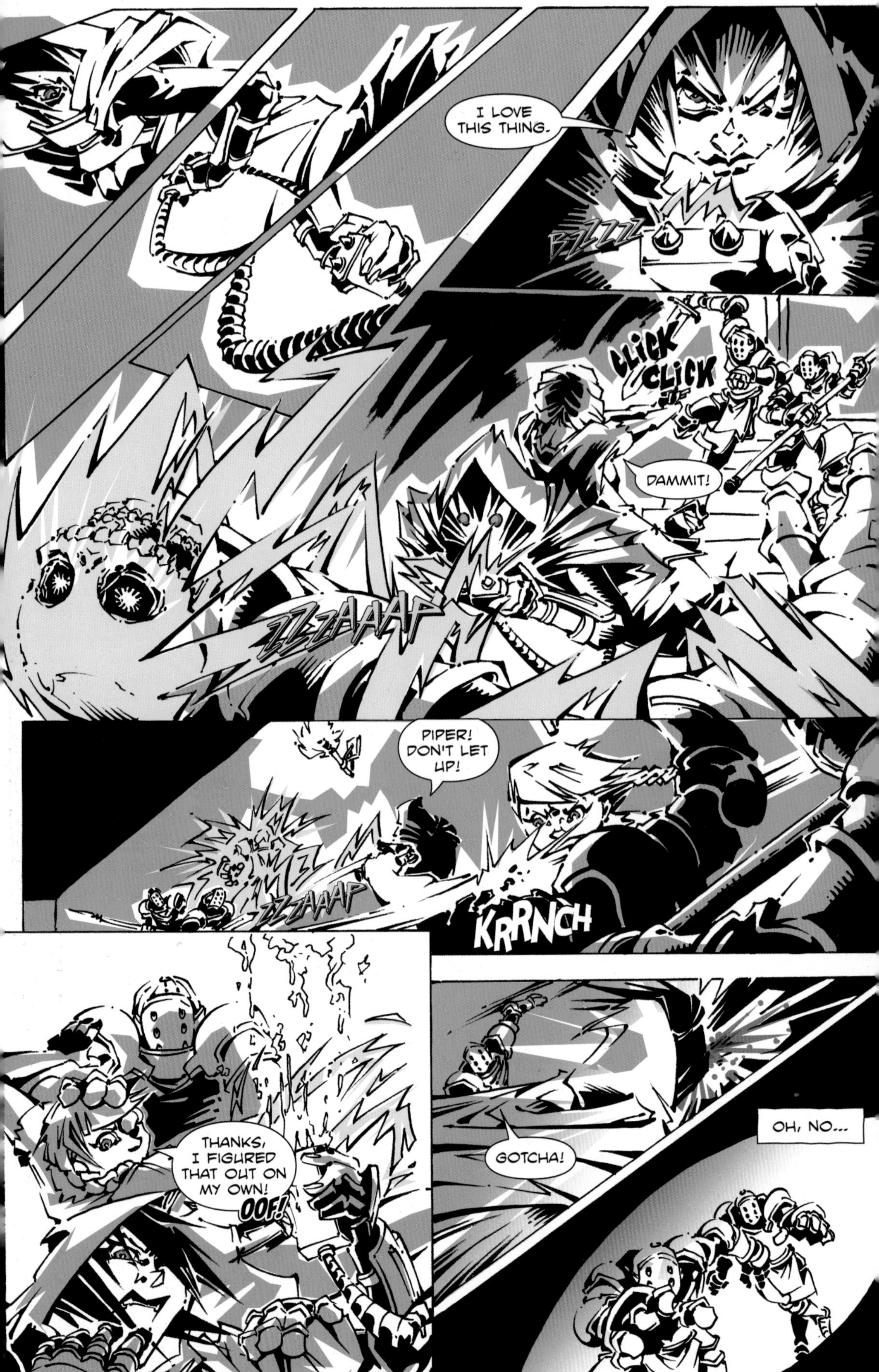
I LOVE THIS THING.
BZZZZZ
CLICK CLICK
DAMMIT!
ZZZZAAAP
PIPER! DON'T LET UP!
ZZZAAAP
KRRNCH
THANKS, I FIGURED THAT OUT ON MY OWN!
OOF!
GOTCHA!
OH, NO...

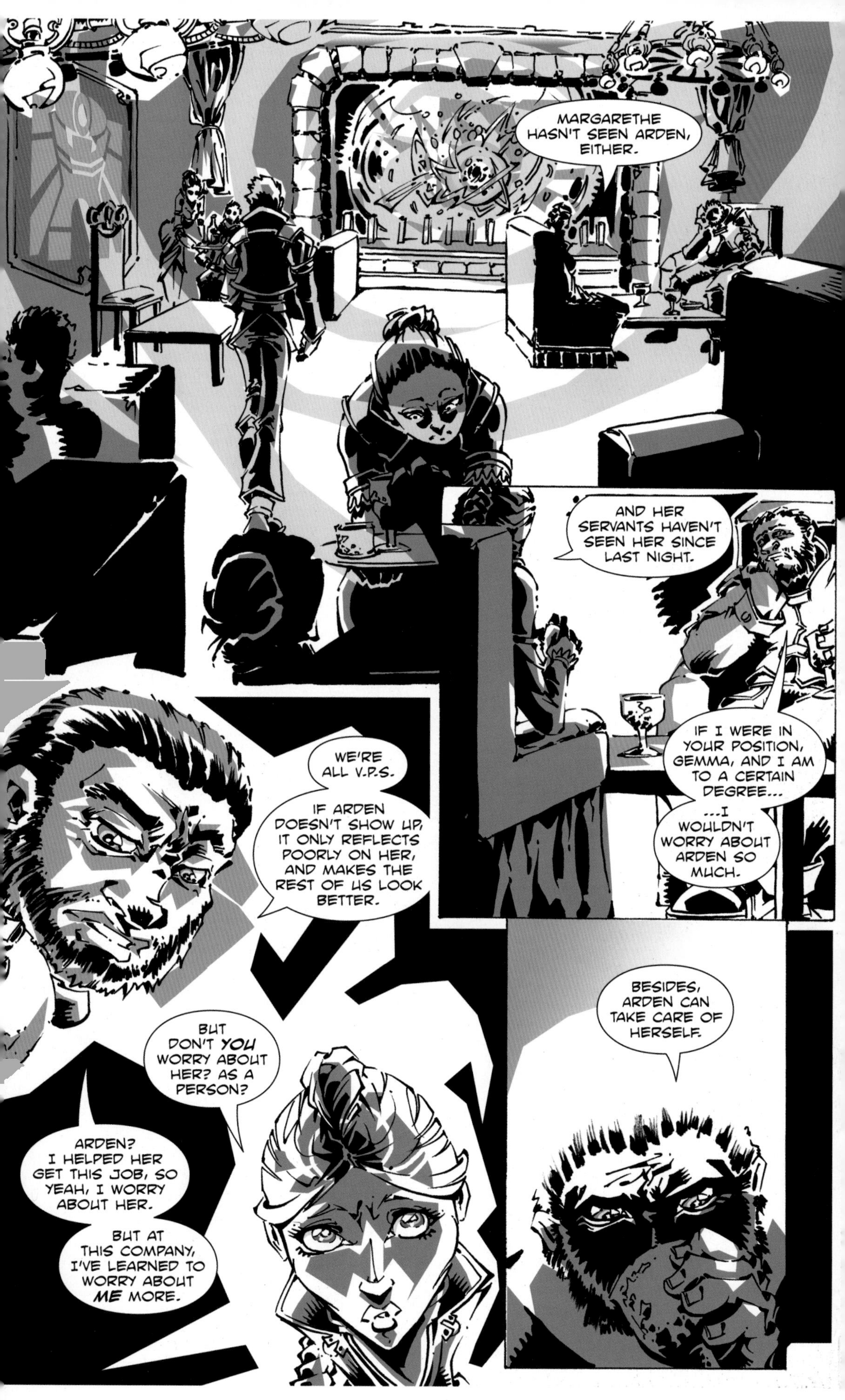
MARGARETHE HASN'T SEEN ARDEN, EITHER.
AND HER SERVANTS HAVEN'T SEEN HER SINCE LAST NIGHT.
IF I WERE IN YOUR POSITION, GEMMA, AND I AM TO A CERTAIN DEGREE...
...I WOULDN'T WORRY ABOUT ARDEN SO MUCH.
WE'RE ALL V.P.S.
IF ARDEN DOESN'T SHOW UP, IT ONLY REFLECTS POORLY ON HER, AND MAKES THE REST OF US LOOK BETTER.
BESIDES, ARDEN CAN TAKE CARE OF HERSELF.
BUT DON'T YOU WORRY ABOUT HER? AS A PERSON?
ARDEN? I HELPED HER GET THIS JOB, SO YEAH, I WORRY ABOUT HER.
BUT AT THIS COMPANY, I'VE LEARNED TO WORRY ABOUT ME MORE.

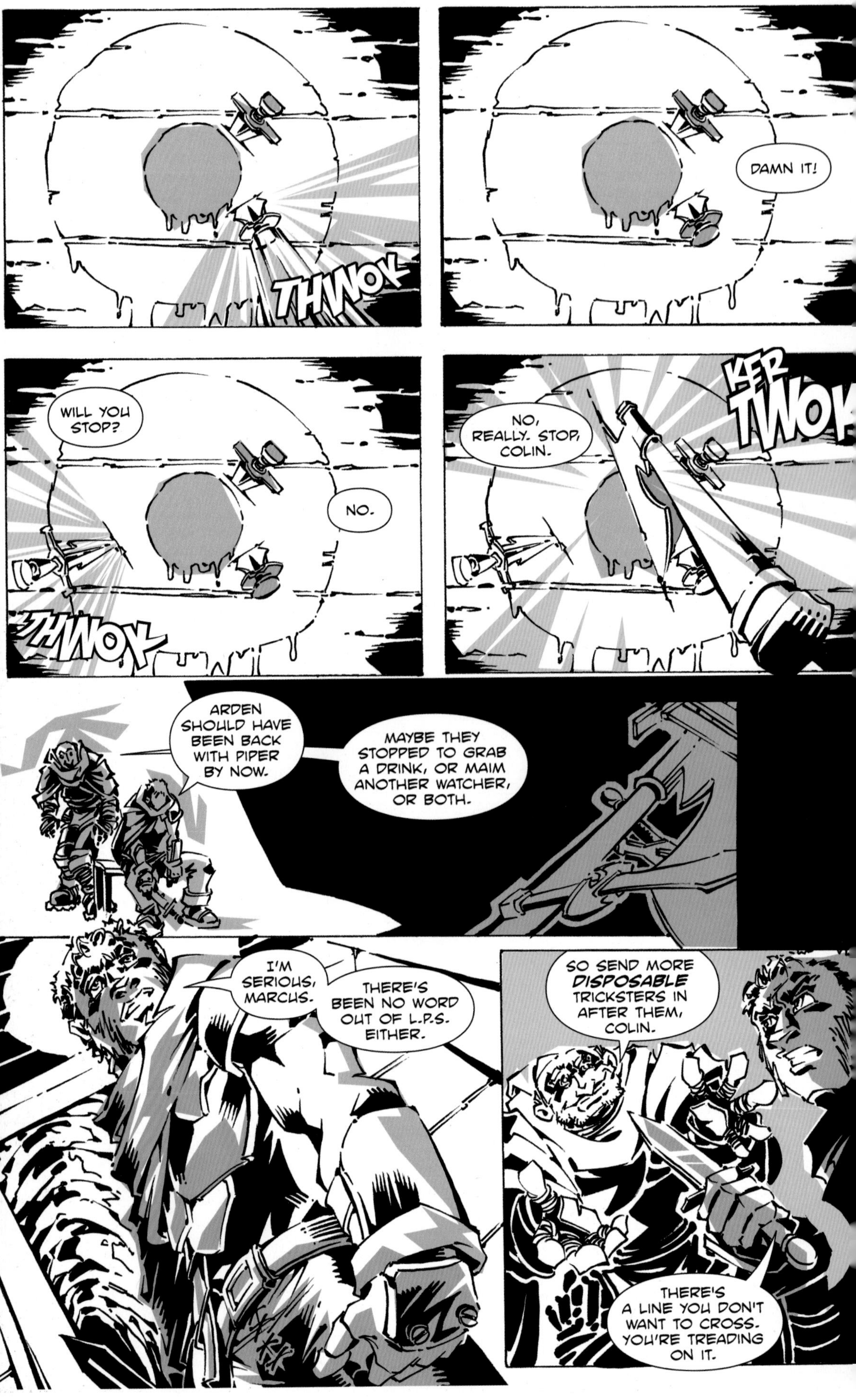
THWOK
DAMN IT!
WILL YOU STOP?
NO.
THWOK
NO, REALLY. STOP, COLIN.
KER TWOK
ARDEN SHOULD HAVE BEEN BACK WITH PIPER BY NOW.
MAYBE THEY STOPPED TO GRAB A DRINK, OR MAIM ANOTHER WATCHER, OR BOTH.
I'M SERIOUS, MARCUS.
THERE'S BEEN NO WORD OUT OF L.P.S. EITHER.
SO SEND MORE *DISPOSABLE* TRICKSTERS IN AFTER THEM, COLIN.
THERE'S A LINE YOU DON'T WANT TO CROSS. YOU'RE TREADING ON IT.

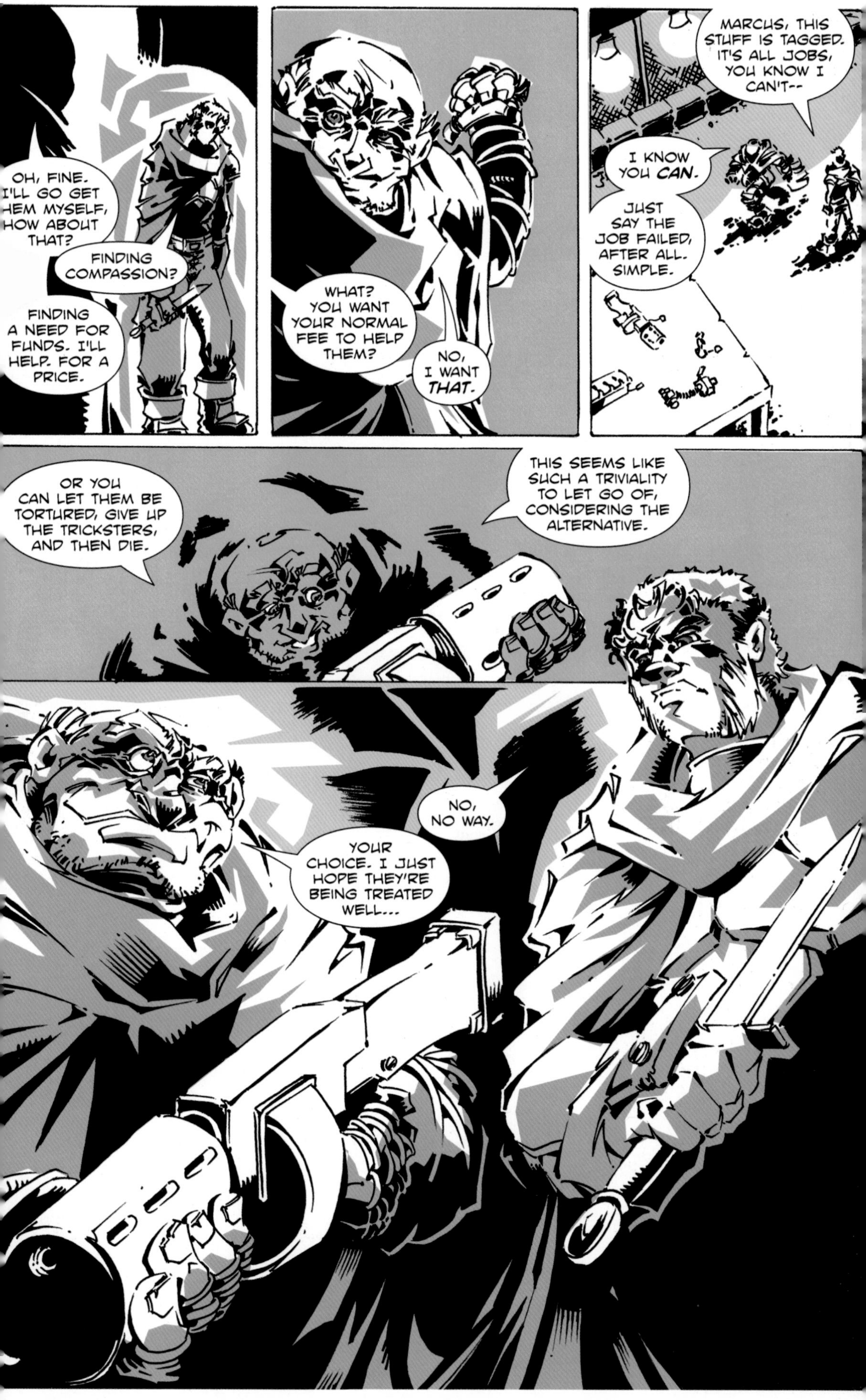

OH, FINE. I'LL GO GET THEM MYSELF, HOW ABOUT THAT?
FINDING COMPASSION?
FINDING A NEED FOR FUNDS. I'LL HELP. FOR A PRICE.
WHAT? YOU WANT YOUR NORMAL FEE TO HELP THEM?
NO, I WANT *THAT*.
MARCUS, THIS STUFF IS TAGGED. IT'S ALL JOBS, YOU KNOW I CAN'T--
I KNOW YOU ***CAN***.
JUST SAY THE JOB FAILED, AFTER ALL. SIMPLE.
OR YOU CAN LET THEM BE TORTURED, GIVE UP THE TRICKSTERS, AND THEN DIE.
THIS SEEMS LIKE SUCH A TRIVIALITY TO LET GO OF, CONSIDERING THE ALTERNATIVE.
NO, NO WAY.
YOUR CHOICE. I JUST HOPE THEY'RE BEING TREATED WELL...

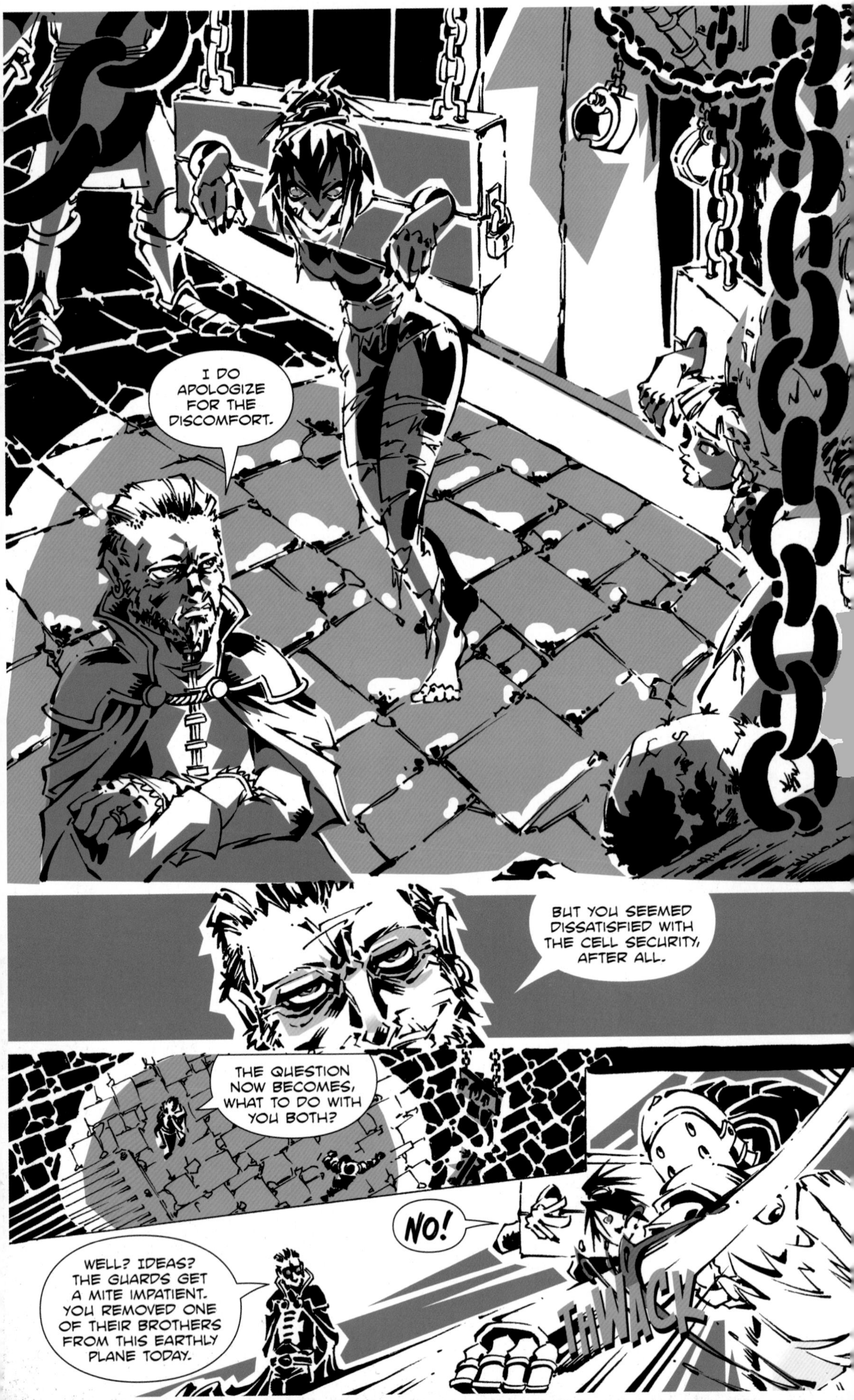
I DO APOLOGIZE FOR THE DISCOMFORT.
BUT YOU SEEMED DISSATISFIED WITH THE CELL SECURITY, AFTER ALL.
THE QUESTION NOW BECOMES, WHAT TO DO WITH YOU BOTH?
NO!
WELL? IDEAS? THE GUARDS GET A MITE IMPATIENT. YOU REMOVED ONE OF THEIR BROTHERS FROM THIS EARTHLY PLANE TODAY.
THWACK

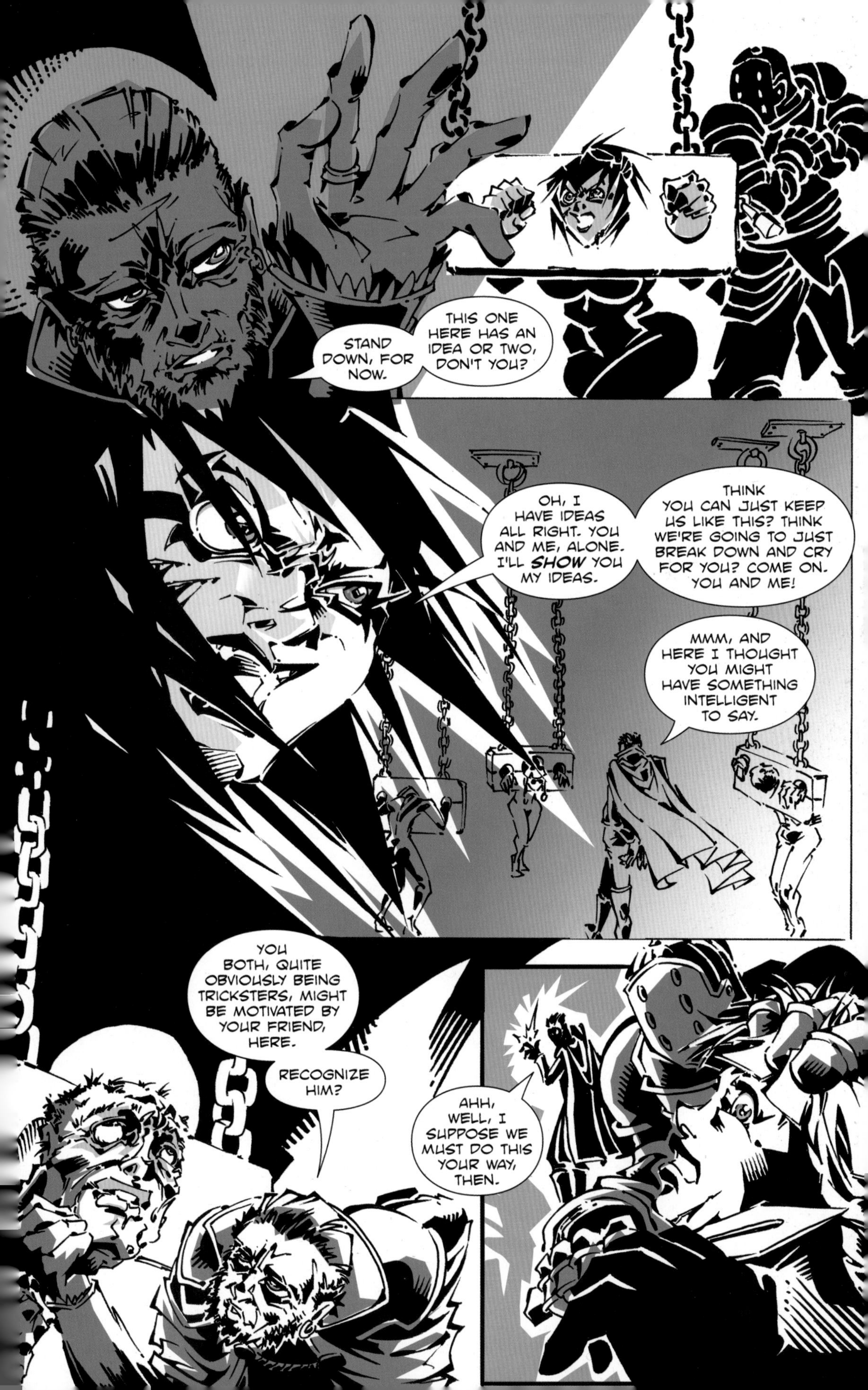
STAND DOWN, FOR NOW.
THIS ONE HERE HAS AN IDEA OR TWO, DON'T YOU?
OH, I HAVE IDEAS ALL RIGHT. YOU AND ME, ALONE. I'LL **SHOW** YOU MY IDEAS.
THINK YOU CAN JUST KEEP US LIKE THIS? THINK WE'RE GOING TO JUST BREAK DOWN AND CRY FOR YOU? COME ON. YOU AND ME!
MMM, AND HERE I THOUGHT YOU MIGHT HAVE SOMETHING INTELLIGENT TO SAY.
YOU BOTH, QUITE OBVIOUSLY BEING TRICKSTERS, MIGHT BE MOTIVATED BY YOUR FRIEND, HERE.
RECOGNIZE HIM?
AHH, WELL, I SUPPOSE WE MUST DO THIS YOUR WAY, THEN.

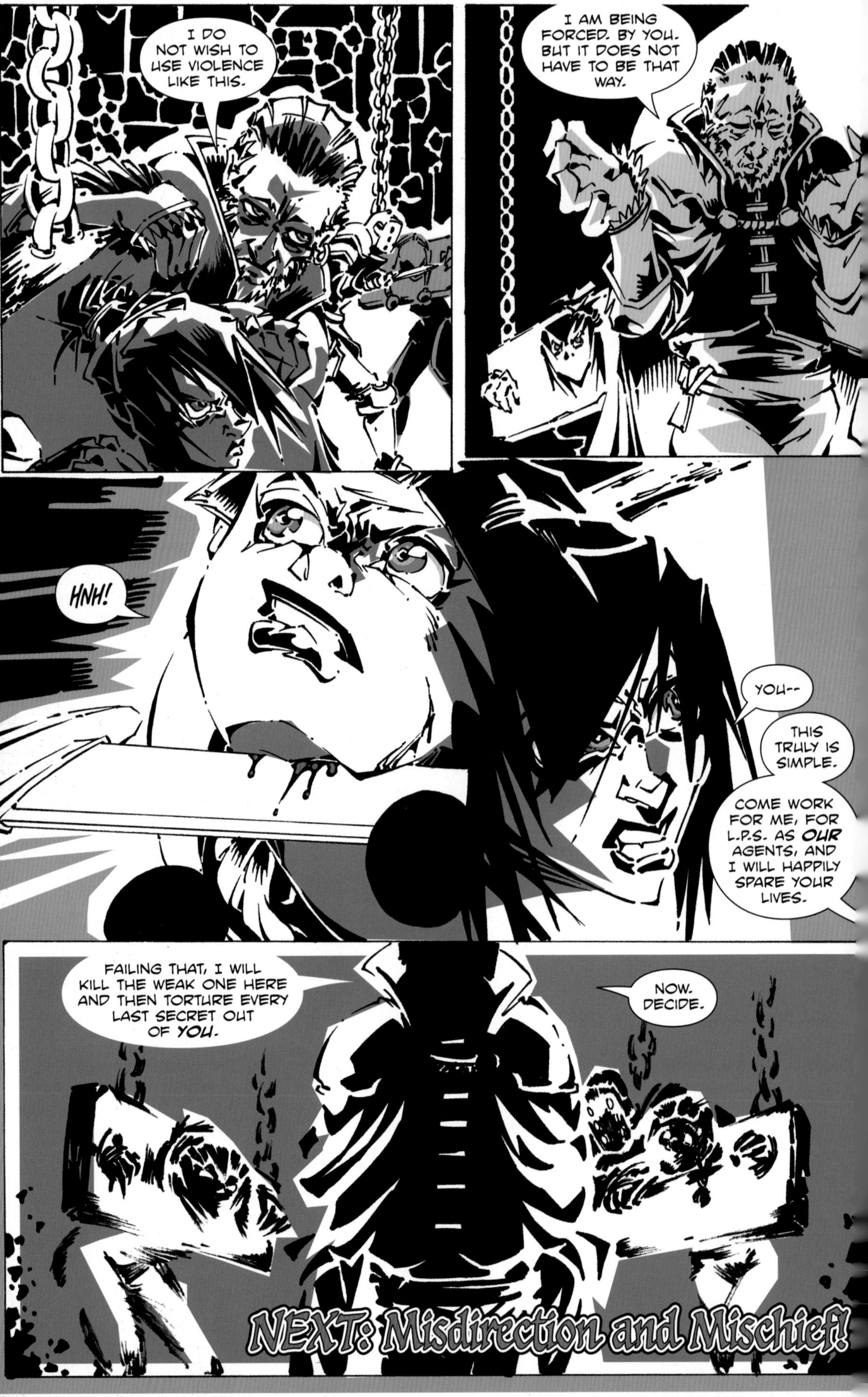
I DO NOT WISH TO USE VIOLENCE LIKE THIS.
I AM BEING FORCED. BY YOU. BUT IT DOES NOT HAVE TO BE THAT WAY.
HNH!
YOU--
THIS TRULY IS SIMPLE.
COME WORK FOR ME, FOR L.P.S. AS OUR AGENTS, AND I WILL HAPPILY SPARE YOUR LIVES.
FAILING THAT, I WILL KILL THE WEAK ONE HERE AND THEN TORTURE EVERY LAST SECRET OUT OF YOU.
NOW. DECIDE.
NEXT: Misdirection and Mischief!

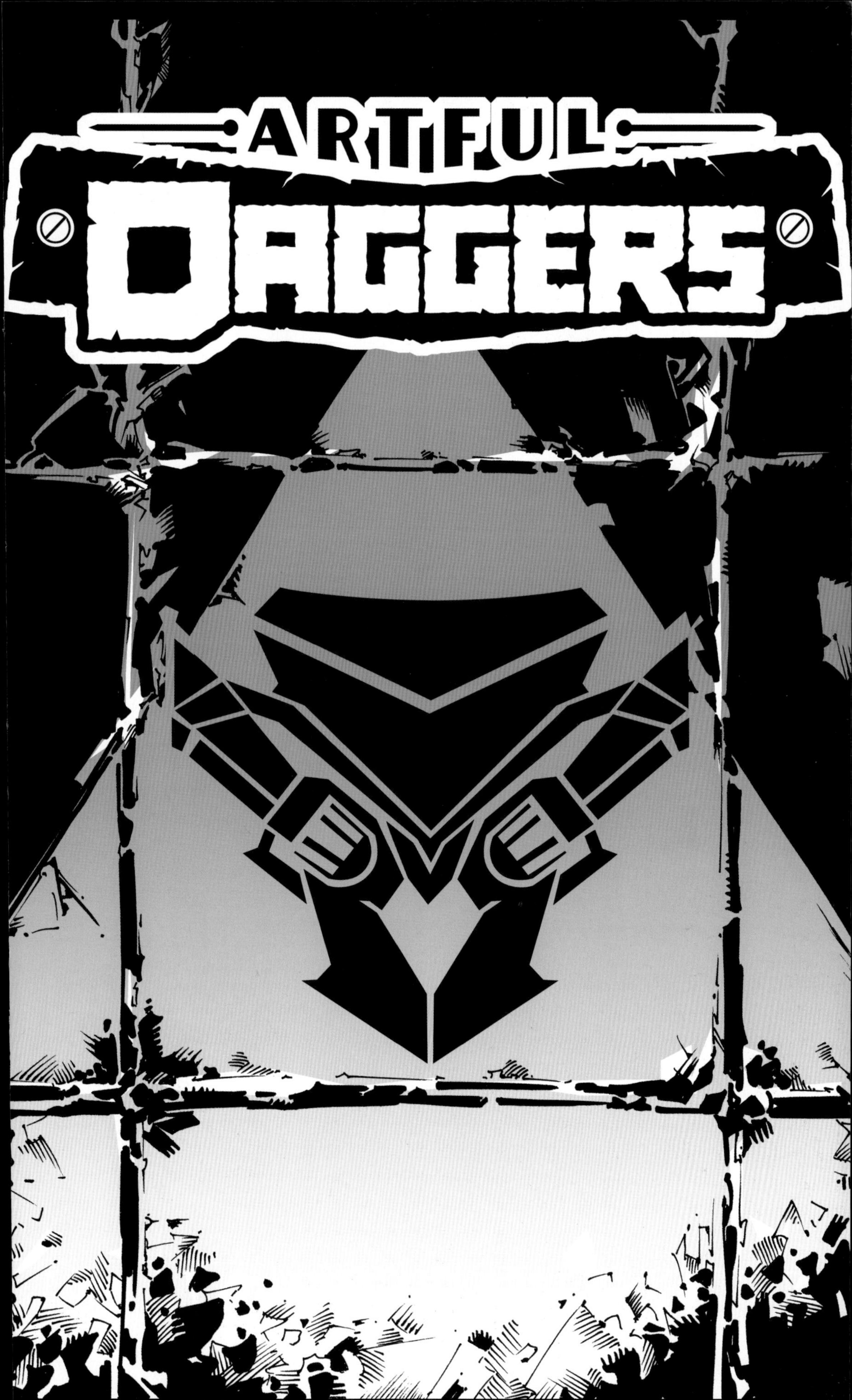
ARTFUL
DAGGERS

ARDEN

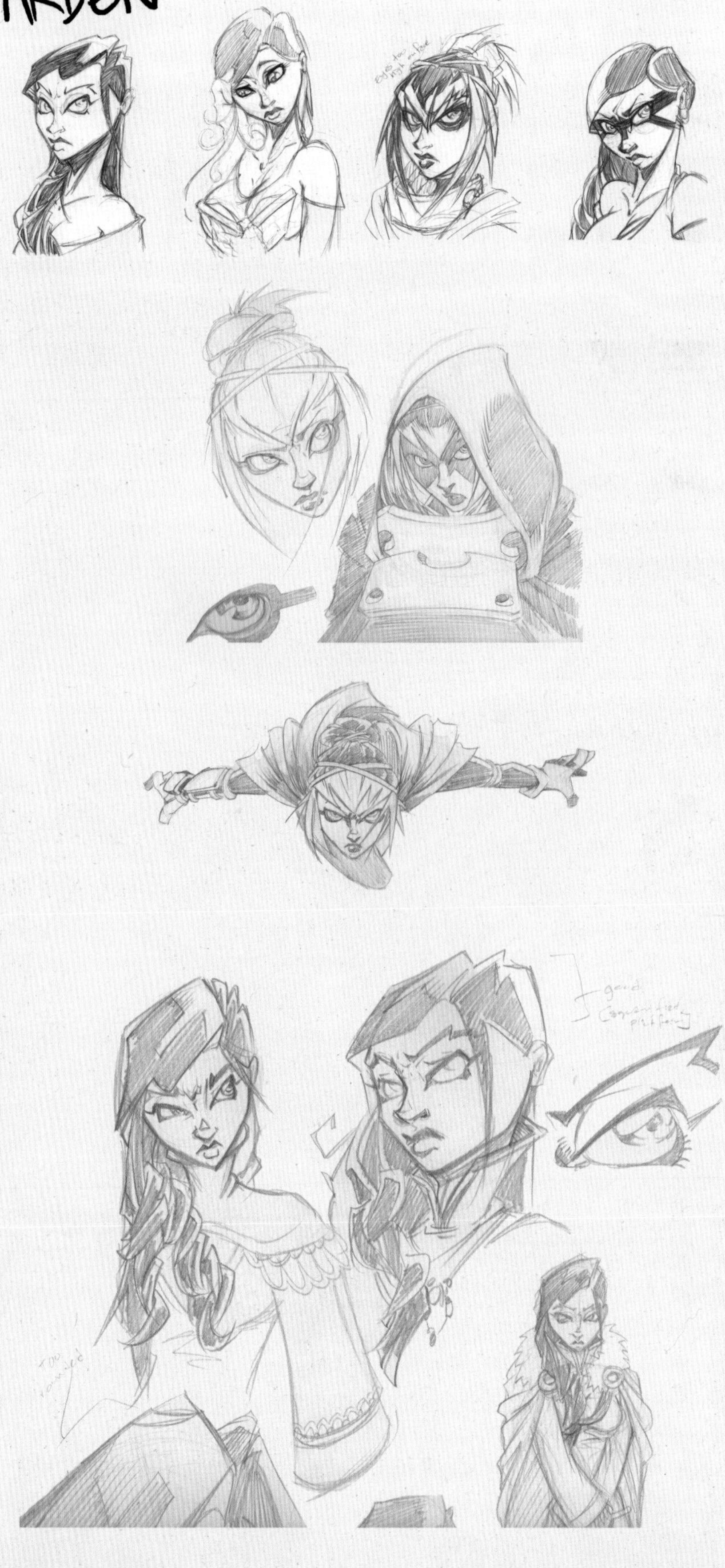
Eyes too high on face
good
[squarified flat faces]
Too rounded

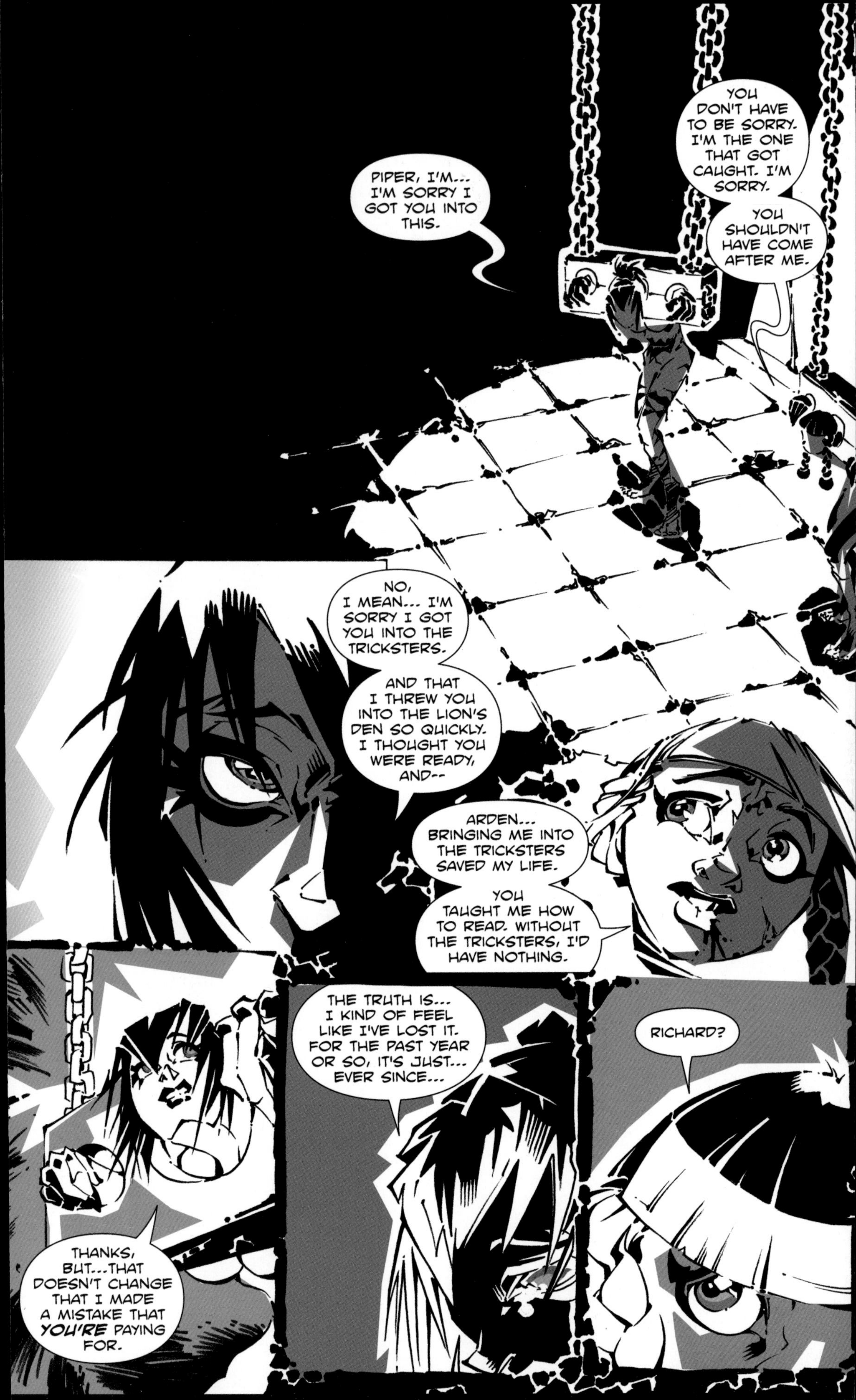
PIPER, I'M... I'M SORRY I GOT YOU INTO THIS.
YOU DON'T HAVE TO BE SORRY. I'M THE ONE THAT GOT CAUGHT. I'M SORRY.
YOU SHOULDN'T HAVE COME AFTER ME.
NO, I MEAN... I'M SORRY I GOT YOU INTO THE TRICKSTERS.
AND THAT I THREW YOU INTO THE LION'S DEN SO QUICKLY. I THOUGHT YOU WERE READY, AND--
ARDEN... BRINGING ME INTO THE TRICKSTERS SAVED MY LIFE.
YOU TAUGHT ME HOW TO READ. WITHOUT THE TRICKSTERS, I'D HAVE NOTHING.
THANKS, BUT...THAT DOESN'T CHANGE THAT I MADE A MISTAKE THAT ***YOU'RE*** PAYING FOR.
THE TRUTH IS... I KIND OF FEEL LIKE I'VE LOST IT. FOR THE PAST YEAR OR SO, IT'S JUST... EVER SINCE...
RICHARD?

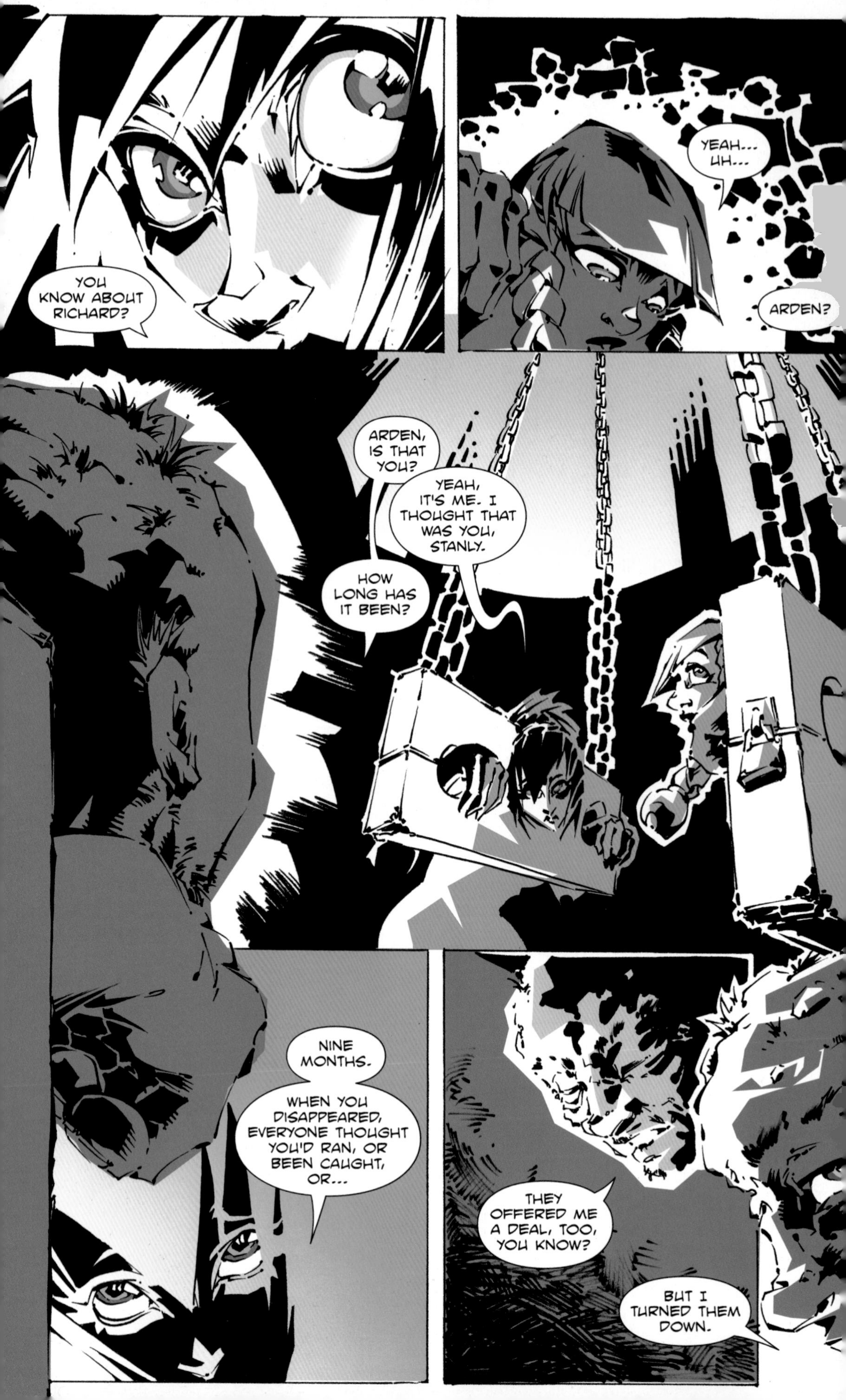
YOU KNOW ABOUT RICHARD?
YEAH... UH...
ARDEN?
ARDEN, IS THAT YOU?
YEAH, IT'S ME. I THOUGHT THAT WAS YOU, STANLY.
HOW LONG HAS IT BEEN?
NINE MONTHS.
WHEN YOU DISAPPEARED, EVERYONE THOUGHT YOU'D RAN, OR BEEN CAUGHT, OR...
THEY OFFERED ME A DEAL, TOO, YOU KNOW?
BUT I TURNED THEM DOWN.

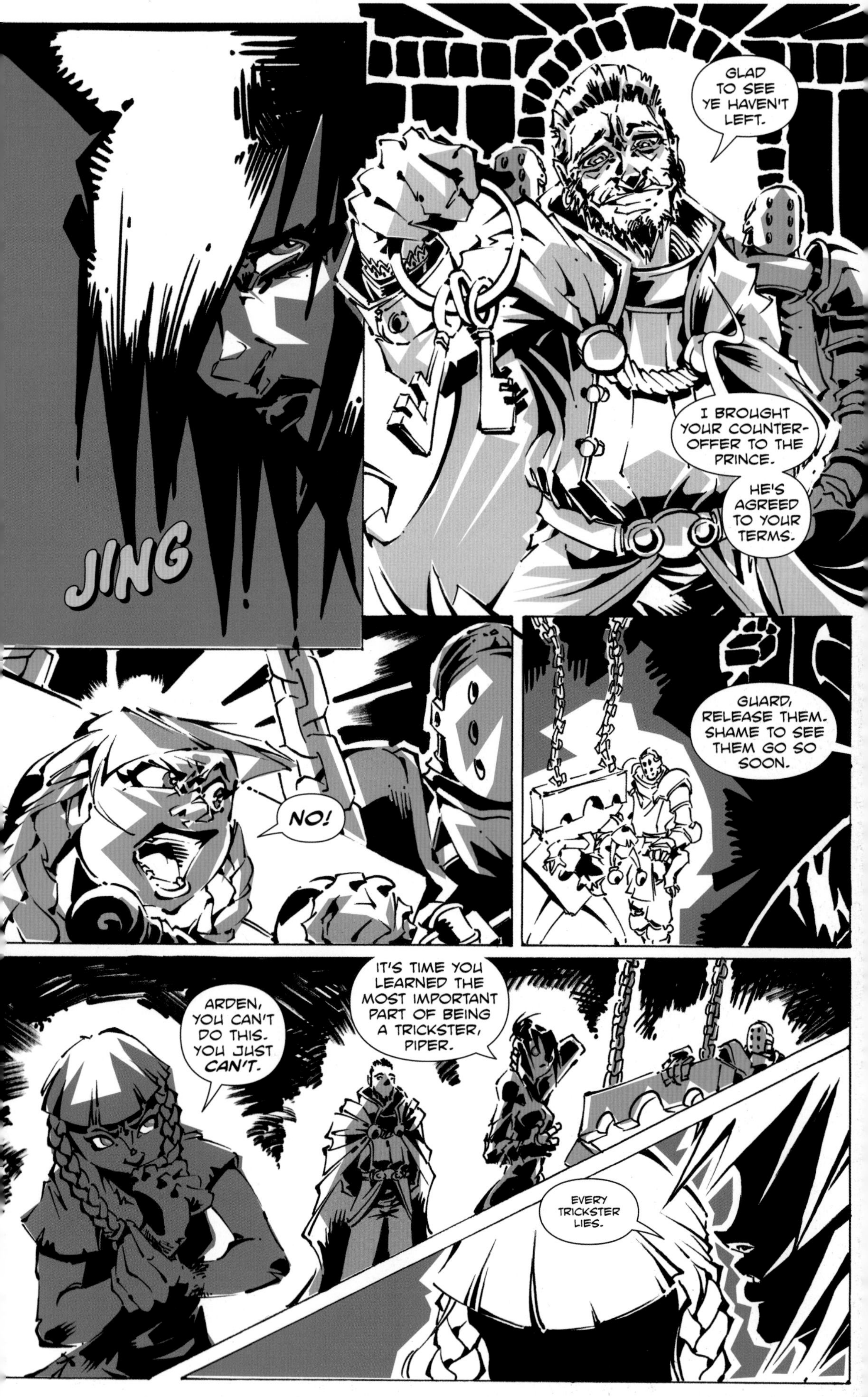
JING
GLAD TO SEE YE HAVEN'T LEFT.
I BROUGHT YOUR COUNTER-OFFER TO THE PRINCE.
HE'S AGREED TO YOUR TERMS.
NO!
GUARD, RELEASE THEM. SHAME TO SEE THEM GO SO SOON.
ARDEN, YOU CAN'T DO THIS. YOU JUST CAN'T.
IT'S TIME YOU LEARNED THE MOST IMPORTANT PART OF BEING A TRICKSTER, PIPER.
EVERY TRICKSTER LIES.

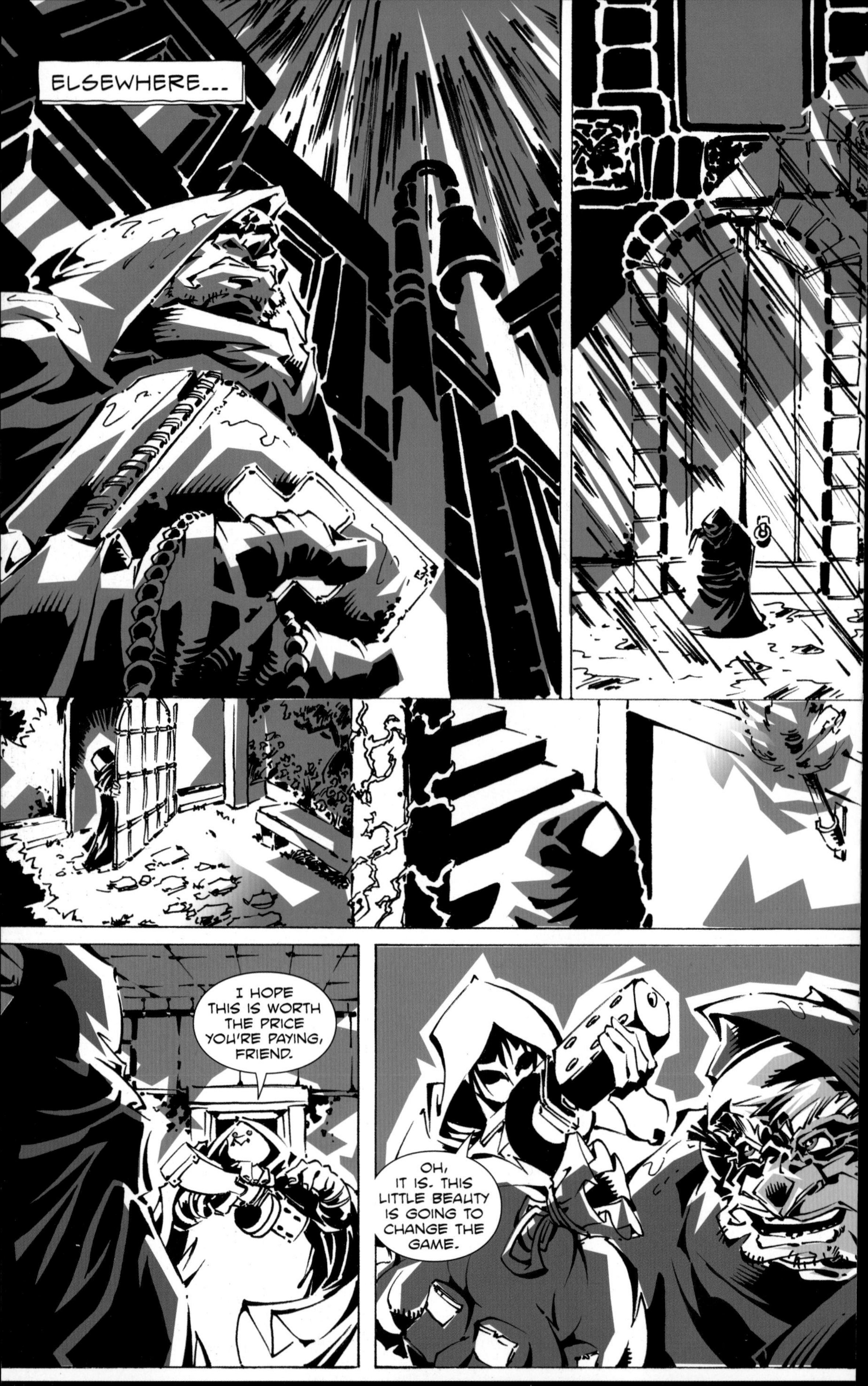
ELSEWHERE...
I HOPE THIS IS WORTH THE PRICE YOU'RE PAYING, FRIEND.
OH, IT IS. THIS LITTLE BEAUTY IS GOING TO CHANGE THE GAME.

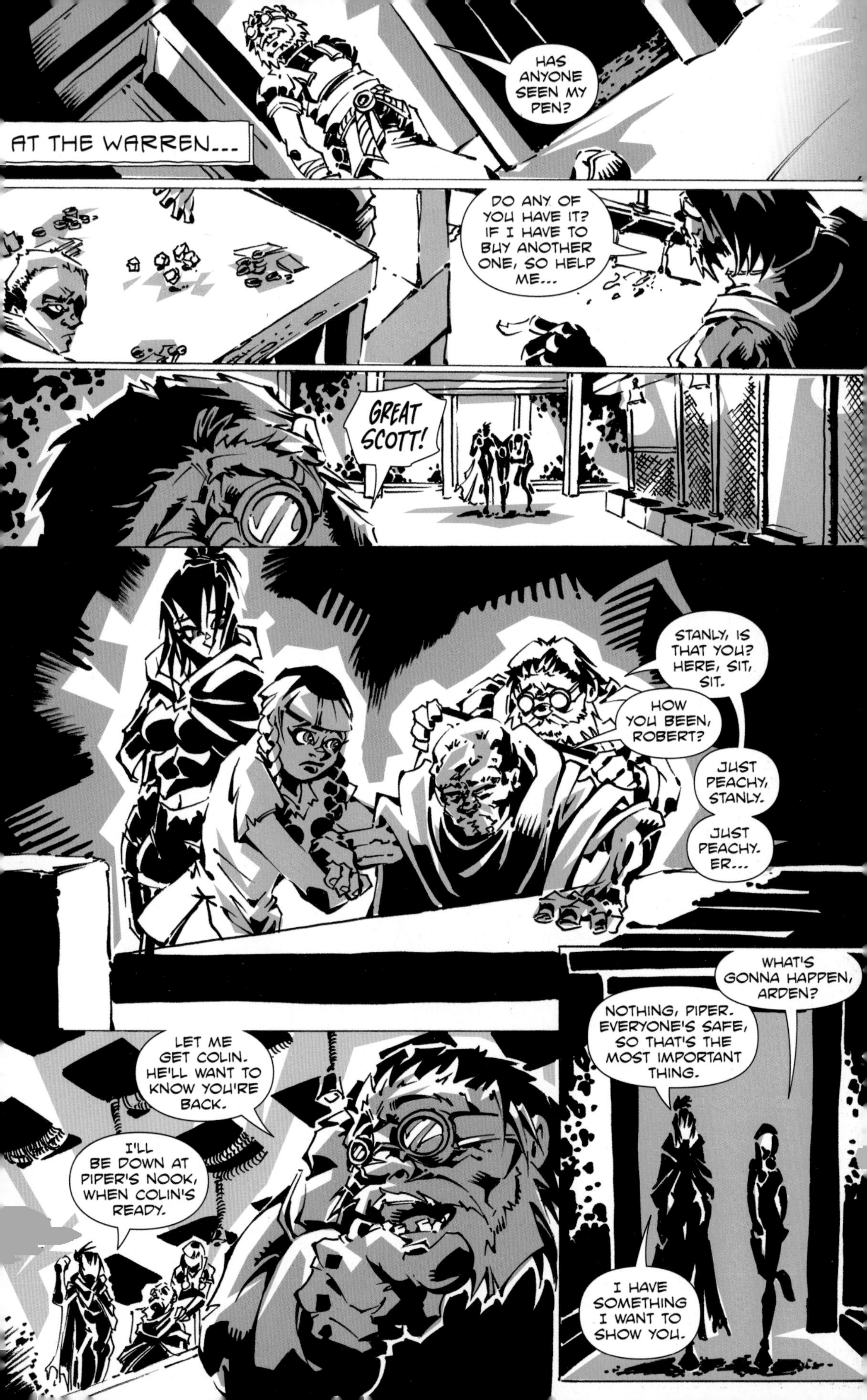

AT THE WARREN...
HAS ANYONE SEEN MY PEN?
DO ANY OF YOU HAVE IT? IF I HAVE TO BUY ANOTHER ONE, SO HELP ME...
GREAT SCOTT!
STANLY, IS THAT YOU? HERE, SIT, SIT.
HOW YOU BEEN, ROBERT?
JUST PEACHY, STANLY.
JUST PEACHY. ER...
LET ME GET COLIN. HE'LL WANT TO KNOW YOU'RE BACK.
I'LL BE DOWN AT PIPER'S NOOK, WHEN COLIN'S READY.
WHAT'S GONNA HAPPEN, ARDEN?
NOTHING, PIPER. EVERYONE'S SAFE, SO THAT'S THE MOST IMPORTANT THING.
I HAVE SOMETHING I WANT TO SHOW YOU.

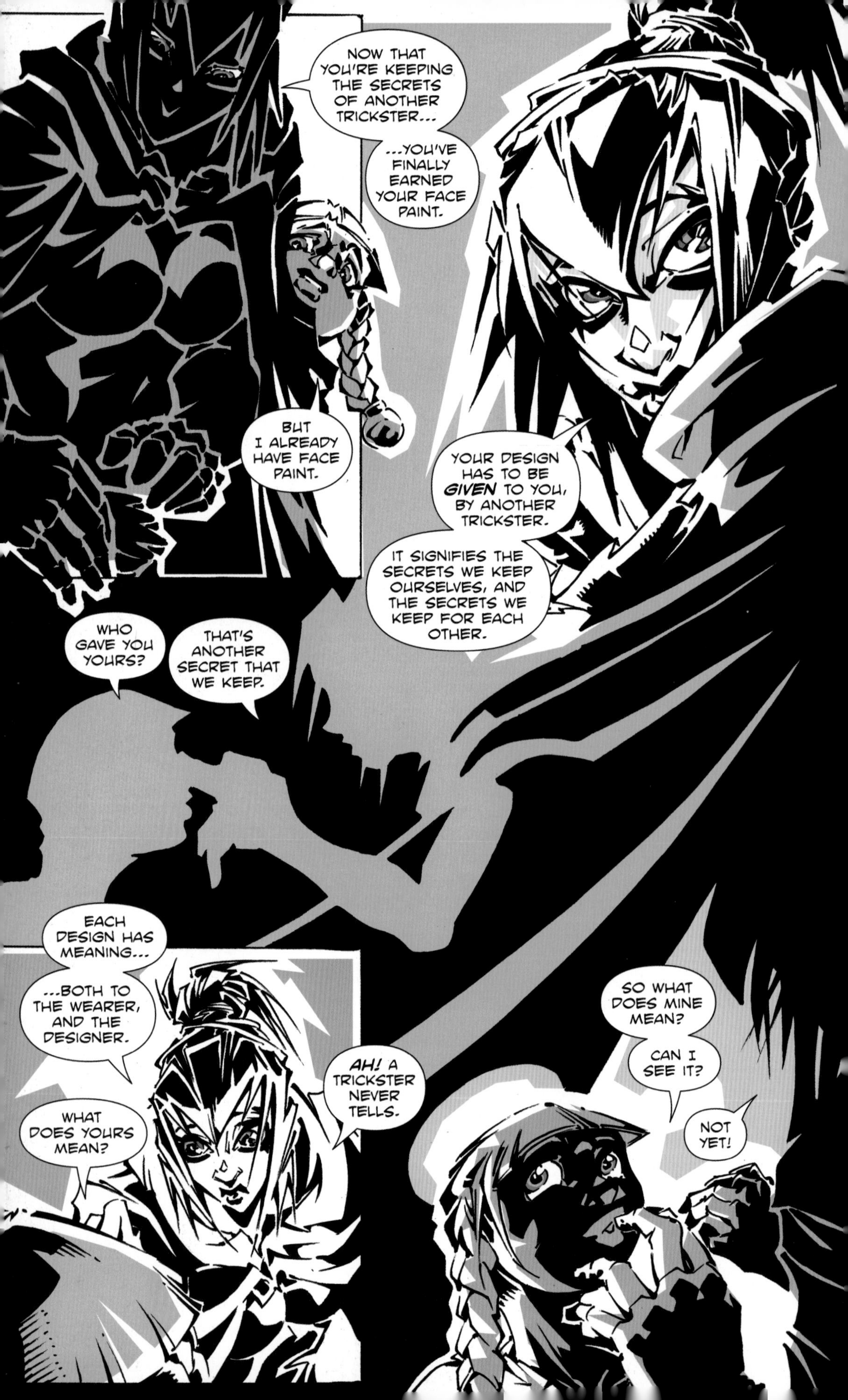

NOW THAT YOU'RE KEEPING THE SECRETS OF ANOTHER TRICKSTER...
...YOU'VE FINALLY EARNED YOUR FACE PAINT.
BUT I ALREADY HAVE FACE PAINT.
YOUR DESIGN HAS TO BE *GIVEN* TO YOU, BY ANOTHER TRICKSTER.
IT SIGNIFIES THE SECRETS WE KEEP OURSELVES, AND THE SECRETS WE KEEP FOR EACH OTHER.
WHO GAVE YOU YOURS?
THAT'S ANOTHER SECRET THAT WE KEEP.
EACH DESIGN HAS MEANING...
...BOTH TO THE WEARER, AND THE DESIGNER.
WHAT DOES YOURS MEAN?
AH! A TRICKSTER NEVER TELLS.
SO WHAT DOES MINE MEAN?
CAN I SEE IT?
NOT YET!

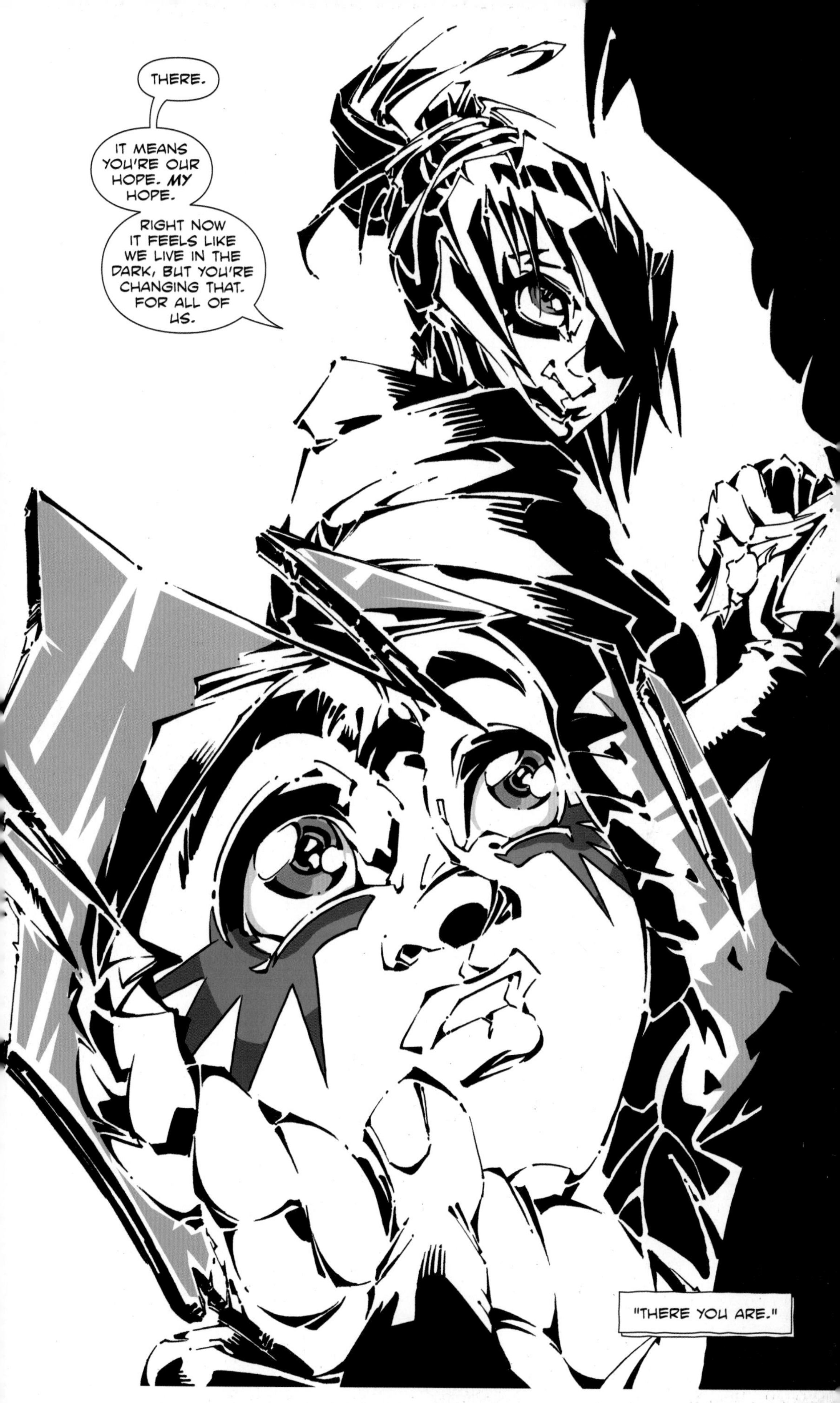
THERE.
IT MEANS YOU'RE OUR HOPE. MY HOPE.
RIGHT NOW IT FEELS LIKE WE LIVE IN THE DARK, BUT YOU'RE CHANGING THAT. FOR ALL OF US.
"THERE YOU ARE."

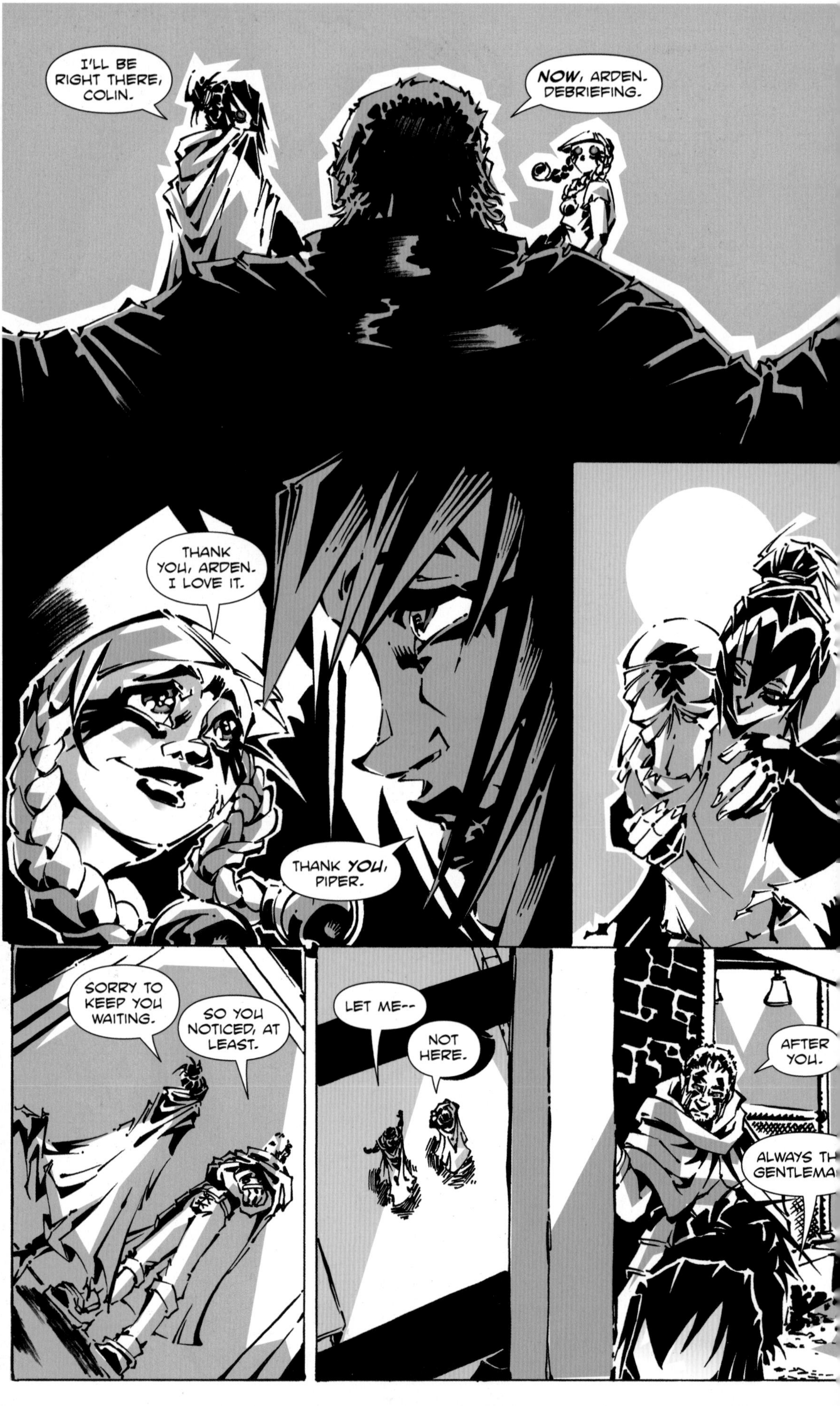
I'LL BE RIGHT THERE, COLIN.
NOW, ARDEN. DEBRIEFING.
THANK YOU, ARDEN. I LOVE IT.
THANK YOU, PIPER.
SORRY TO KEEP YOU WAITING.
SO YOU NOTICED, AT LEAST.
LET ME--
NOT HERE.
AFTER YOU.
ALWAYS TH
GENTLEMA

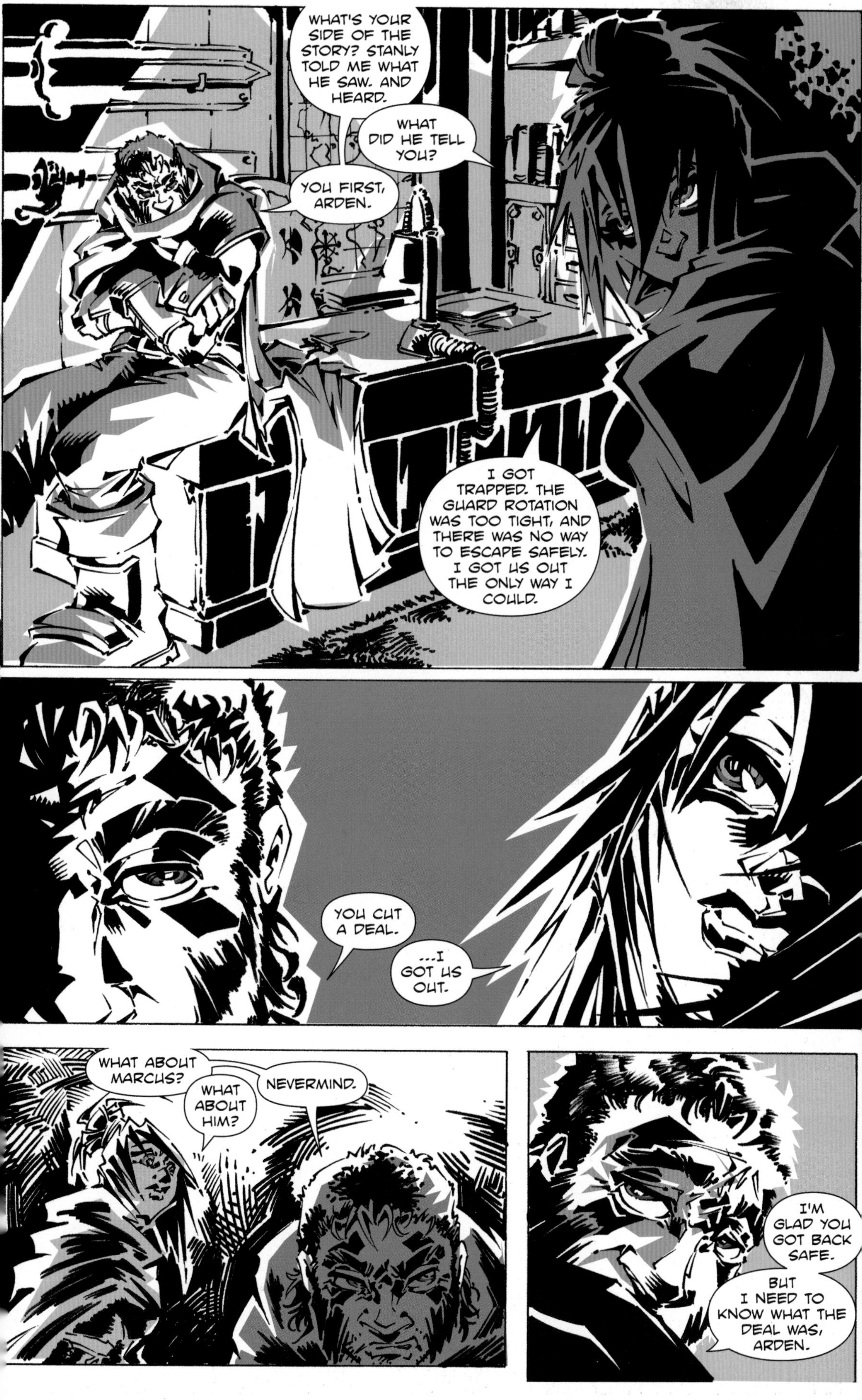
WHAT'S YOUR SIDE OF THE STORY? STANLY TOLD ME WHAT HE SAW. AND HEARD.
WHAT DID HE TELL YOU?
YOU FIRST, ARDEN.
I GOT TRAPPED. THE GUARD ROTATION WAS TOO TIGHT, AND THERE WAS NO WAY TO ESCAPE SAFELY. I GOT US OUT THE ONLY WAY I COULD.
YOU CUT A DEAL.
...I GOT US OUT.
WHAT ABOUT MARCUS?
WHAT ABOUT HIM?
NEVERMIND.
I'M GLAD YOU GOT BACK SAFE.
BUT I NEED TO KNOW WHAT THE DEAL WAS, ARDEN.

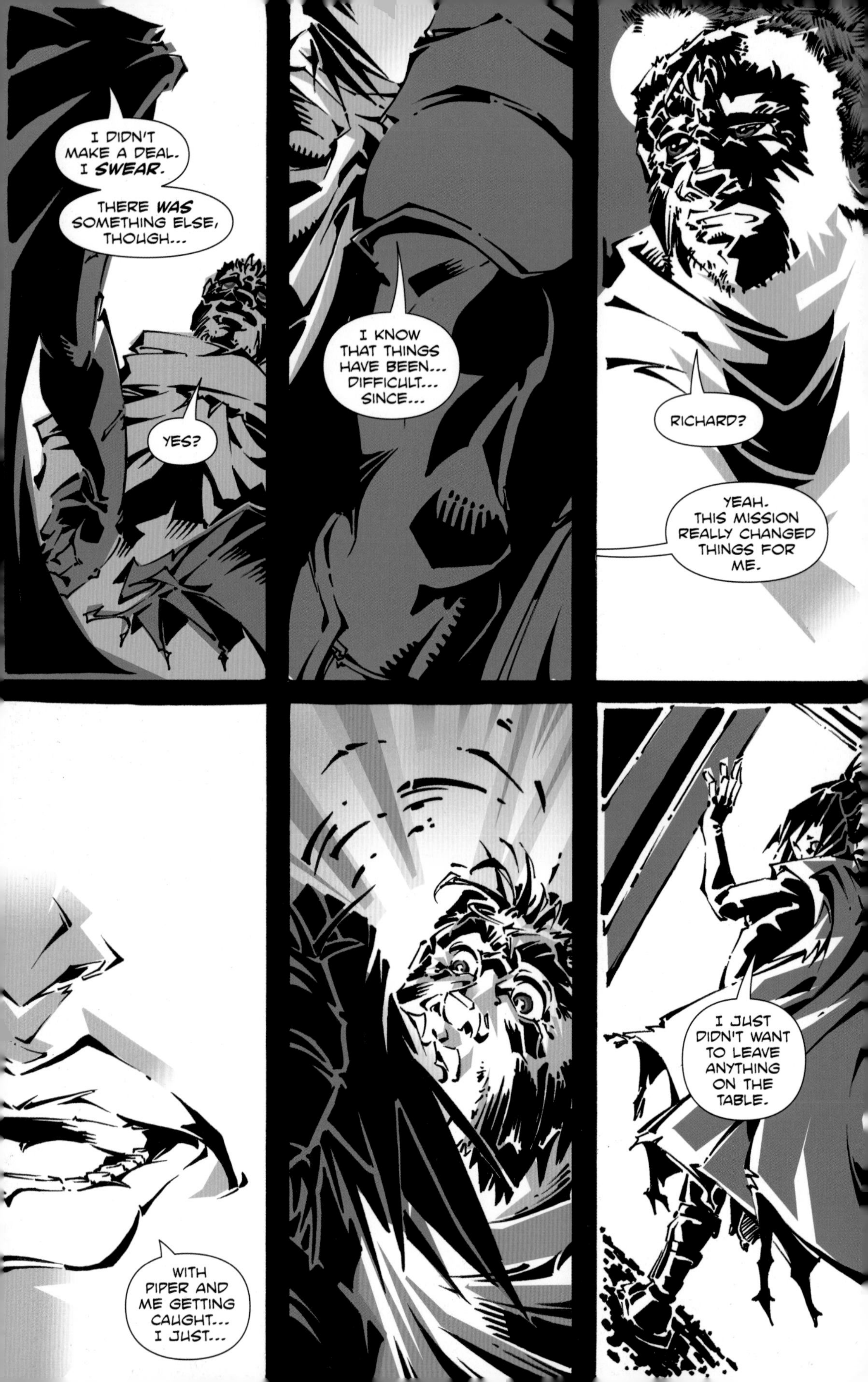
I DIDN'T MAKE A DEAL. I SWEAR.
THERE WAS SOMETHING ELSE, THOUGH...
YES?
I KNOW THAT THINGS HAVE BEEN... DIFFICULT... SINCE...
RICHARD?
YEAH. THIS MISSION REALLY CHANGED THINGS FOR ME.
WITH PIPER AND ME GETTING CAUGHT... I JUST...
I JUST DIDN'T WANT TO LEAVE ANYTHING ON THE TABLE.

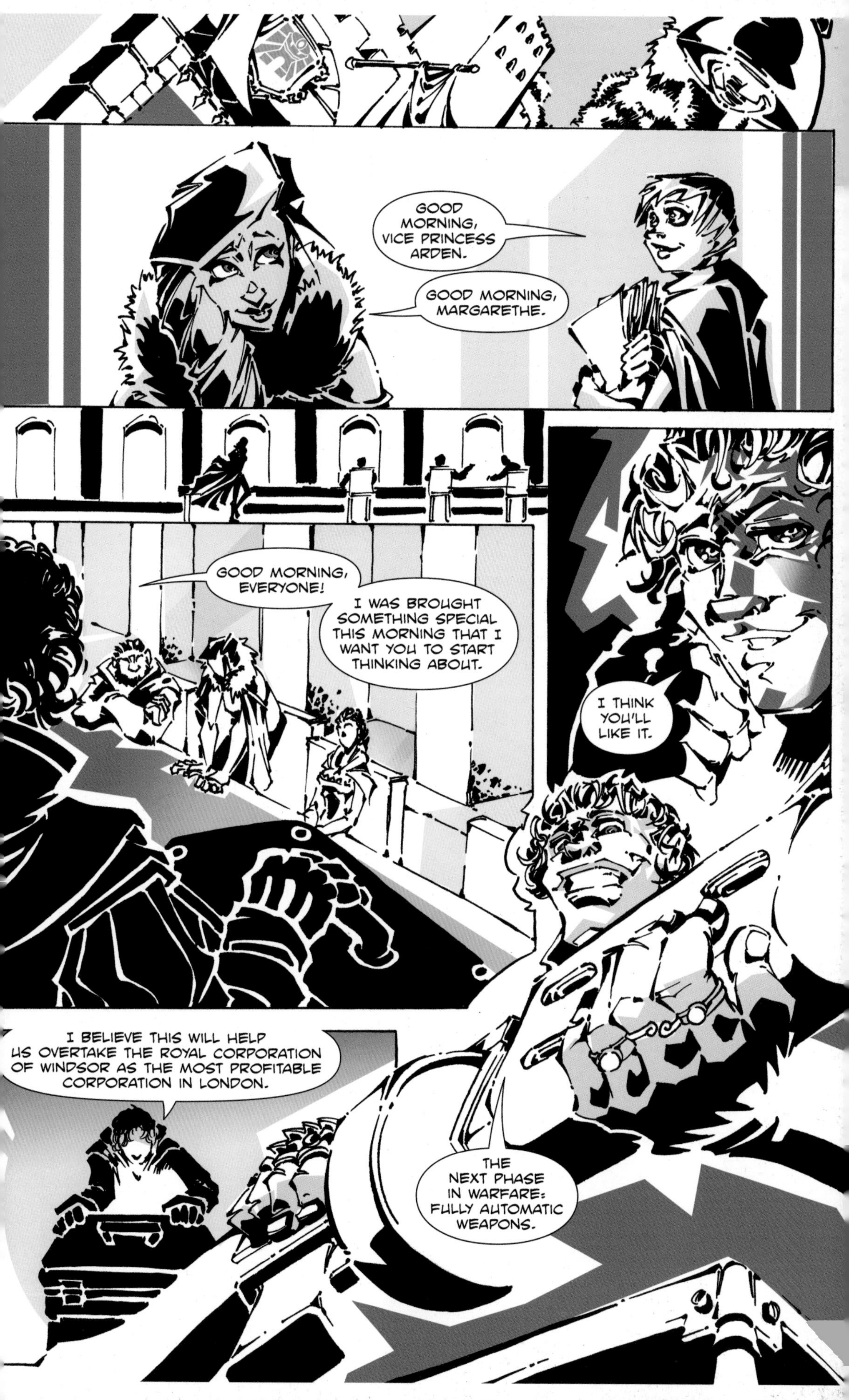
GOOD MORNING, VICE PRINCESS ARDEN.
GOOD MORNING, MARGARETHE.
GOOD MORNING, EVERYONE!
I WAS BROUGHT SOMETHING SPECIAL THIS MORNING THAT I WANT YOU TO START THINKING ABOUT.
I THINK YOU'LL LIKE IT.
I BELIEVE THIS WILL HELP US OVERTAKE THE ROYAL CORPORATION OF WINDSOR AS THE MOST PROFITABLE CORPORATION IN LONDON.
THE NEXT PHASE IN WARFARE: FULLY AUTOMATIC WEAPONS.

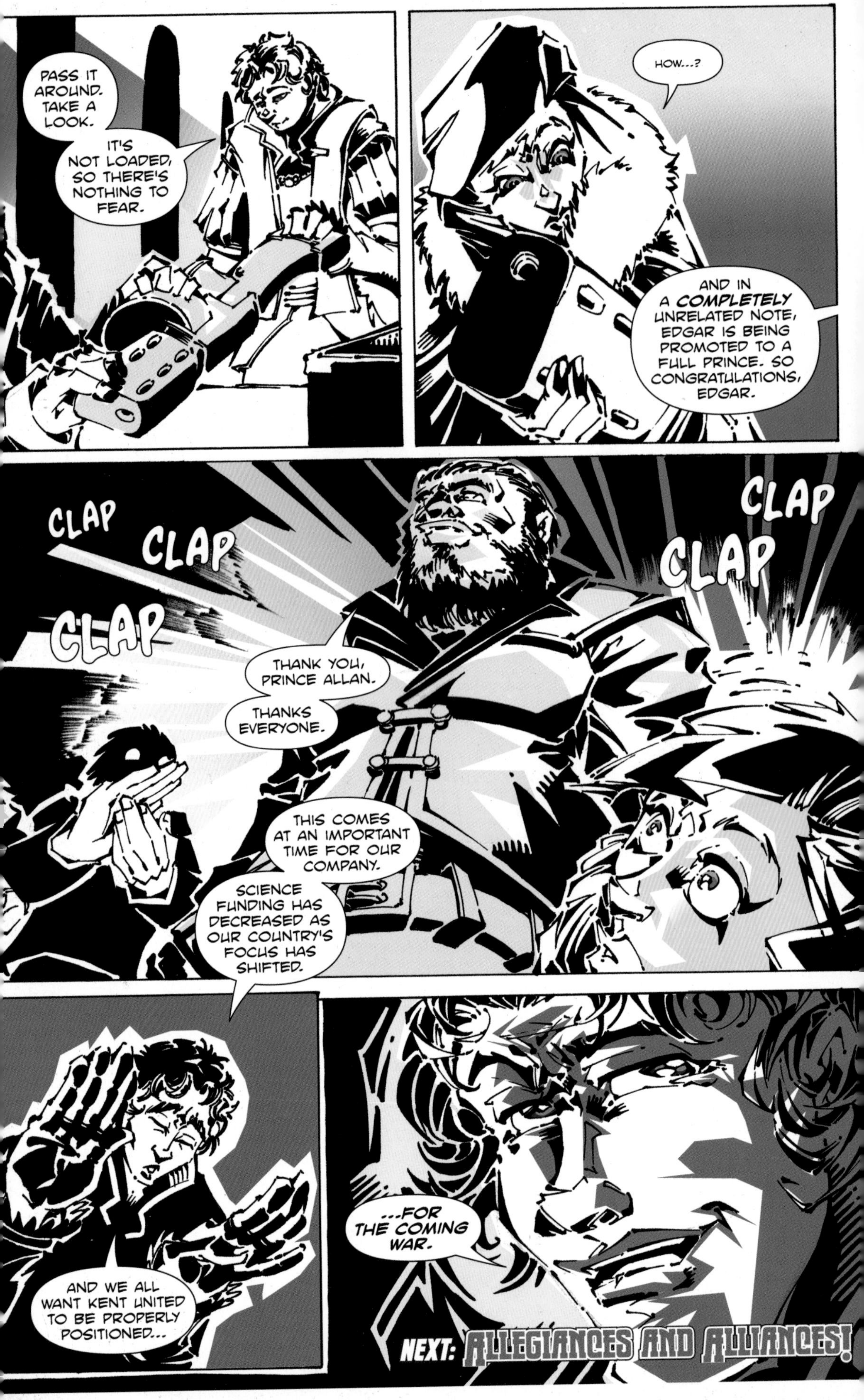
PASS IT AROUND. TAKE A LOOK.
IT'S NOT LOADED, SO THERE'S NOTHING TO FEAR.
HOW...?
AND IN A COMPLETELY UNRELATED NOTE, EDGAR IS BEING PROMOTED TO A FULL PRINCE. SO CONGRATULATIONS, EDGAR.
CLAP
CLAP
CLAP
CLAP
CLAP
THANK YOU, PRINCE ALLAN.
THANKS EVERYONE.
THIS COMES AT AN IMPORTANT TIME FOR OUR COMPANY.
SCIENCE FUNDING HAS DECREASED AS OUR COUNTRY'S FOCUS HAS SHIFTED.
AND WE ALL WANT KENT UNITED TO BE PROPERLY POSITIONED...
...FOR THE COMING WAR.
NEXT: ALLEGIANCES AND ALLIANCES!

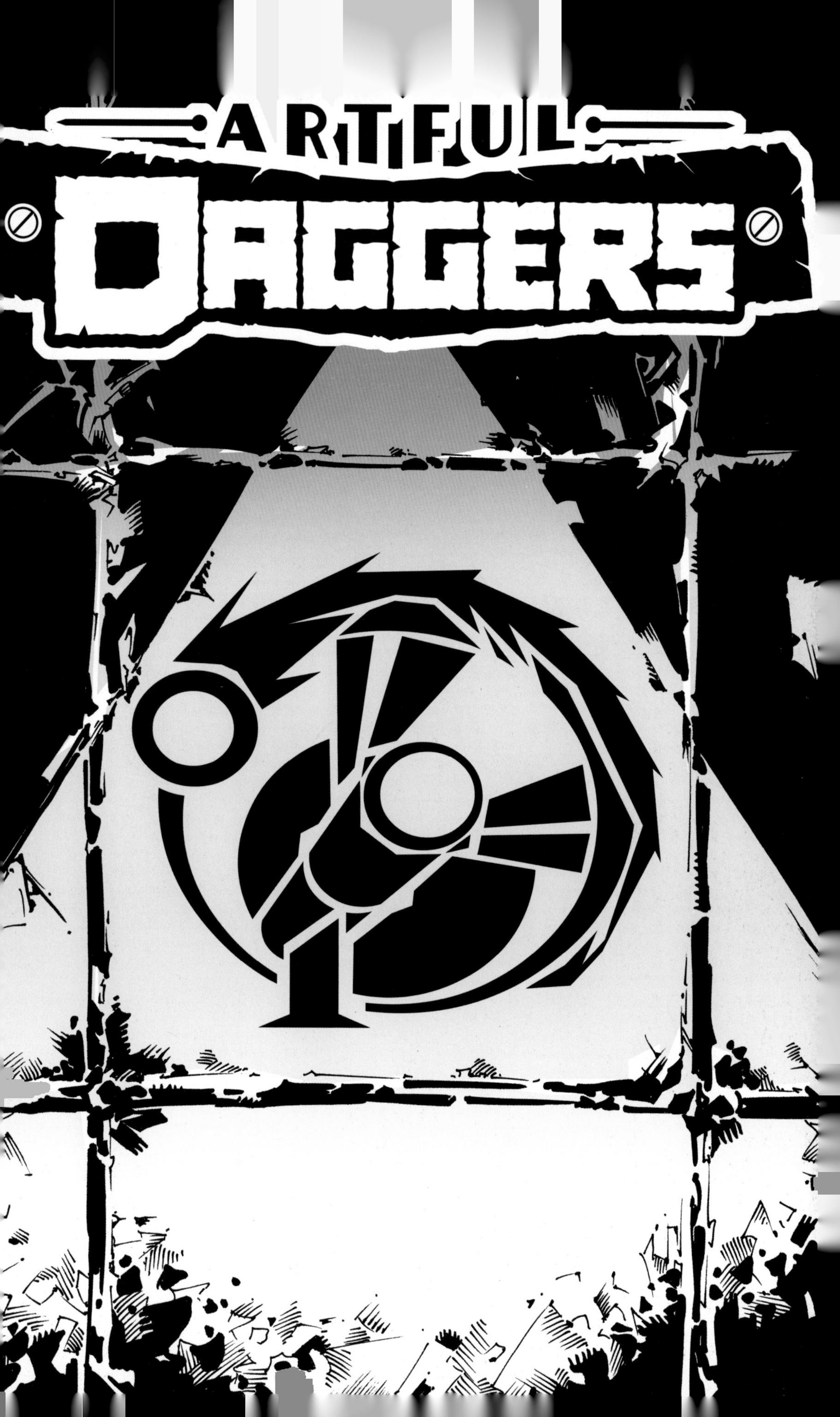
ARTFUL
DAGGERS

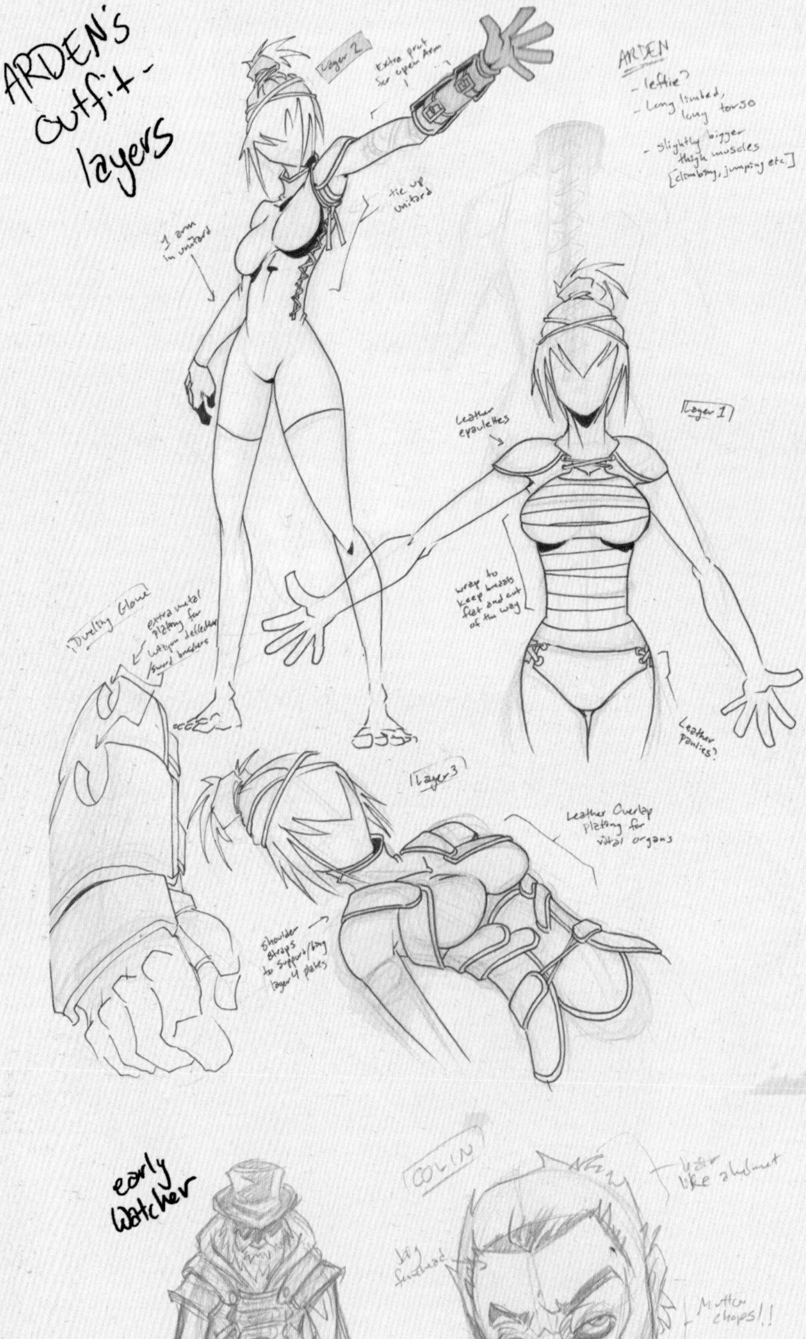

ARDEN's outfit layers
Layer 2
ARDEN
- leftie?
- Long limbed, long torso
- slightly bigger thigh muscles [climbing, jumping etc.]
tie up unitard
1 arm in unitard
Leather epaulettes
Layer 1
wrap to keep breasts flat and out of the way
Dueling Glove
Leather panties?
Layer 3
Leather Overlap plating for vital organs

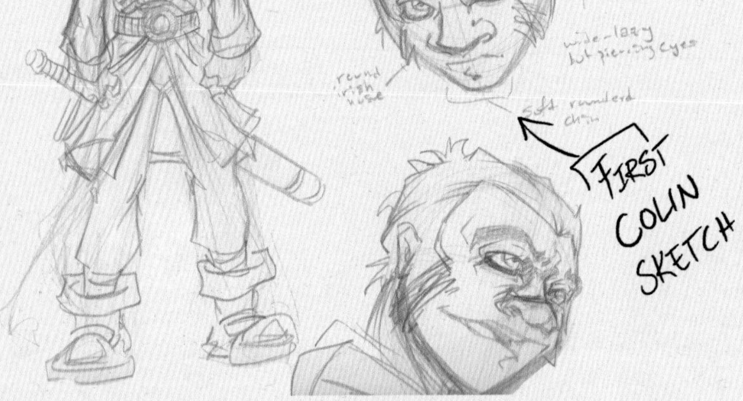

early Watcher
COLIN
big forehead
Mutton chops!!
wide-lazy but piercing eyes
round irish nose
soft rounded chin
FIRST COLIN SKETCH

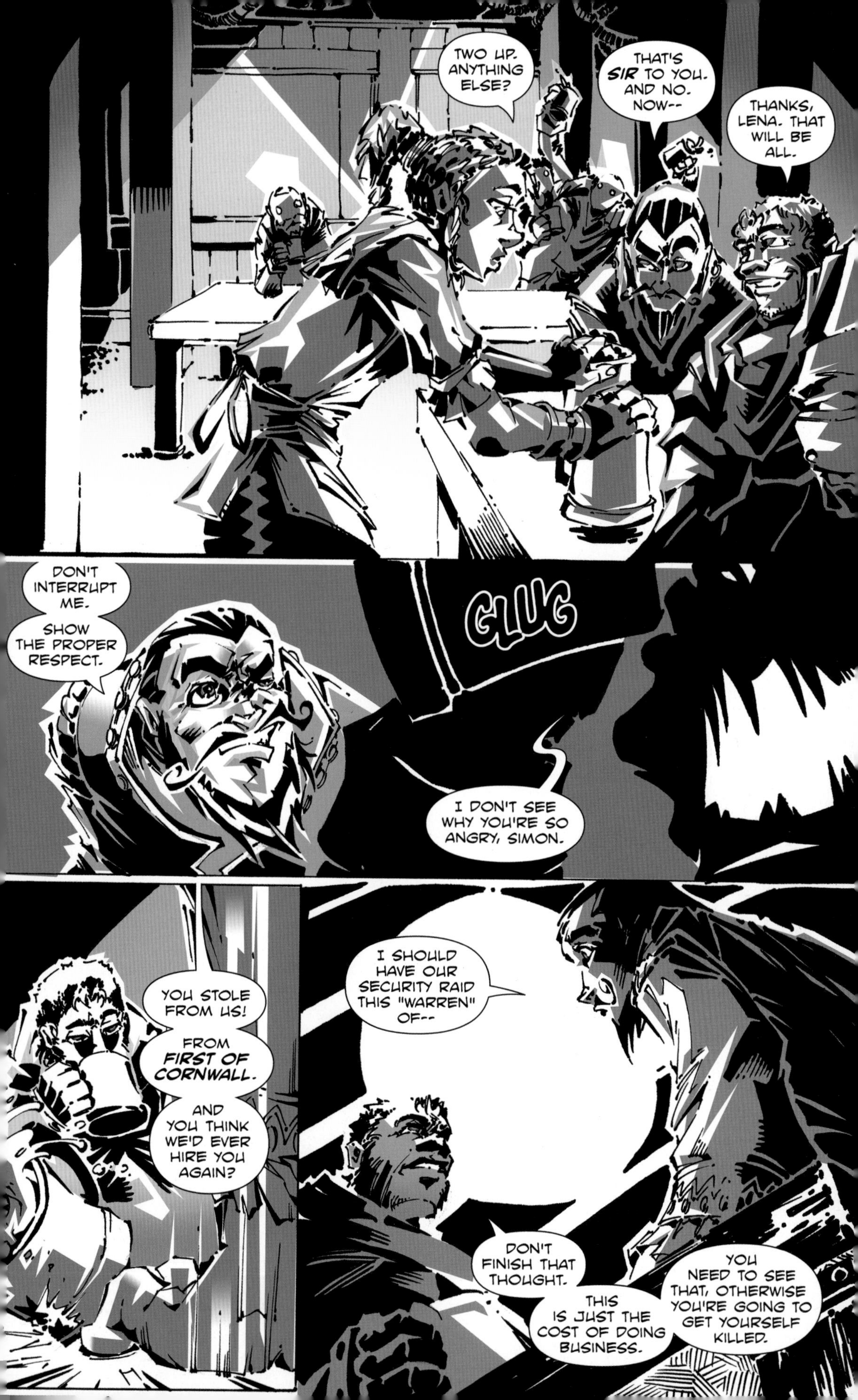
TWO UP. ANYTHING ELSE?
THAT'S SIR TO YOU. AND NO. NOW--
THANKS, LENA. THAT WILL BE ALL.
DON'T INTERRUPT ME.
SHOW THE PROPER RESPECT.
GLUG
I DON'T SEE WHY YOU'RE SO ANGRY, SIMON.
YOU STOLE FROM US!
FROM FIRST OF CORNWALL.
AND YOU THINK WE'D EVER HIRE YOU AGAIN?
I SHOULD HAVE OUR SECURITY RAID THIS "WARREN" OF--
DON'T FINISH THAT THOUGHT.
THIS IS JUST THE COST OF DOING BUSINESS.
YOU NEED TO SEE THAT, OTHERWISE YOU'RE GOING TO GET YOURSELF KILLED.

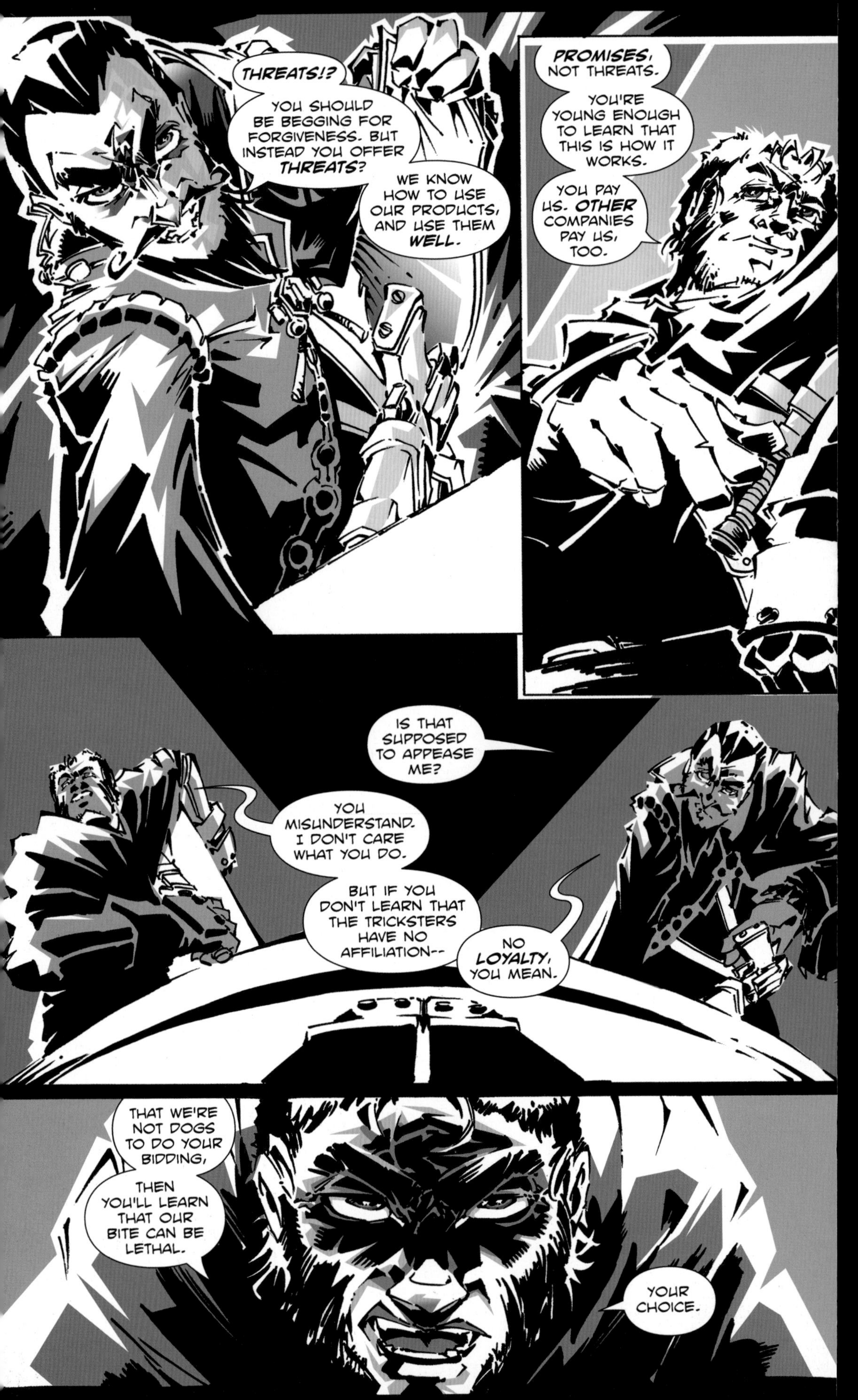
THREATS!?
YOU SHOULD BE BEGGING FOR FORGIVENESS. BUT INSTEAD YOU OFFER THREATS?
WE KNOW HOW TO USE OUR PRODUCTS, AND USE THEM WELL.
PROMISES, NOT THREATS.
YOU'RE YOUNG ENOUGH TO LEARN THAT THIS IS HOW IT WORKS.
YOU PAY US. OTHER COMPANIES PAY US, TOO.
IS THAT SUPPOSED TO APPEASE ME?
YOU MISUNDERSTAND. I DON'T CARE WHAT YOU DO.
BUT IF YOU DON'T LEARN THAT THE TRICKSTERS HAVE NO AFFILIATION--
NO LOYALTY, YOU MEAN.
THAT WE'RE NOT DOGS TO DO YOUR BIDDING,
THEN YOU'LL LEARN THAT OUR BITE CAN BE LETHAL.
YOUR CHOICE.

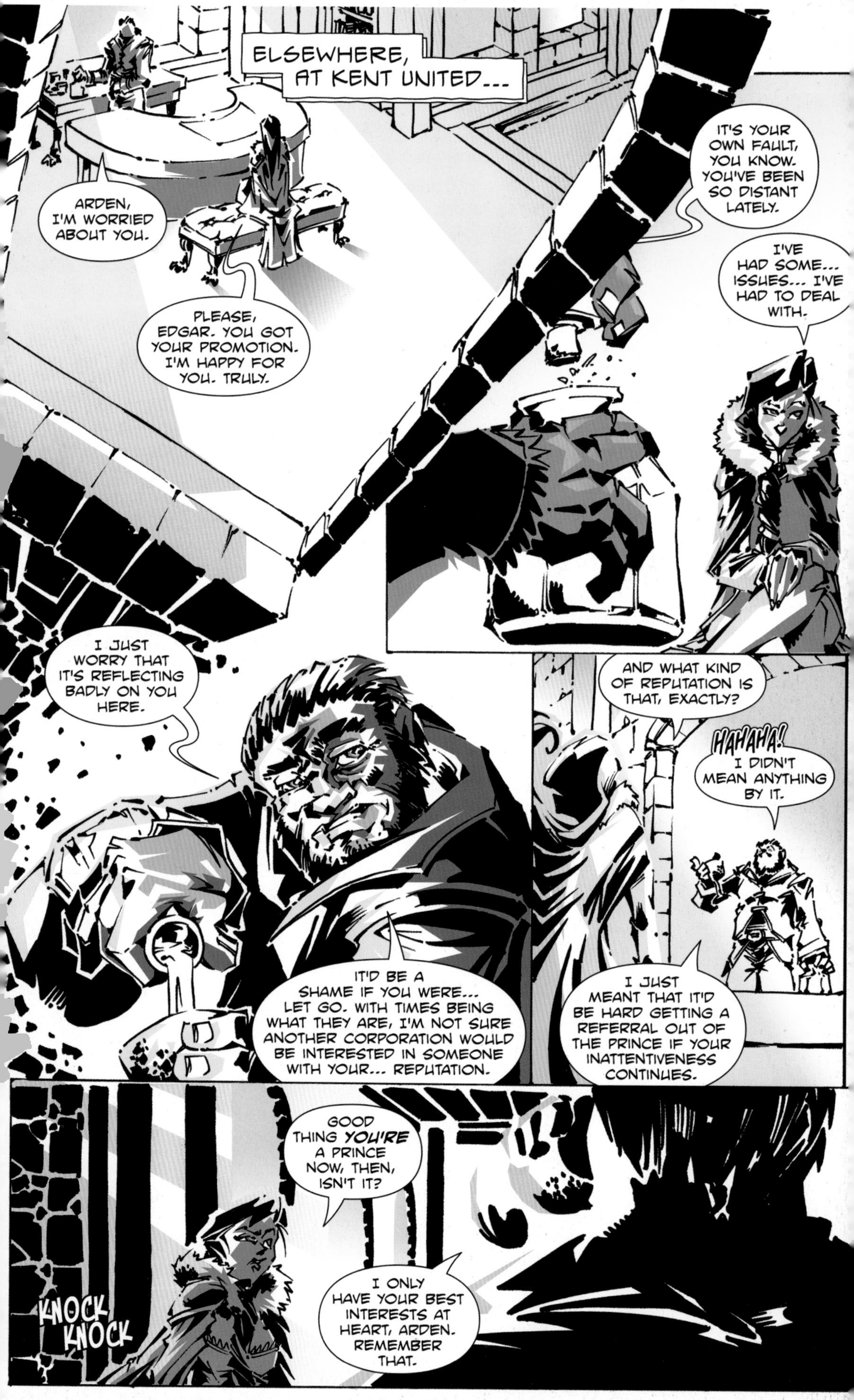
ELSEWHERE, AT KENT UNITED...
ARDEN, I'M WORRIED ABOUT YOU.
PLEASE, EDGAR. YOU GOT YOUR PROMOTION. I'M HAPPY FOR YOU. TRULY.
IT'S YOUR OWN FAULT, YOU KNOW. YOU'VE BEEN SO DISTANT LATELY.
I'VE HAD SOME... ISSUES... I'VE HAD TO DEAL WITH.
I JUST WORRY THAT IT'S REFLECTING BADLY ON YOU HERE.
IT'D BE A SHAME IF YOU WERE... LET GO. WITH TIMES BEING WHAT THEY ARE, I'M NOT SURE ANOTHER CORPORATION WOULD BE INTERESTED IN SOMEONE WITH YOUR... REPUTATION.
AND WHAT KIND OF REPUTATION IS THAT, EXACTLY?
HAHAHA!
I DIDN'T MEAN ANYTHING BY IT.
I JUST MEANT THAT IT'D BE HARD GETTING A REFERRAL OUT OF THE PRINCE IF YOUR INATTENTIVENESS CONTINUES.
GOOD THING YOU'RE A PRINCE NOW, THEN, ISN'T IT?
I ONLY HAVE YOUR BEST INTERESTS AT HEART, ARDEN. REMEMBER THAT.
KNOCK KNOCK

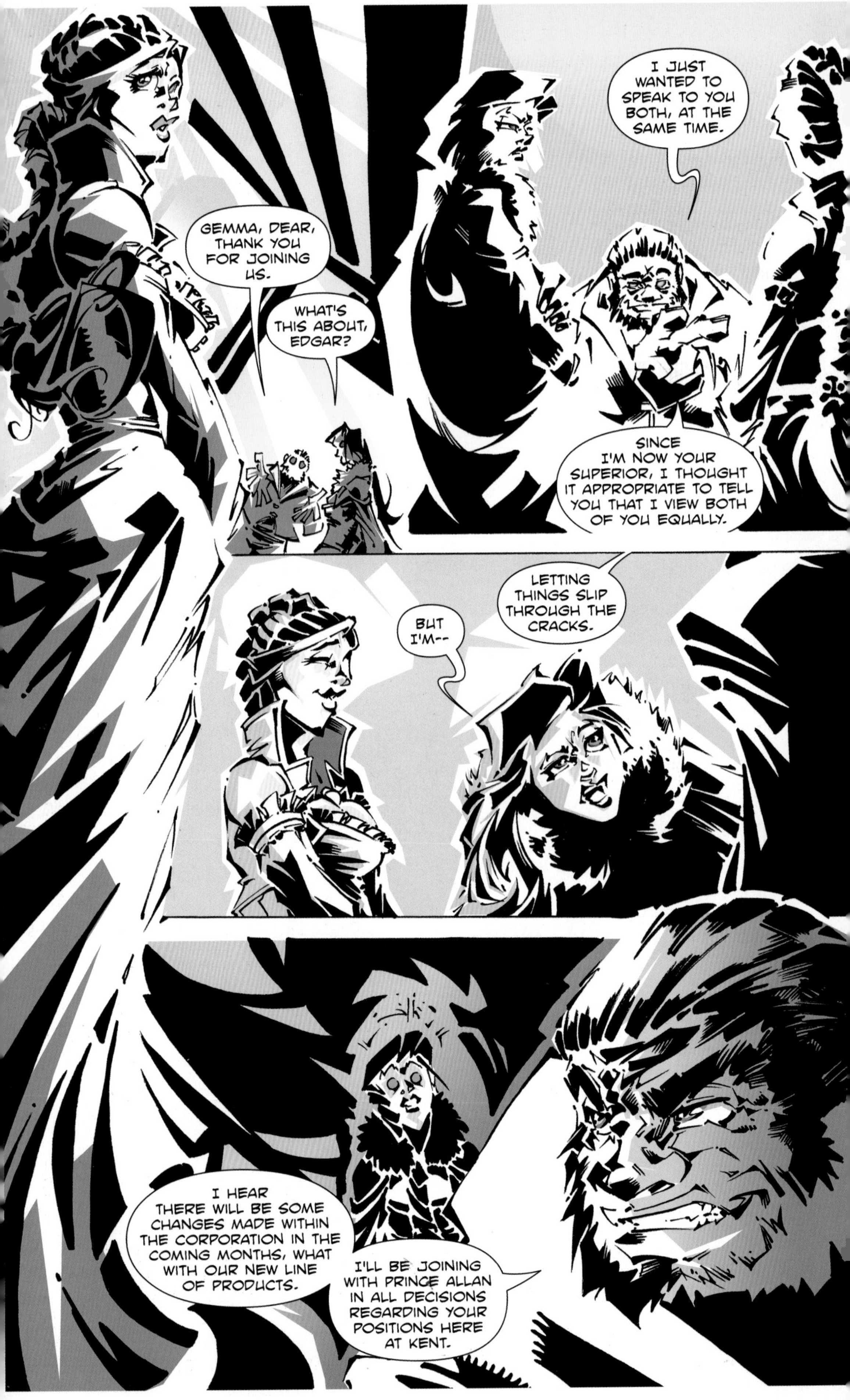
GEMMA, DEAR, THANK YOU FOR JOINING US.
WHAT'S THIS ABOUT, EDGAR?
I JUST WANTED TO SPEAK TO YOU BOTH, AT THE SAME TIME.
SINCE I'M NOW YOUR SUPERIOR, I THOUGHT IT APPROPRIATE TO TELL YOU THAT I VIEW BOTH OF YOU EQUALLY.
LETTING THINGS SLIP THROUGH THE CRACKS.
BUT I'M--
I HEAR THERE WILL BE SOME CHANGES MADE WITHIN THE CORPORATION IN THE COMING MONTHS, WHAT WITH OUR NEW LINE OF PRODUCTS.
I'LL BE JOINING WITH PRINCE ALLAN IN ALL DECISIONS REGARDING YOUR POSITIONS HERE AT KENT.

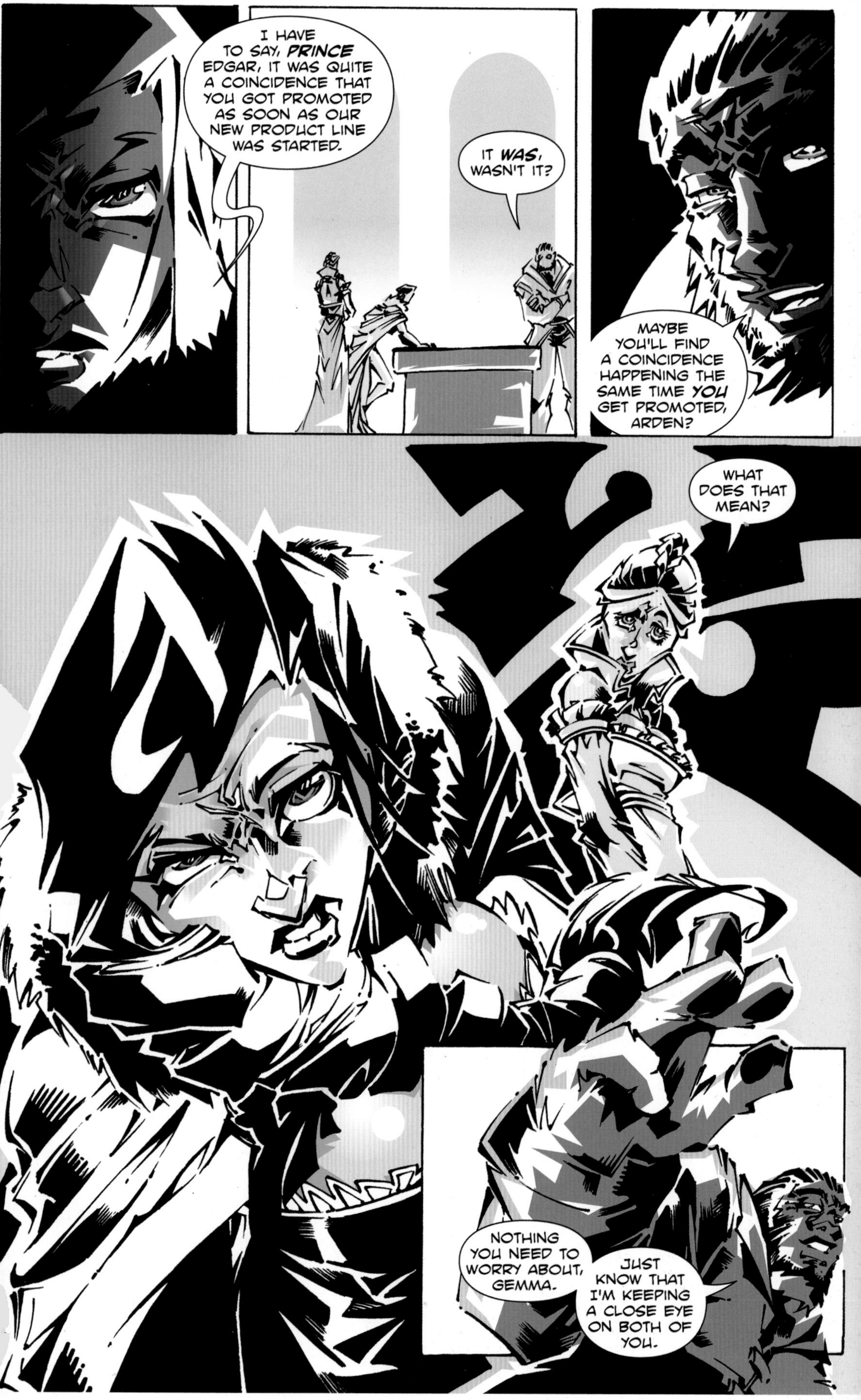
I HAVE TO SAY, PRINCE EDGAR, IT WAS QUITE A COINCIDENCE THAT YOU GOT PROMOTED AS SOON AS OUR NEW PRODUCT LINE WAS STARTED.
IT WAS, WASN'T IT?
MAYBE YOU'LL FIND A COINCIDENCE HAPPENING THE SAME TIME YOU GET PROMOTED, ARDEN?
WHAT DOES THAT MEAN?
NOTHING YOU NEED TO WORRY ABOUT, GEMMA.
JUST KNOW THAT I'M KEEPING A CLOSE EYE ON BOTH OF YOU.

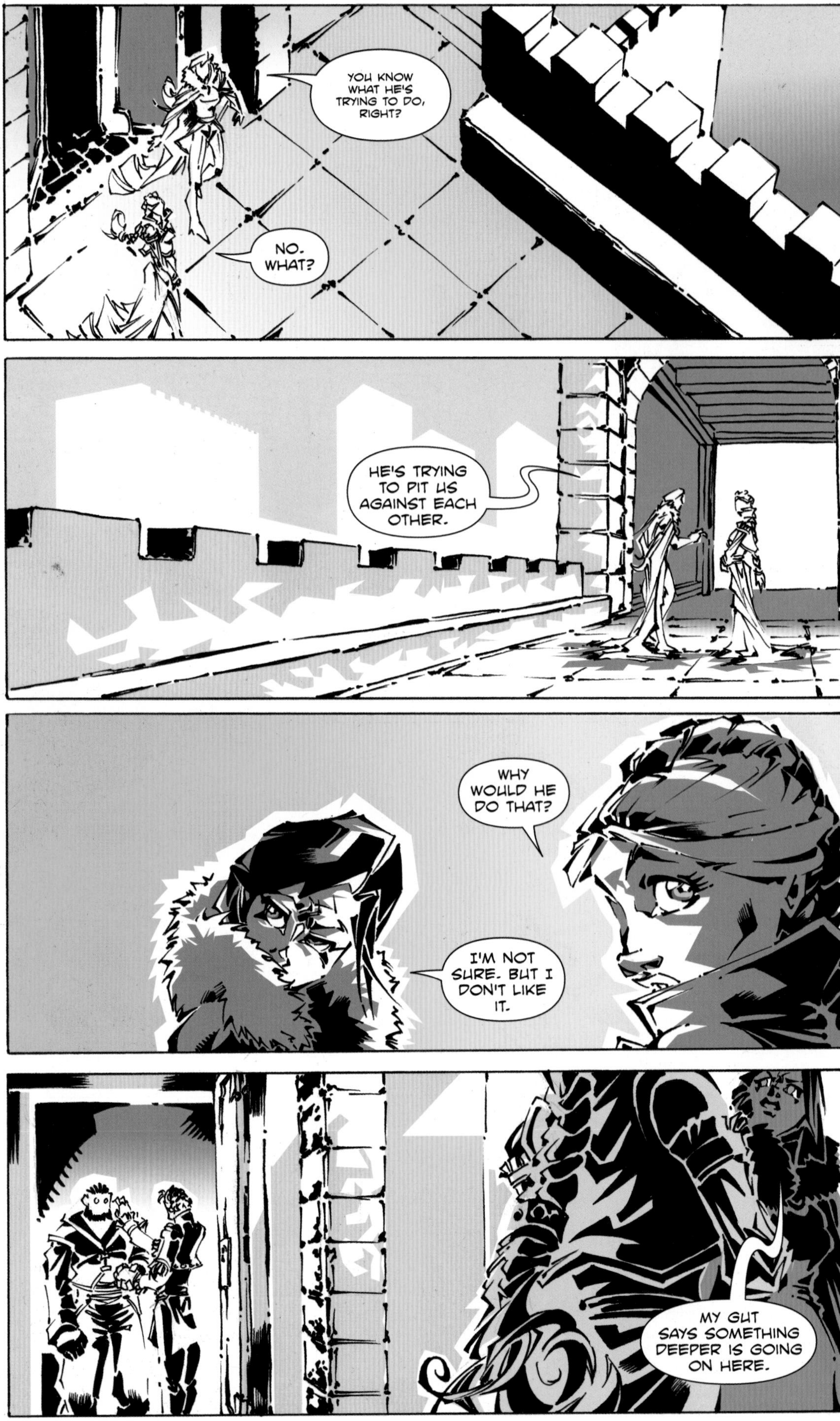
YOU KNOW WHAT HE'S TRYING TO DO, RIGHT?
NO. WHAT?
HE'S TRYING TO PIT US AGAINST EACH OTHER.
WHY WOULD HE DO THAT?
I'M NOT SURE. BUT I DON'T LIKE IT.
MY GUT SAYS SOMETHING DEEPER IS GOING ON HERE.

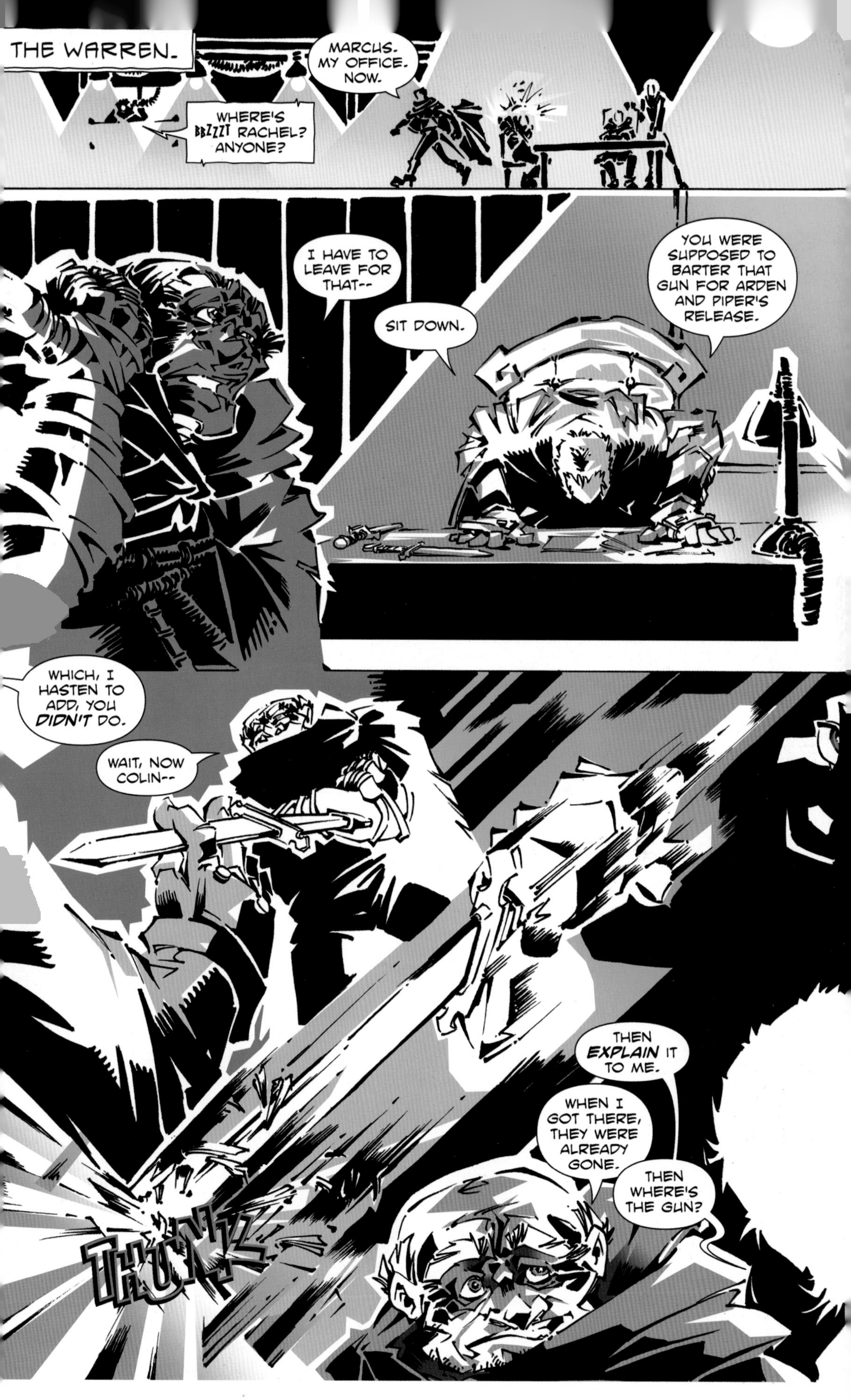
THE WARREN.
MARCUS. MY OFFICE. NOW.
WHERE'S BBZZZT RACHEL? ANYONE?
I HAVE TO LEAVE FOR THAT--
SIT DOWN.
YOU WERE SUPPOSED TO BARTER THAT GUN FOR ARDEN AND PIPER'S RELEASE.
WHICH, I HASTEN TO ADD, YOU *DIDN'T* DO.
WAIT, NOW COLIN--
THUNK
THEN *EXPLAIN* IT TO ME.
WHEN I GOT THERE, THEY WERE ALREADY GONE.
THEN WHERE'S THE GUN?

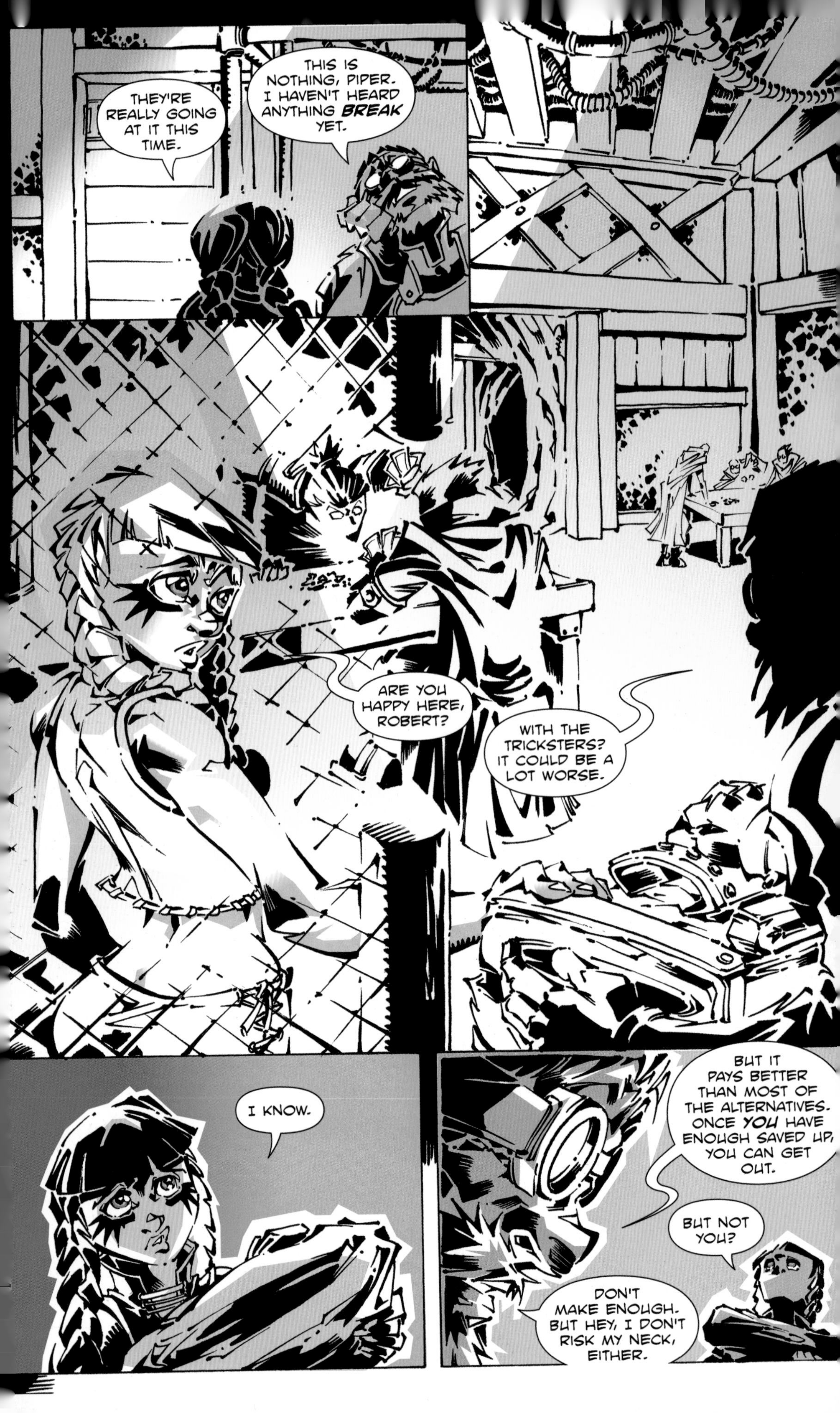
THEY'RE REALLY GOING AT IT THIS TIME.
THIS IS NOTHING, PIPER. I HAVEN'T HEARD ANYTHING BREAK YET.
ARE YOU HAPPY HERE, ROBERT?
WITH THE TRICKSTERS? IT COULD BE A LOT WORSE.
I KNOW.
BUT IT PAYS BETTER THAN MOST OF THE ALTERNATIVES. ONCE YOU HAVE ENOUGH SAVED UP, YOU CAN GET OUT.
BUT NOT YOU?
DON'T MAKE ENOUGH. BUT HEY, I DON'T RISK MY NECK, EITHER.

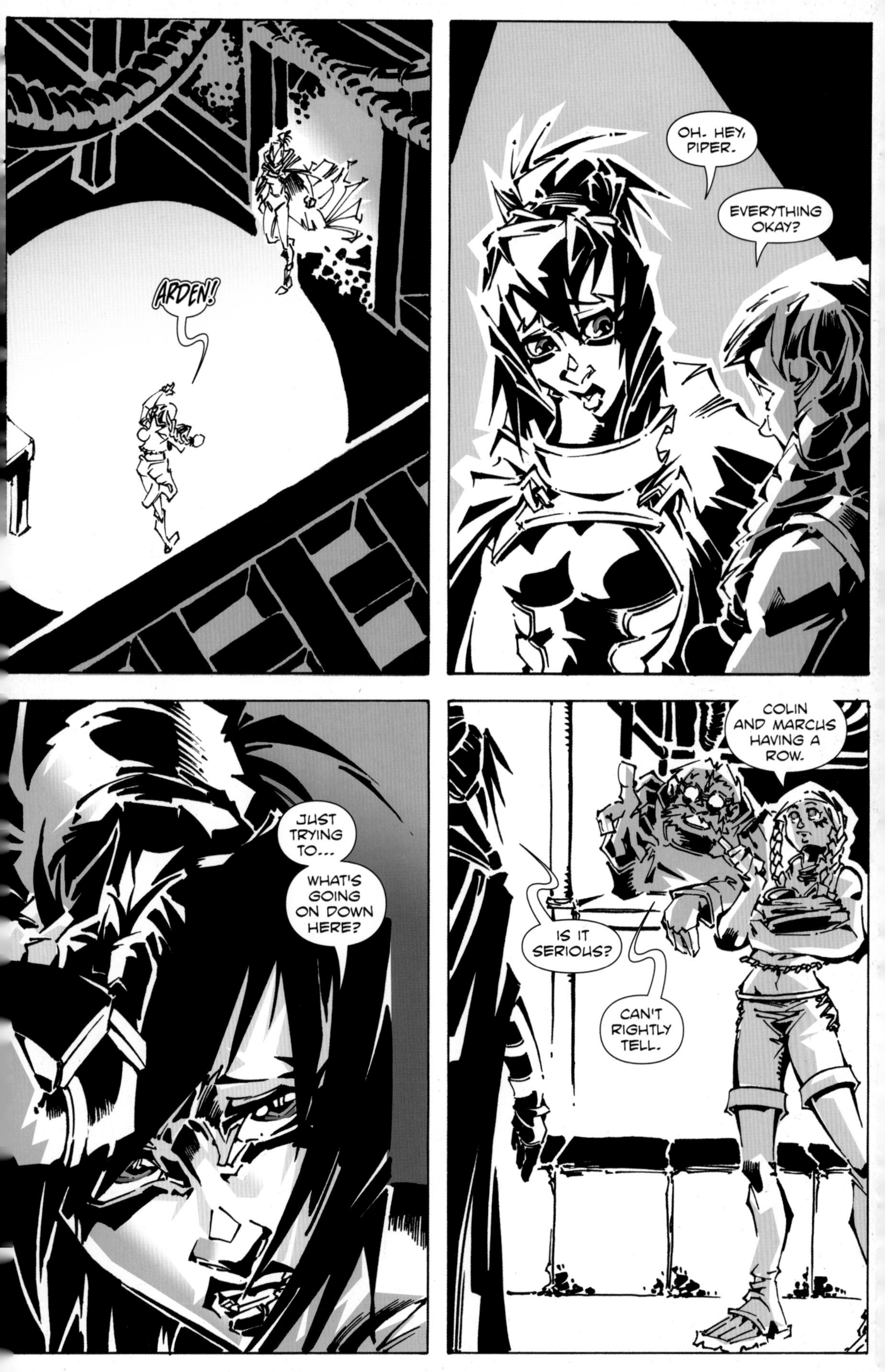
ARDEN!
OH. HEY, PIPER.
EVERYTHING OKAY?
JUST TRYING TO...
WHAT'S GOING ON DOWN HERE?
COLIN AND MARCUS HAVING A ROW.
IS IT SERIOUS?
CAN'T RIGHTLY TELL.

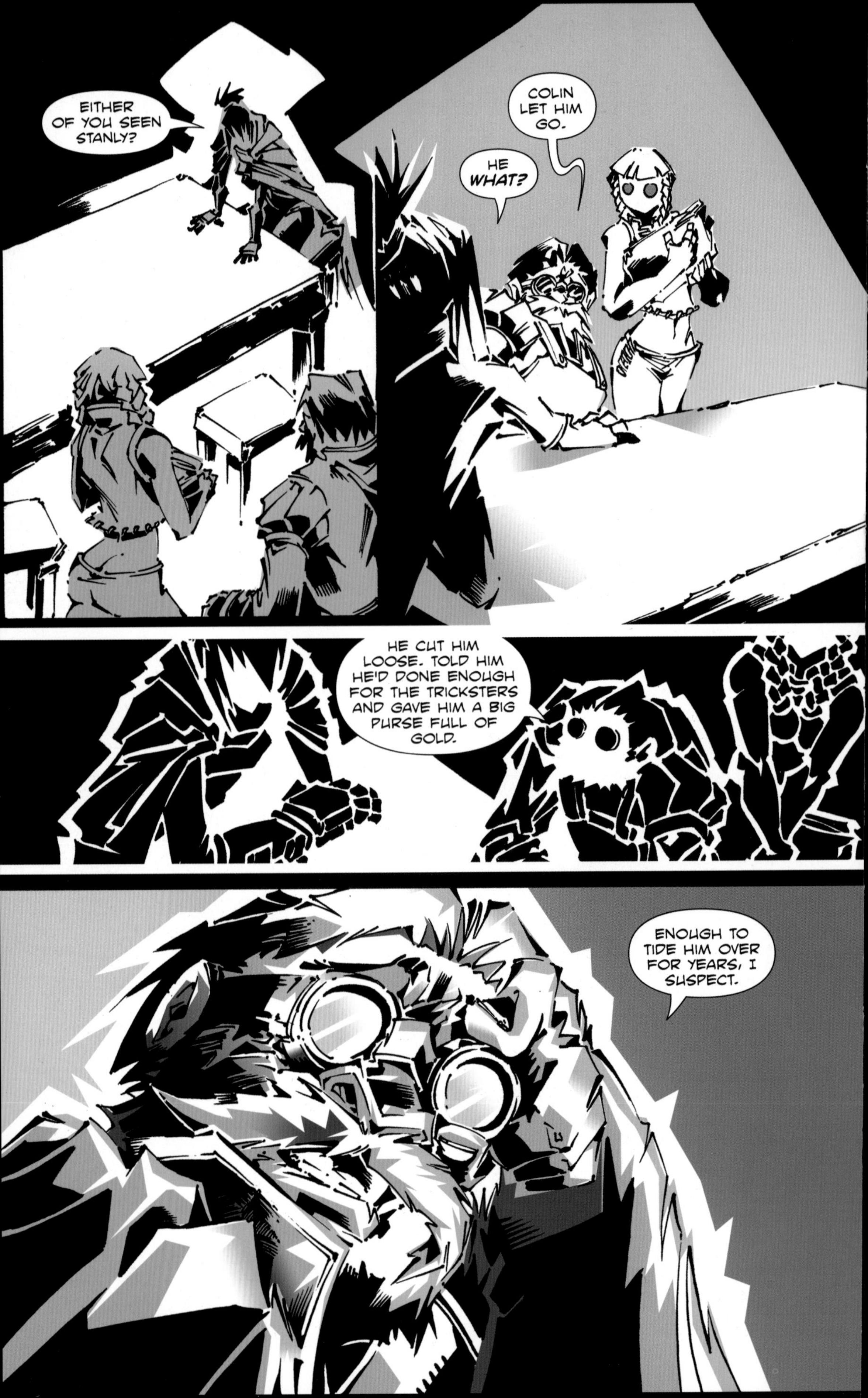
EITHER OF YOU SEEN STANLY?
COLIN LET HIM GO.
HE WHAT?
HE CUT HIM LOOSE. TOLD HIM HE'D DONE ENOUGH FOR THE TRICKSTERS AND GAVE HIM A BIG PURSE FULL OF GOLD.
ENOUGH TO TIDE HIM OVER FOR YEARS, I SUSPECT.

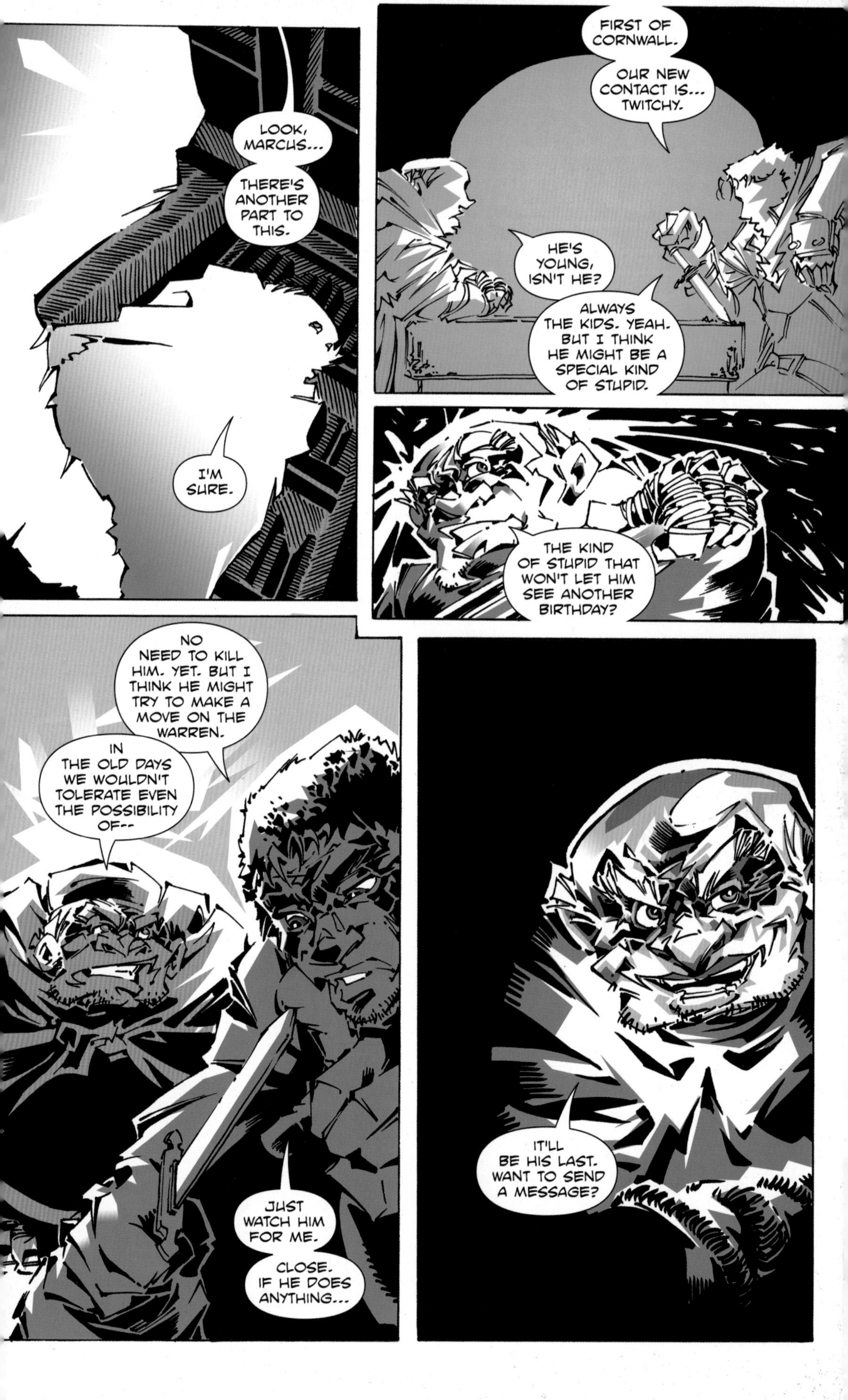
LOOK, MARCUS...
THERE'S ANOTHER PART TO THIS.
I'M SURE.
FIRST OF CORNWALL.
OUR NEW CONTACT IS... TWITCHY.
HE'S YOUNG, ISN'T HE?
ALWAYS THE KIDS. YEAH. BUT I THINK HE MIGHT BE A SPECIAL KIND OF STUPID.
THE KIND OF STUPID THAT WON'T LET HIM SEE ANOTHER BIRTHDAY?
NO NEED TO KILL HIM. YET. BUT I THINK HE MIGHT TRY TO MAKE A MOVE ON THE WARREN.
IN THE OLD DAYS WE WOULDN'T TOLERATE EVEN THE POSSIBILITY OF--
JUST WATCH HIM FOR ME.
CLOSE. IF HE DOES ANYTHING...
IT'LL BE HIS LAST. WANT TO SEND A MESSAGE?

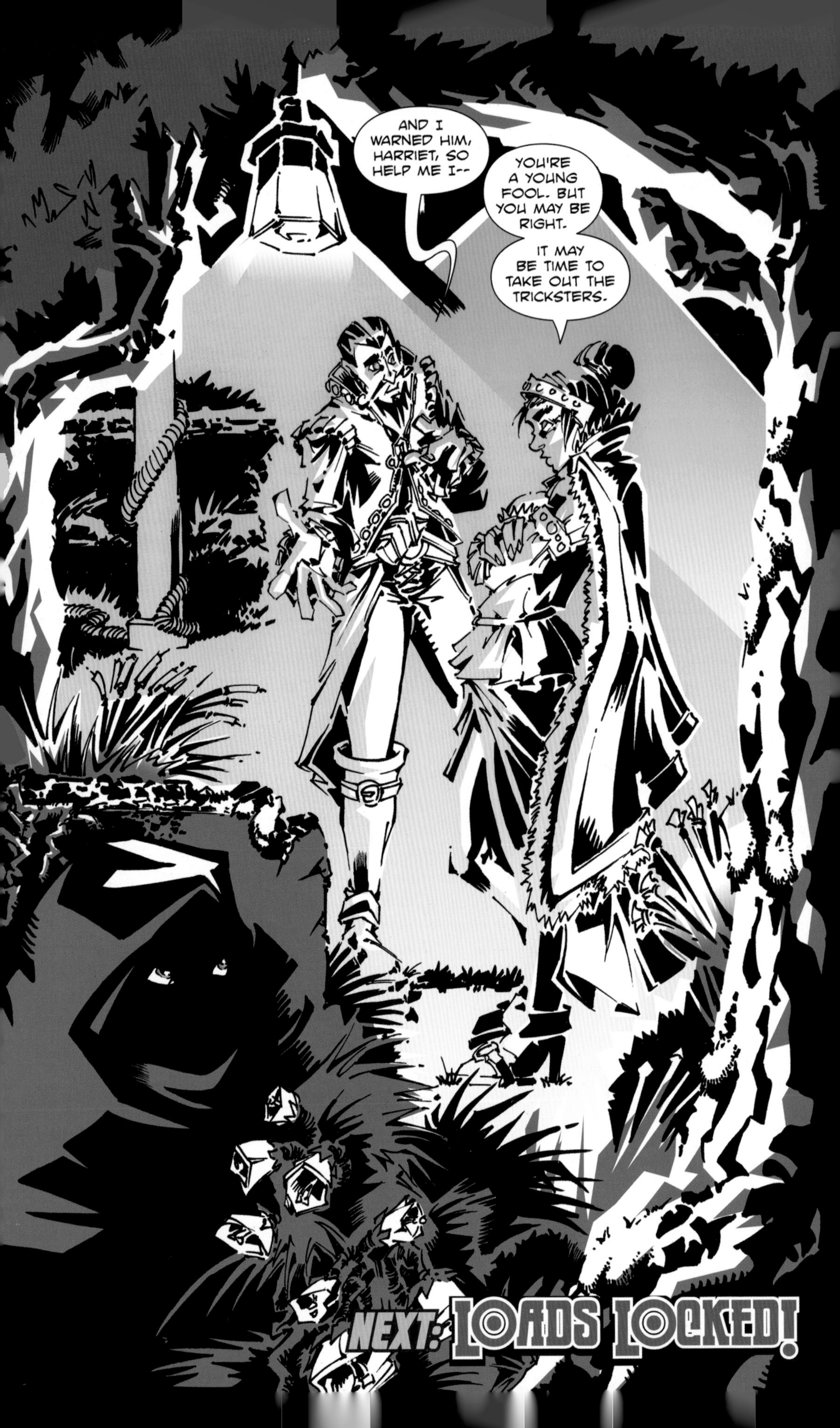
AND I WARNED HIM, HARRIET, SO HELP ME I--
YOU'RE A YOUNG FOOL. BUT YOU MAY BE RIGHT.
IT MAY BE TIME TO TAKE OUT THE TRICKSTERS.
NEXT: LOADS LOCKED!

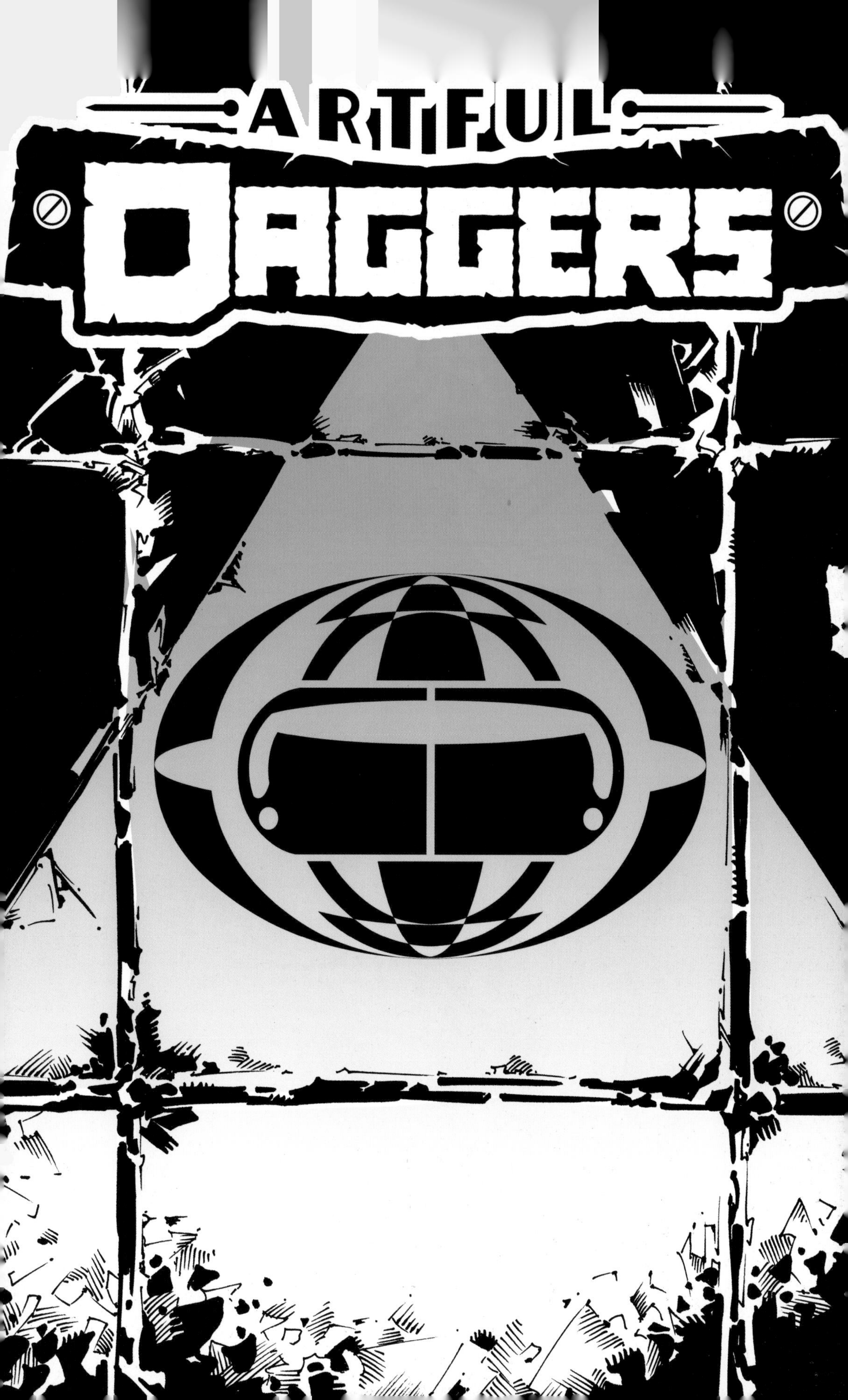
ARTFUL
DAGGERS

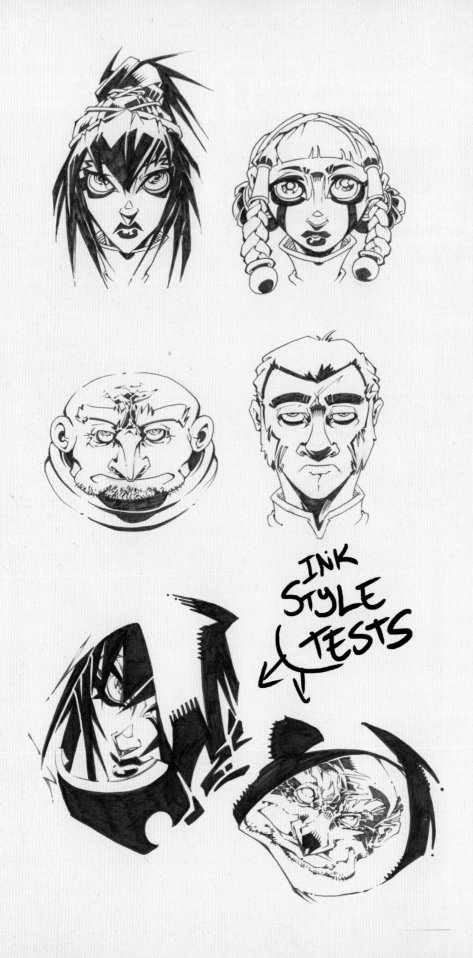

INK
STYLE
TESTS

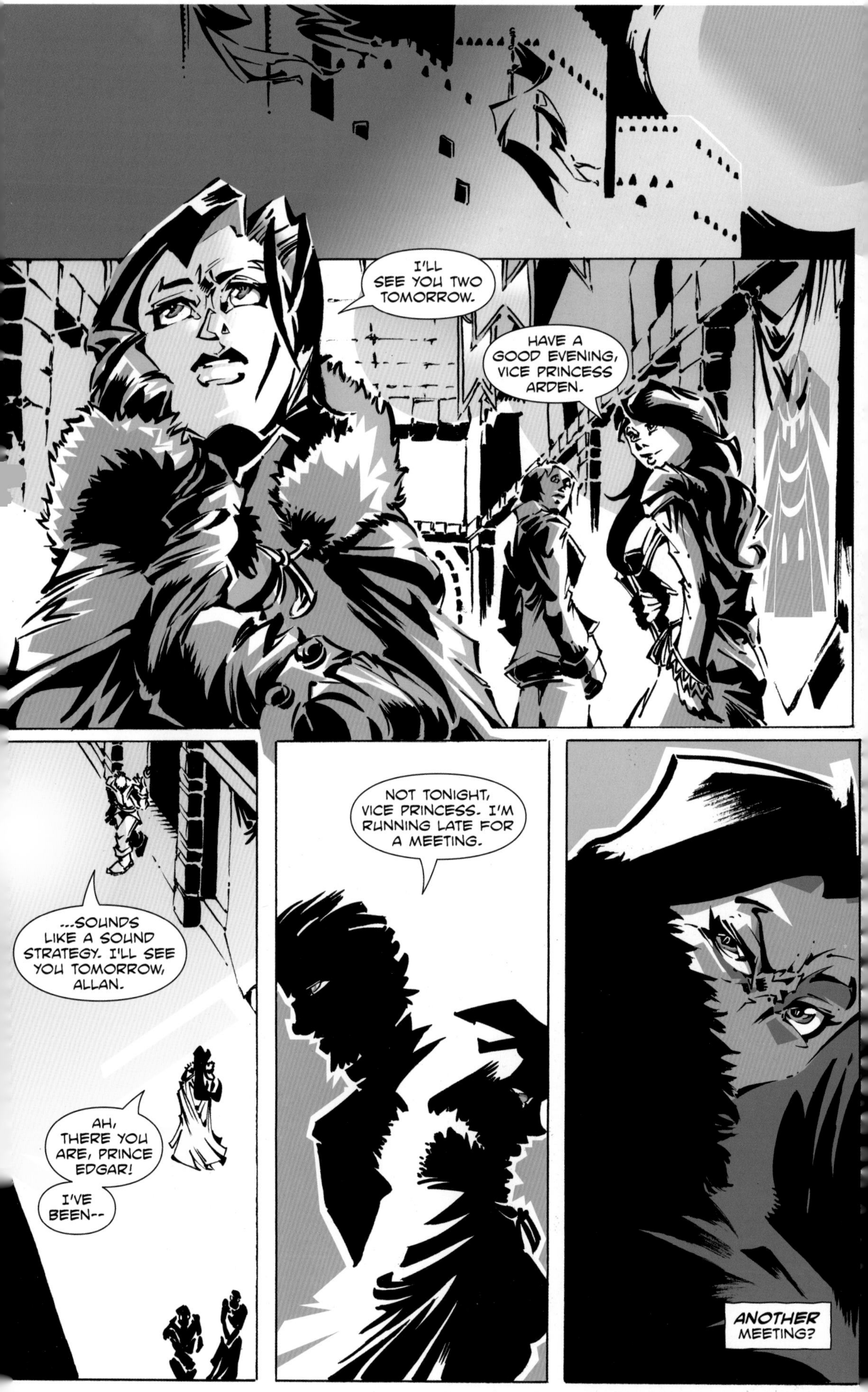
I'LL SEE YOU TWO TOMORROW.
HAVE A GOOD EVENING, VICE PRINCESS ARDEN.
...SOUNDS LIKE A SOUND STRATEGY. I'LL SEE YOU TOMORROW, ALLAN.
AH, THERE YOU ARE, PRINCE EDGAR!
I'VE BEEN--
NOT TONIGHT, VICE PRINCESS. I'M RUNNING LATE FOR A MEETING.
ANOTHER MEETING?

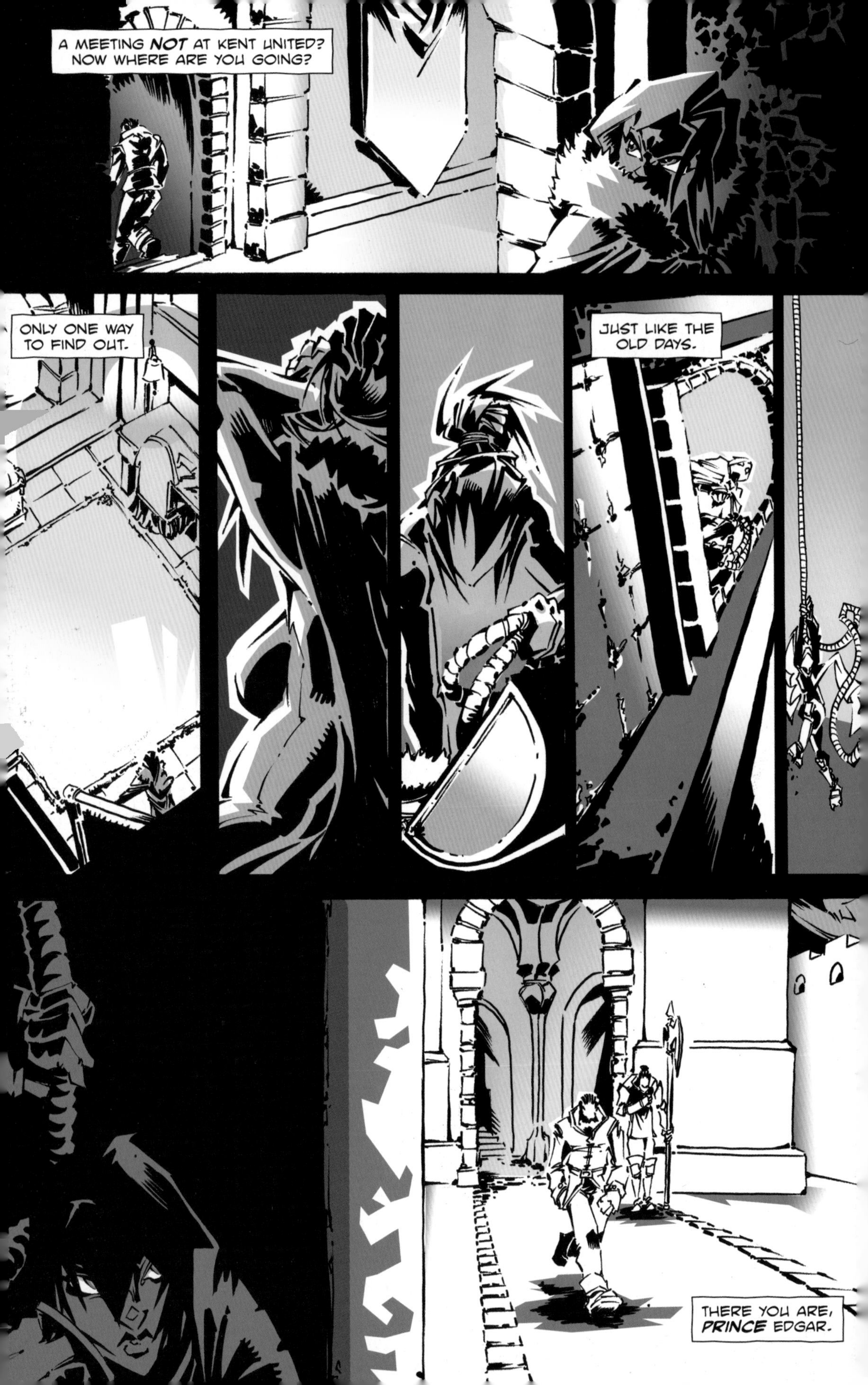
A MEETING NOT AT KENT UNITED? NOW WHERE ARE YOU GOING?
ONLY ONE WAY TO FIND OUT.
JUST LIKE THE OLD DAYS.
THERE YOU ARE, PRINCE EDGAR.

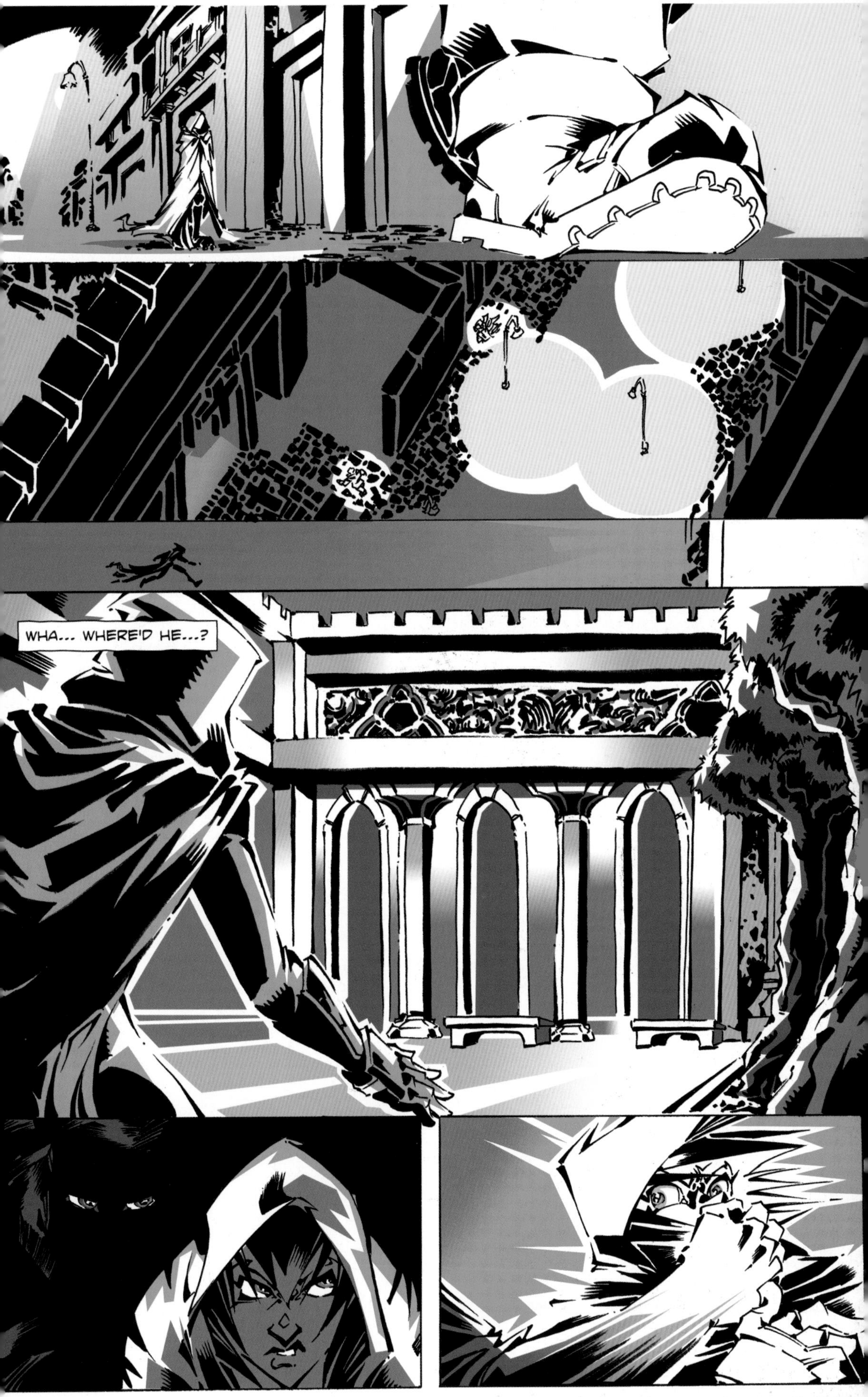

WHA... WHERE'D HE...?

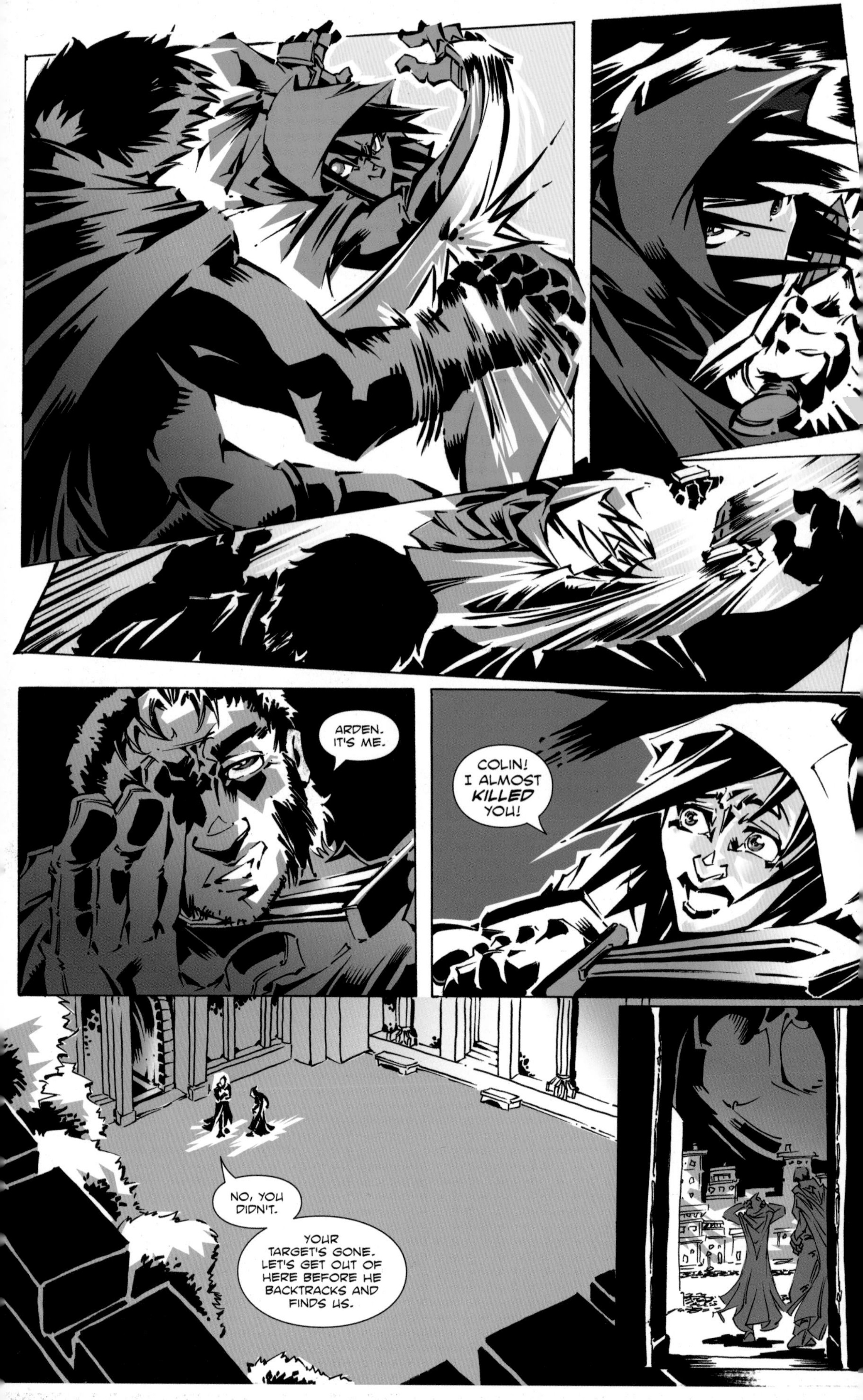
ARDEN. IT'S ME.
COLIN! I ALMOST *KILLED* YOU!
NO, YOU DIDN'T.
YOUR TARGET'S GONE. LET'S GET OUT OF HERE BEFORE HE BACKTRACKS AND FINDS US.

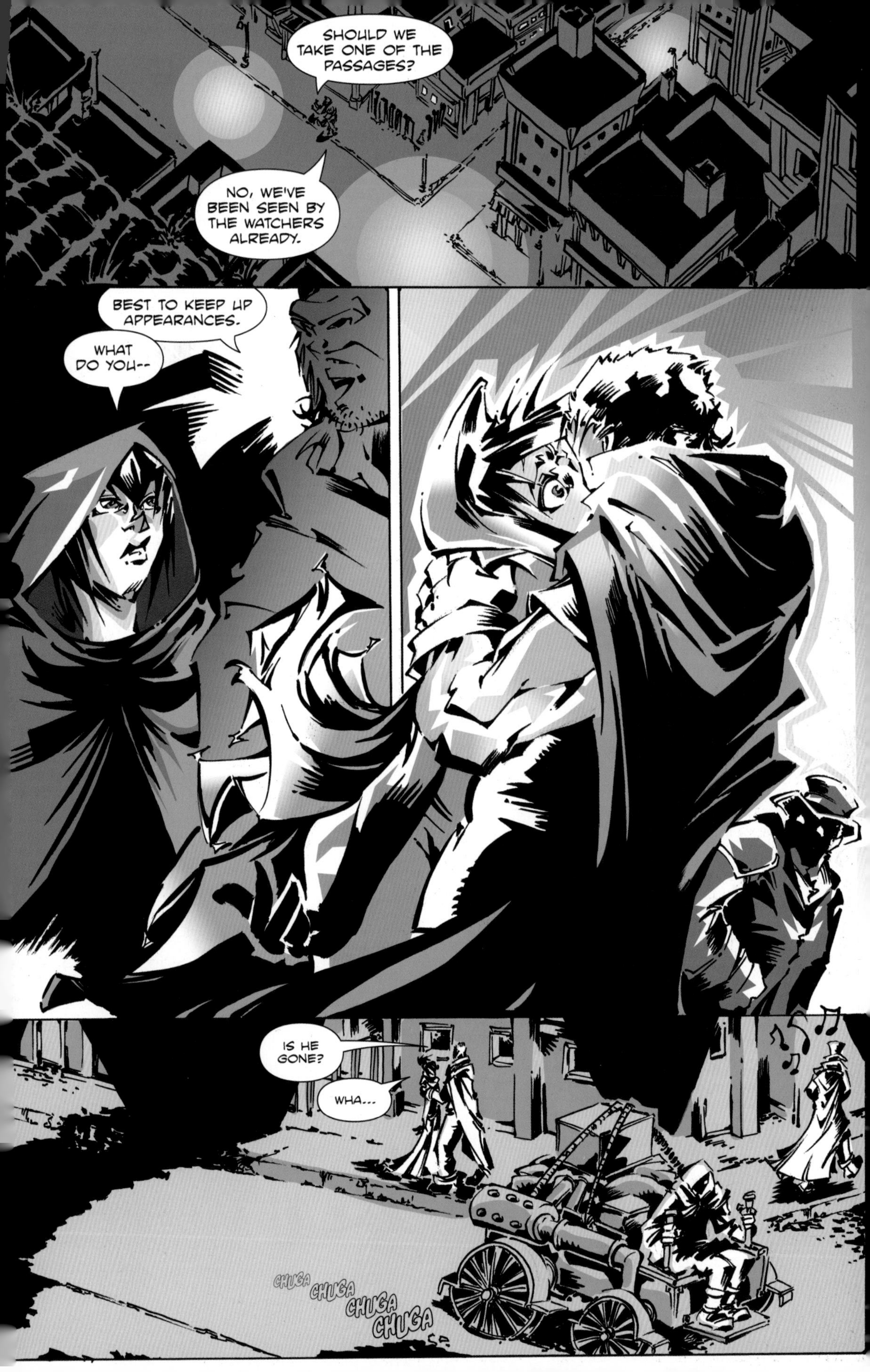

SHOULD WE TAKE ONE OF THE PASSAGES?
NO, WE'VE BEEN SEEN BY THE WATCHERS ALREADY.
BEST TO KEEP UP APPEARANCES.
WHAT DO YOU--
IS HE GONE?
WHA...
CHUGA CHUGA CHUGA CHUGA

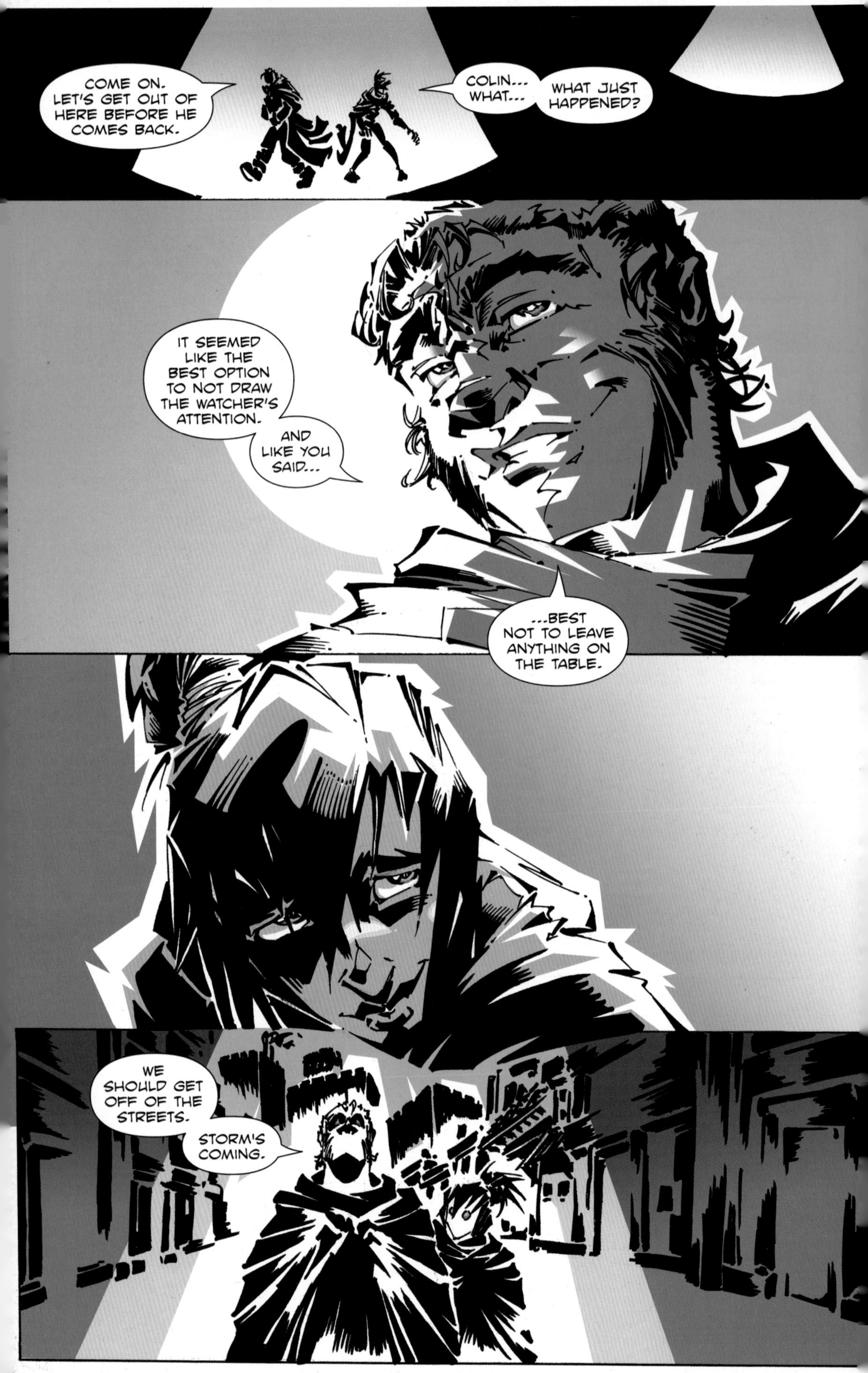
COME ON. LET'S GET OUT OF HERE BEFORE HE COMES BACK.
COLIN... WHAT...
WHAT JUST HAPPENED?
IT SEEMED LIKE THE BEST OPTION TO NOT DRAW THE WATCHER'S ATTENTION.
AND LIKE YOU SAID...
...BEST NOT TO LEAVE ANYTHING ON THE TABLE.
WE SHOULD GET OFF OF THE STREETS.
STORM'S COMING.

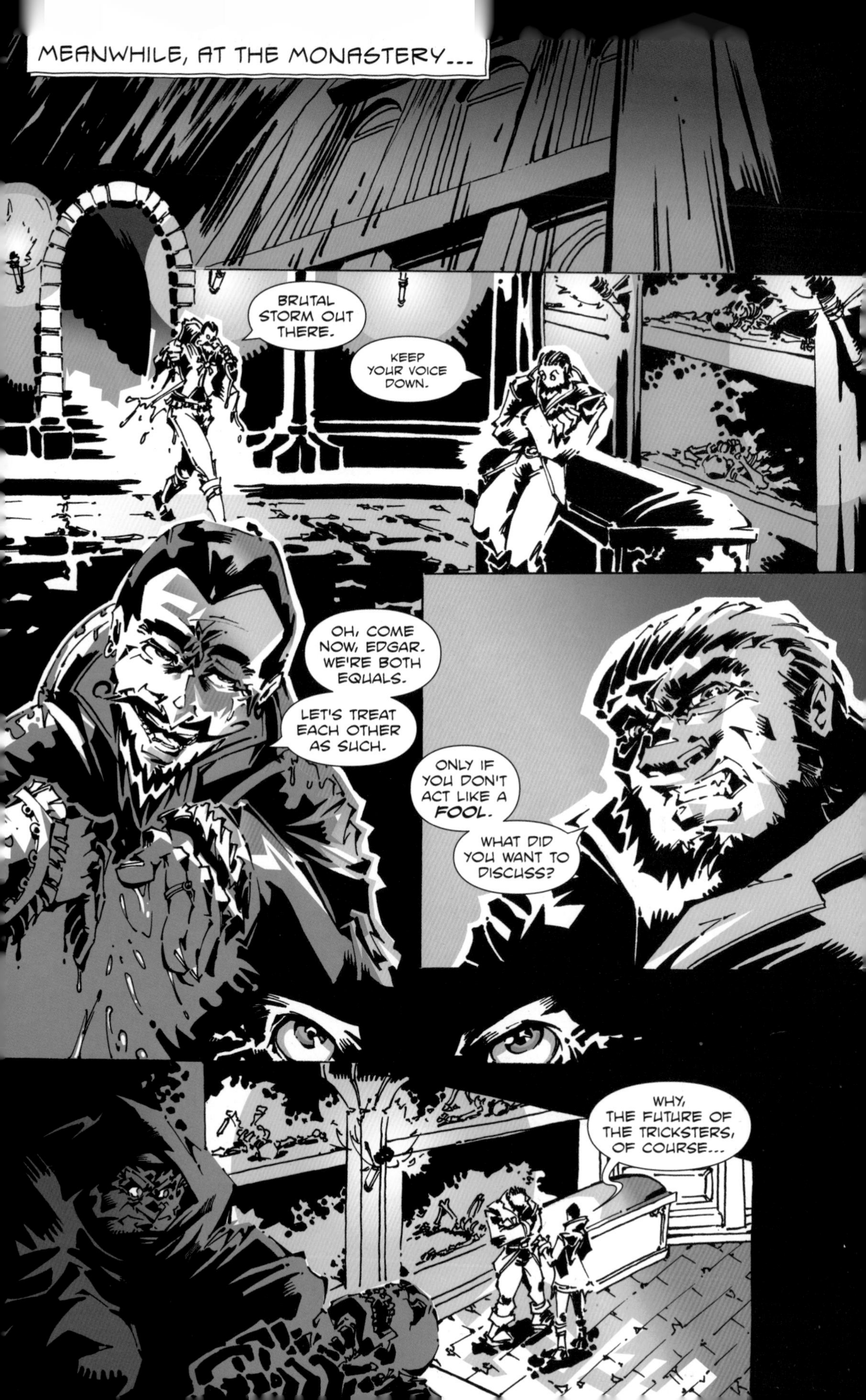
MEANWHILE, AT THE MONASTERY...
BRUTAL STORM OUT THERE.
KEEP YOUR VOICE DOWN.
OH, COME NOW, EDGAR. WE'RE BOTH EQUALS.
LET'S TREAT EACH OTHER AS SUCH.
ONLY IF YOU DON'T ACT LIKE A FOOL.
WHAT DID YOU WANT TO DISCUSS?
WHY, THE FUTURE OF THE TRICKSTERS, OF COURSE...

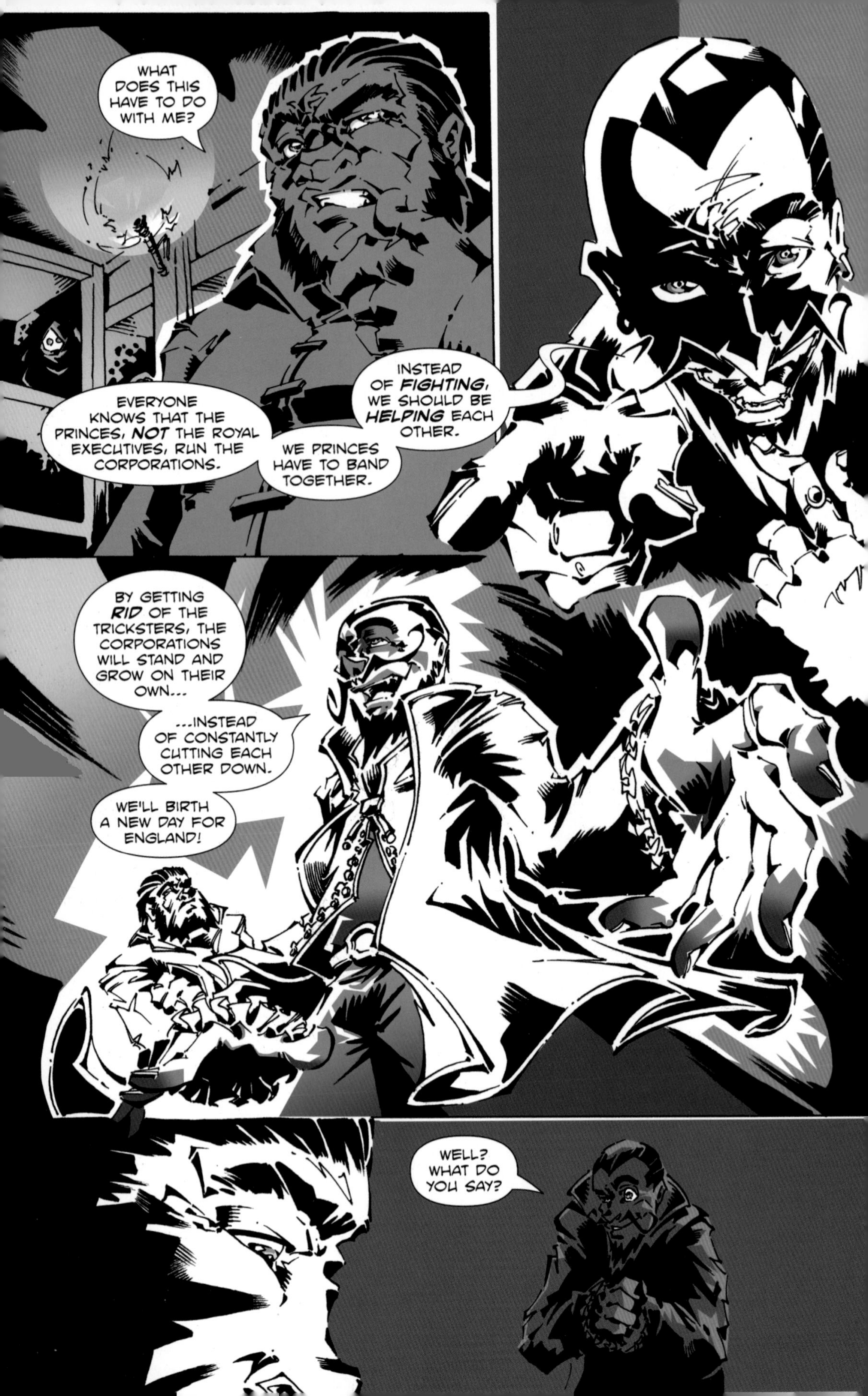
WHAT DOES THIS HAVE TO DO WITH ME?
EVERYONE KNOWS THAT THE PRINCES, NOT THE ROYAL EXECUTIVES, RUN THE CORPORATIONS.
WE PRINCES HAVE TO BAND TOGETHER.
INSTEAD OF FIGHTING, WE SHOULD BE HELPING EACH OTHER.
BY GETTING RID OF THE TRICKSTERS, THE CORPORATIONS WILL STAND AND GROW ON THEIR OWN...
...INSTEAD OF CONSTANTLY CUTTING EACH OTHER DOWN.
WE'LL BIRTH A NEW DAY FOR ENGLAND!
WELL? WHAT DO YOU SAY?

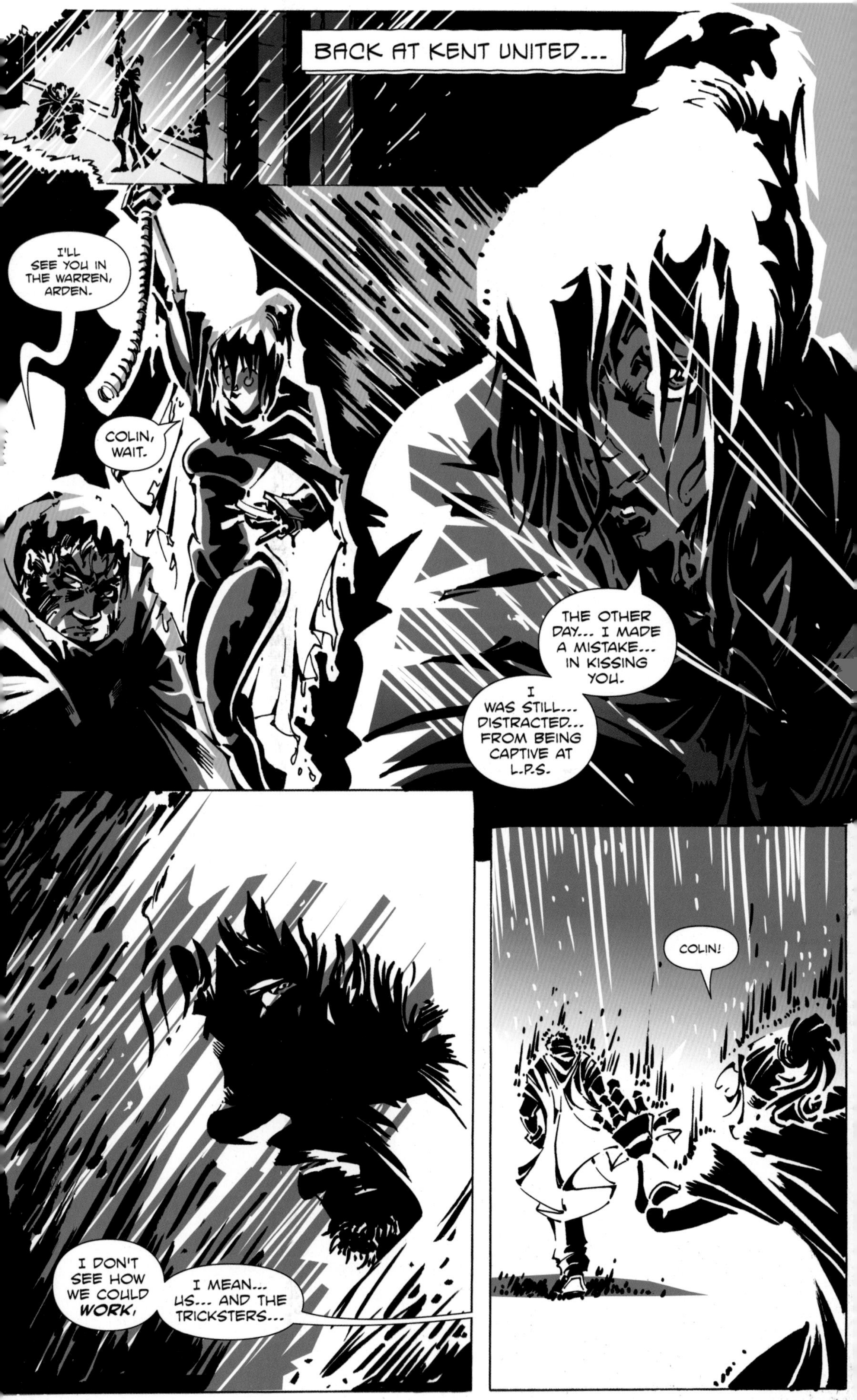
BACK AT KENT UNITED...
I'LL SEE YOU IN THE WARREN, ARDEN.
COLIN, WAIT.
THE OTHER DAY... I MADE A MISTAKE... IN KISSING YOU.
I WAS STILL... DISTRACTED... FROM BEING CAPTIVE AT L.P.S.
I DON'T SEE HOW WE COULD *WORK*,
I MEAN... US... AND THE TRICKSTERS...
COLIN!

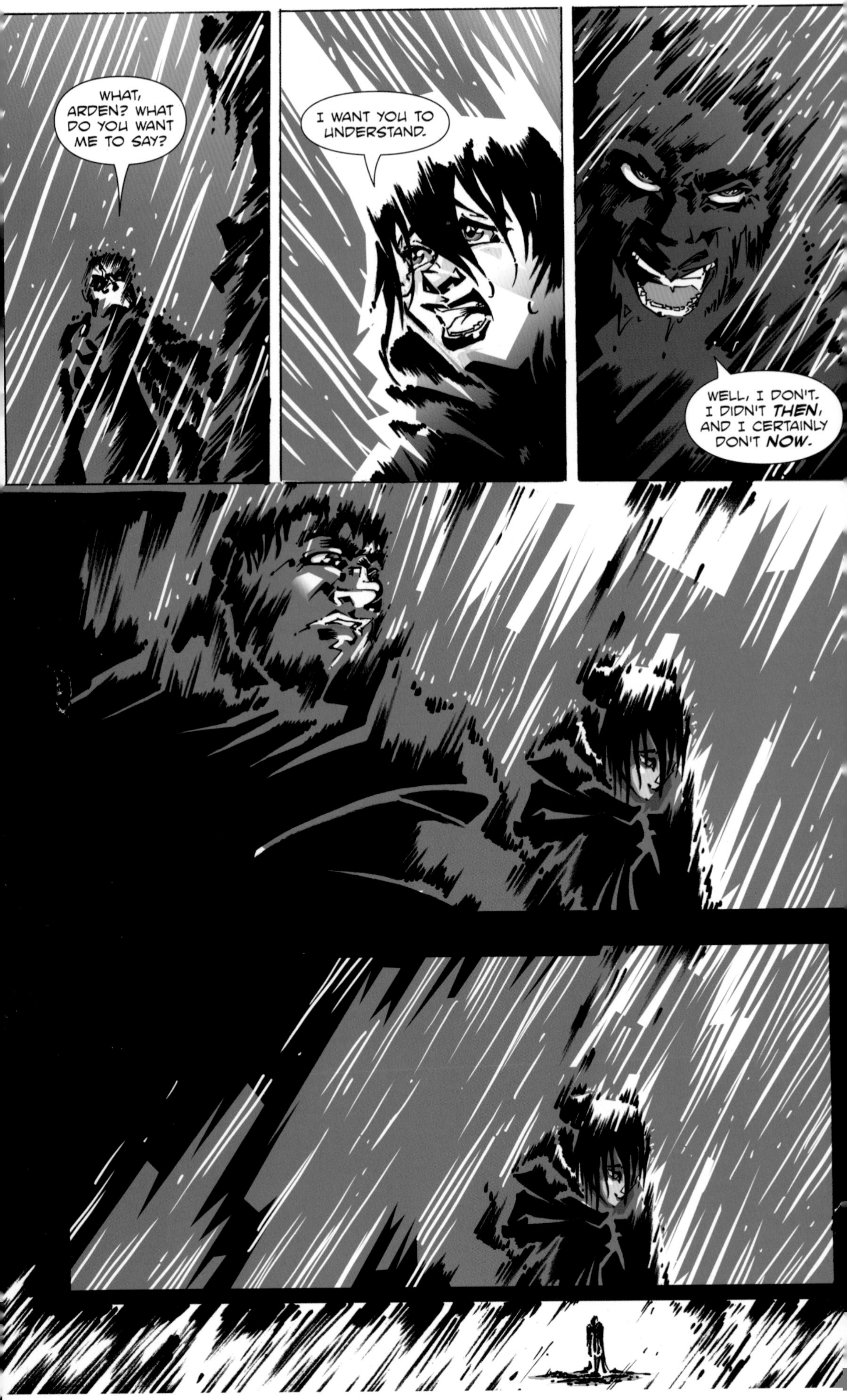
WHAT, ARDEN? WHAT DO YOU WANT ME TO SAY?
I WANT YOU TO UNDERSTAND.
WELL, I DON'T. I DIDN'T *THEN*, AND I CERTAINLY DON'T *NOW*.

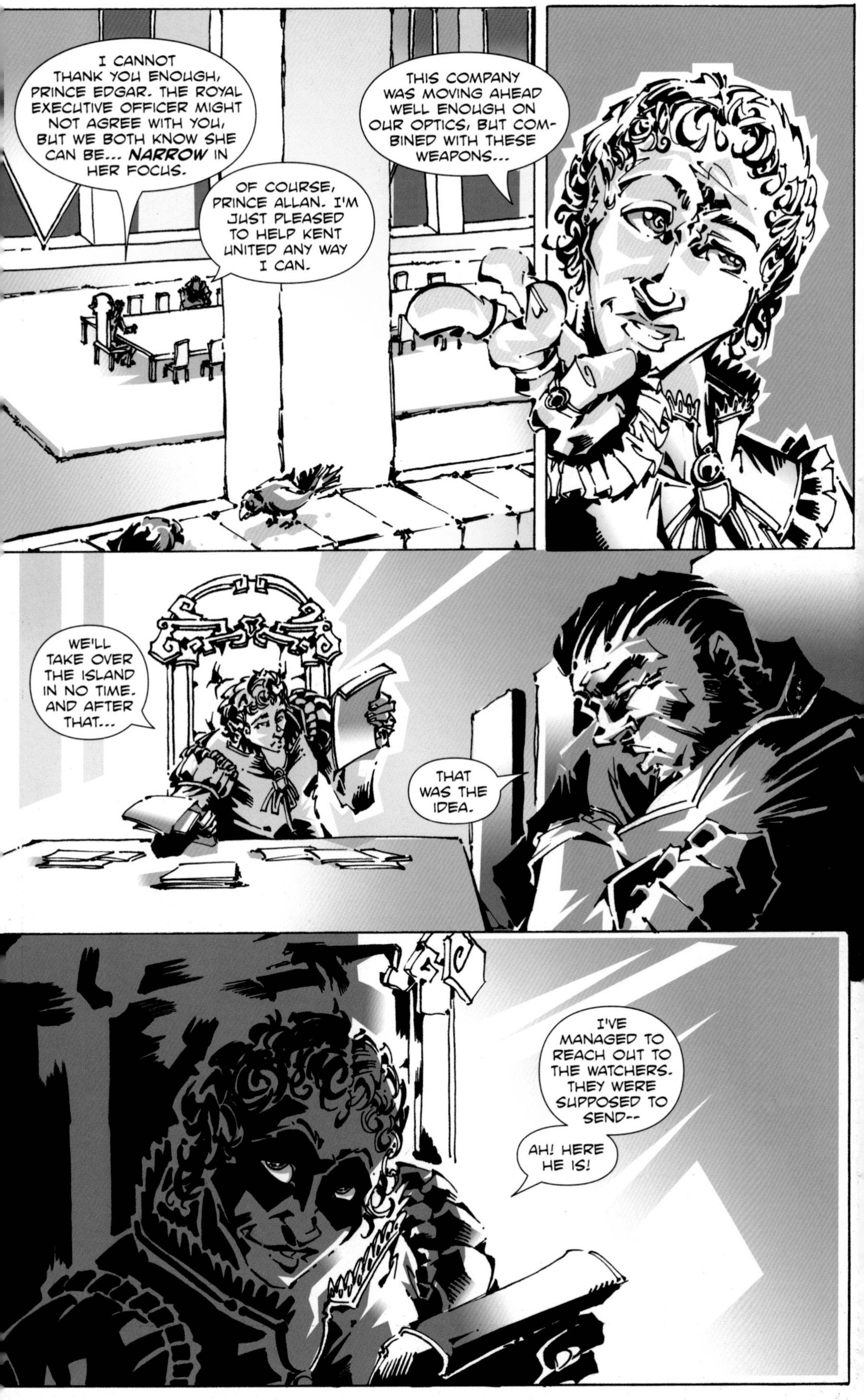
I CANNOT THANK YOU ENOUGH, PRINCE EDGAR. THE ROYAL EXECUTIVE OFFICER MIGHT NOT AGREE WITH YOU, BUT WE BOTH KNOW SHE CAN BE... *NARROW* IN HER FOCUS.
OF COURSE, PRINCE ALLAN. I'M JUST PLEASED TO HELP KENT UNITED ANY WAY I CAN.
THIS COMPANY WAS MOVING AHEAD WELL ENOUGH ON OUR OPTICS, BUT COMBINED WITH THESE WEAPONS...
WE'LL TAKE OVER THE ISLAND IN NO TIME. AND AFTER THAT...
THAT WAS THE IDEA.
I'VE MANAGED TO REACH OUT TO THE WATCHERS. THEY WERE SUPPOSED TO SEND--
AH! HERE HE IS!

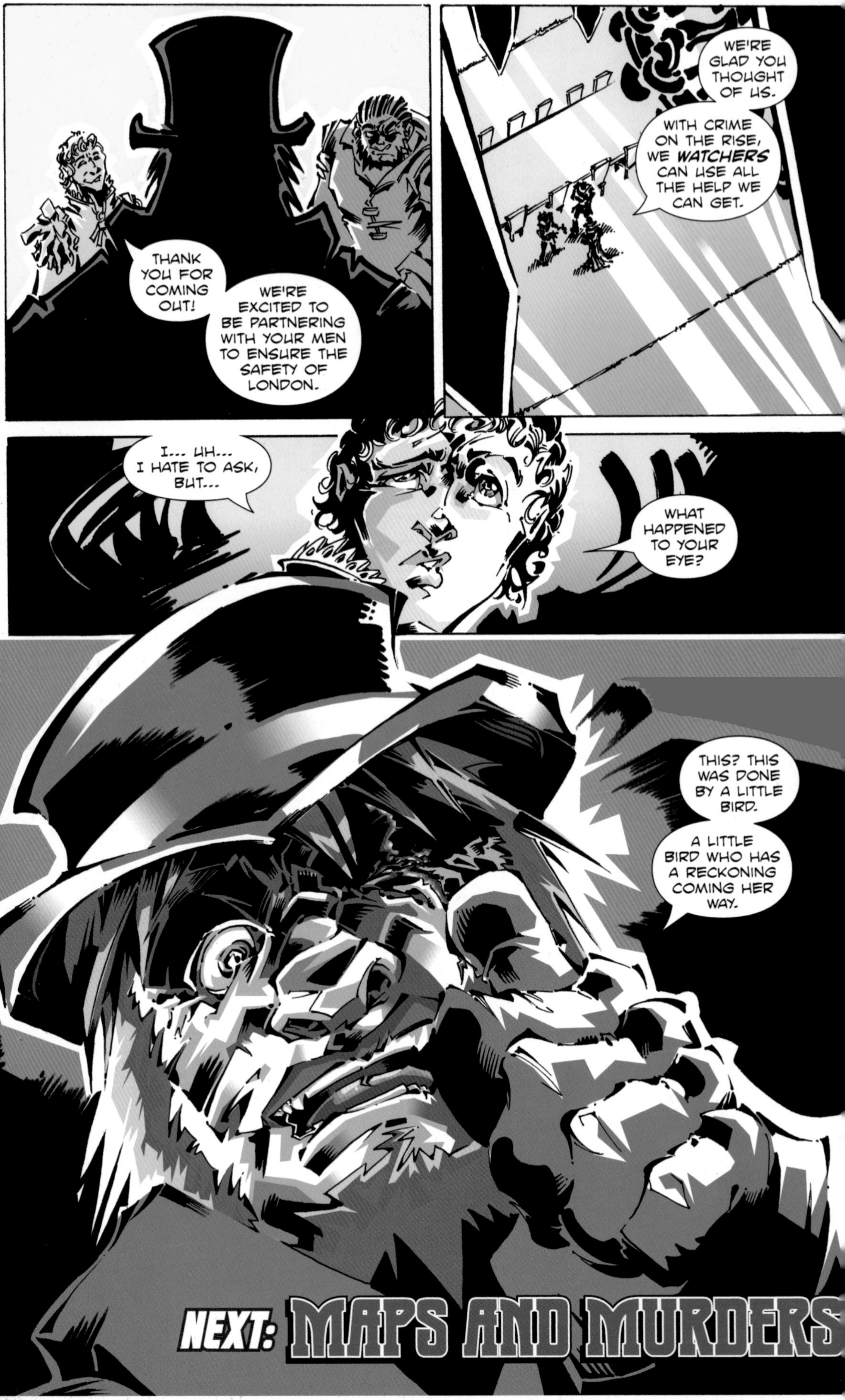
THANK YOU FOR COMING OUT!
WE'RE EXCITED TO BE PARTNERING WITH YOUR MEN TO ENSURE THE SAFETY OF LONDON.
WE'RE GLAD YOU THOUGHT OF US.
WITH CRIME ON THE RISE, WE *WATCHERS* CAN USE ALL THE HELP WE CAN GET.
I... UH... I HATE TO ASK, BUT...
WHAT HAPPENED TO YOUR EYE?
THIS? THIS WAS DONE BY A LITTLE BIRD.
A LITTLE BIRD WHO HAS A RECKONING COMING HER WAY.
NEXT: MAPS AND MURDERS

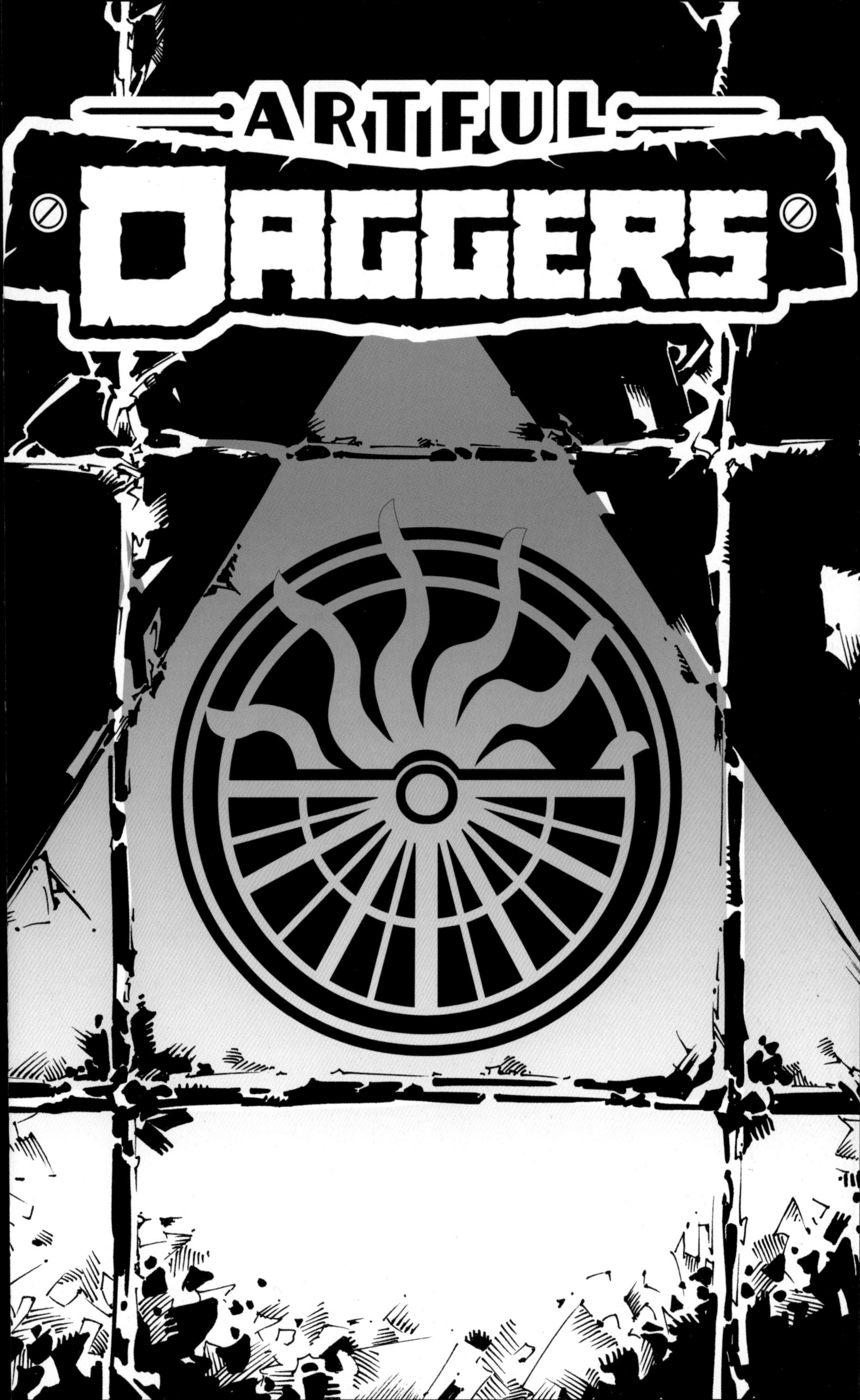
ARTFUL
DAGGERS

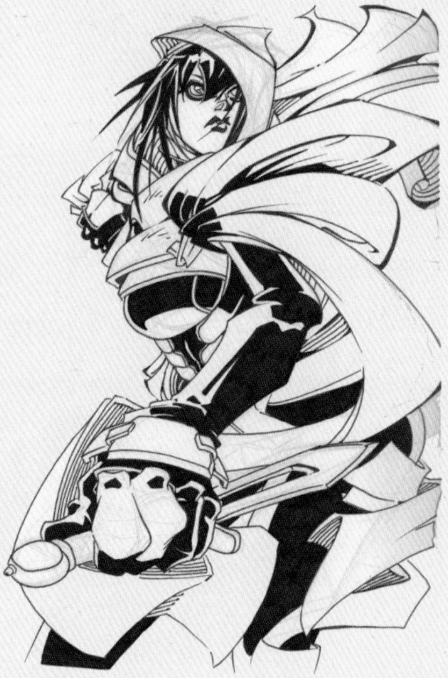

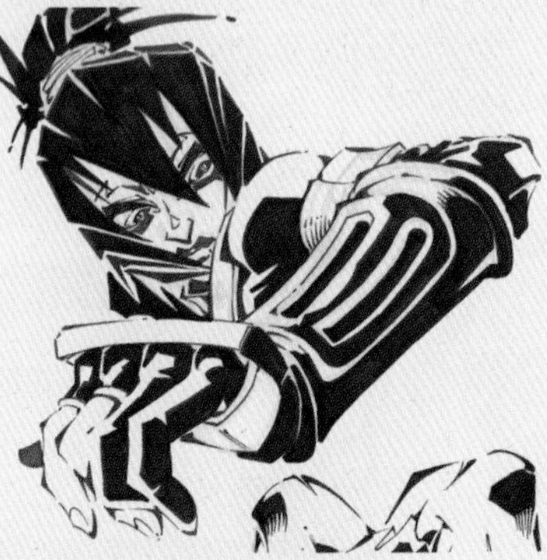

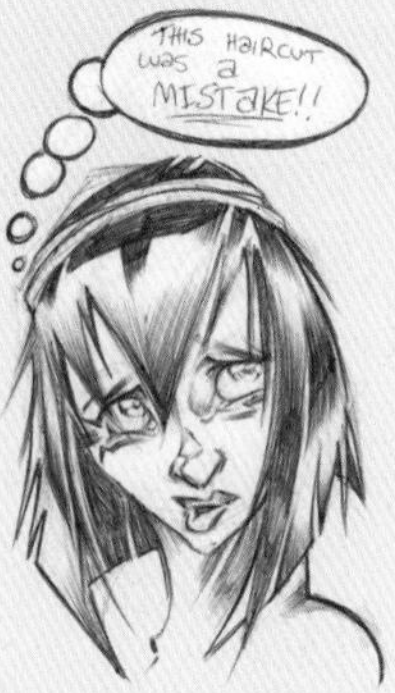
THIS HAIRCUT was a MISTAKE!!

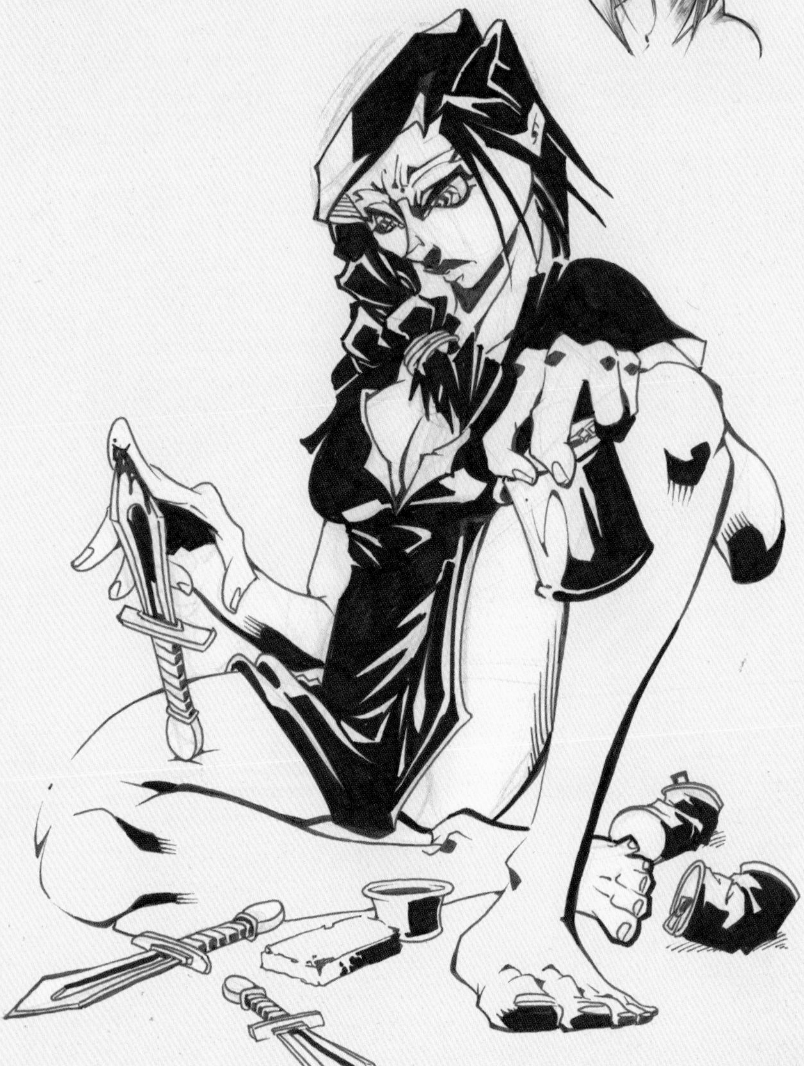

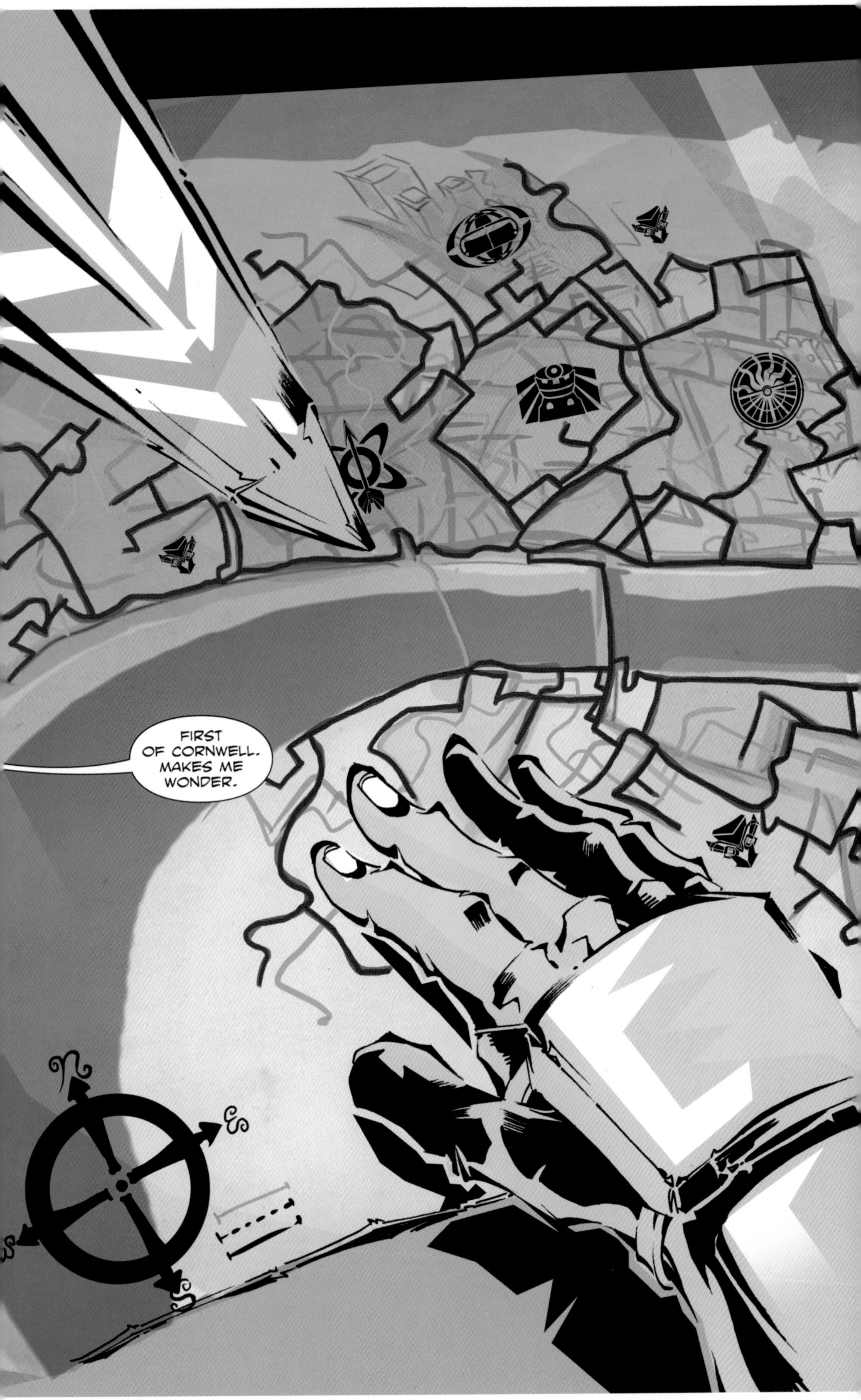
FIRST OF CORNWELL. MAKES ME WONDER.

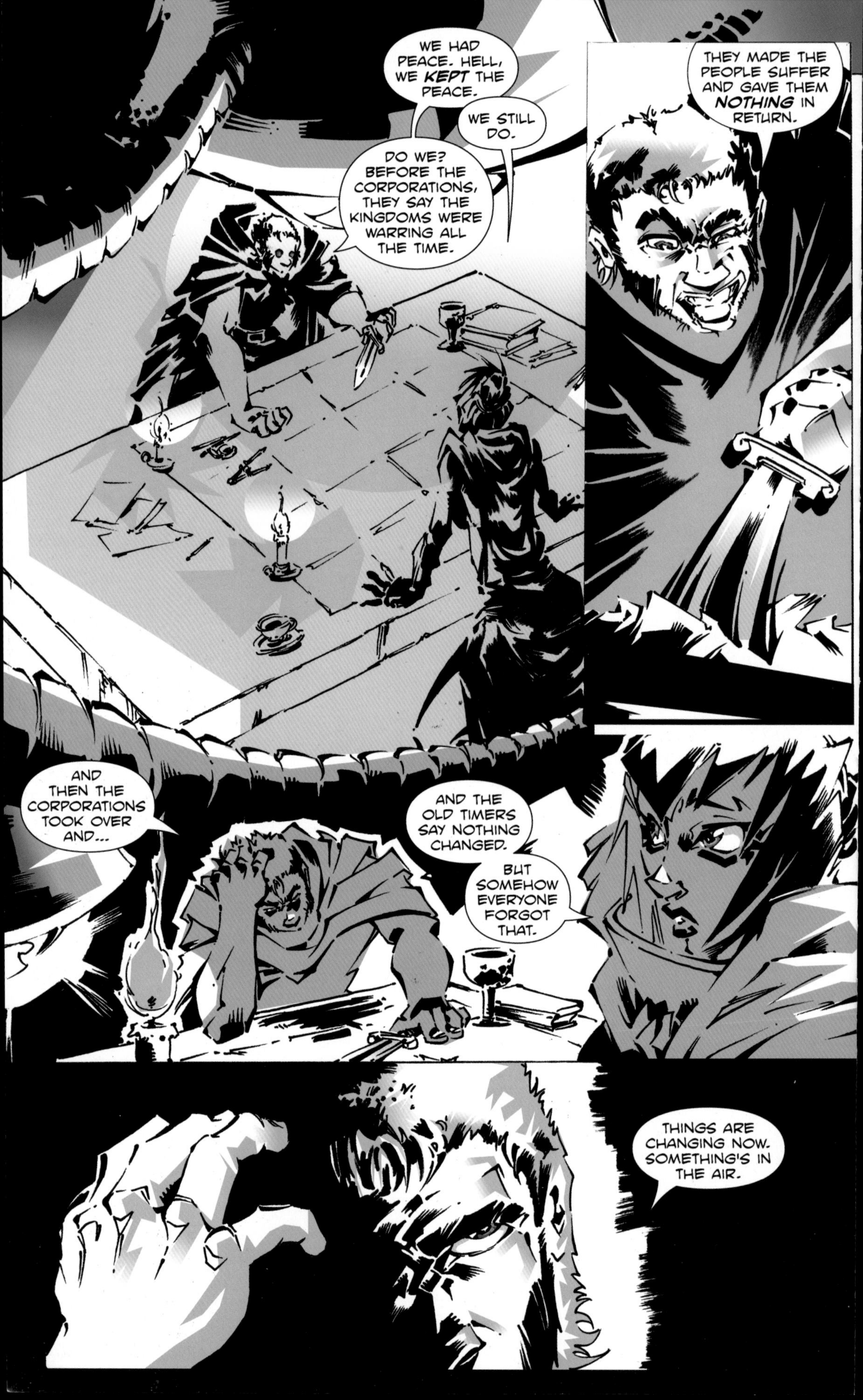
WE HAD PEACE. HELL, WE *KEPT* THE PEACE.
WE STILL DO.
DO WE? BEFORE THE CORPORATIONS, THEY SAY THE KINGDOMS WERE WARRING ALL THE TIME.
THEY MADE THE PEOPLE SUFFER AND GAVE THEM ***NOTHING*** IN RETURN.
AND THEN THE CORPORATIONS TOOK OVER AND...
AND THE OLD TIMERS SAY NOTHING CHANGED.
BUT SOMEHOW EVERYONE FORGOT THAT.
THINGS ARE CHANGING NOW. SOMETHING'S IN THE AIR.

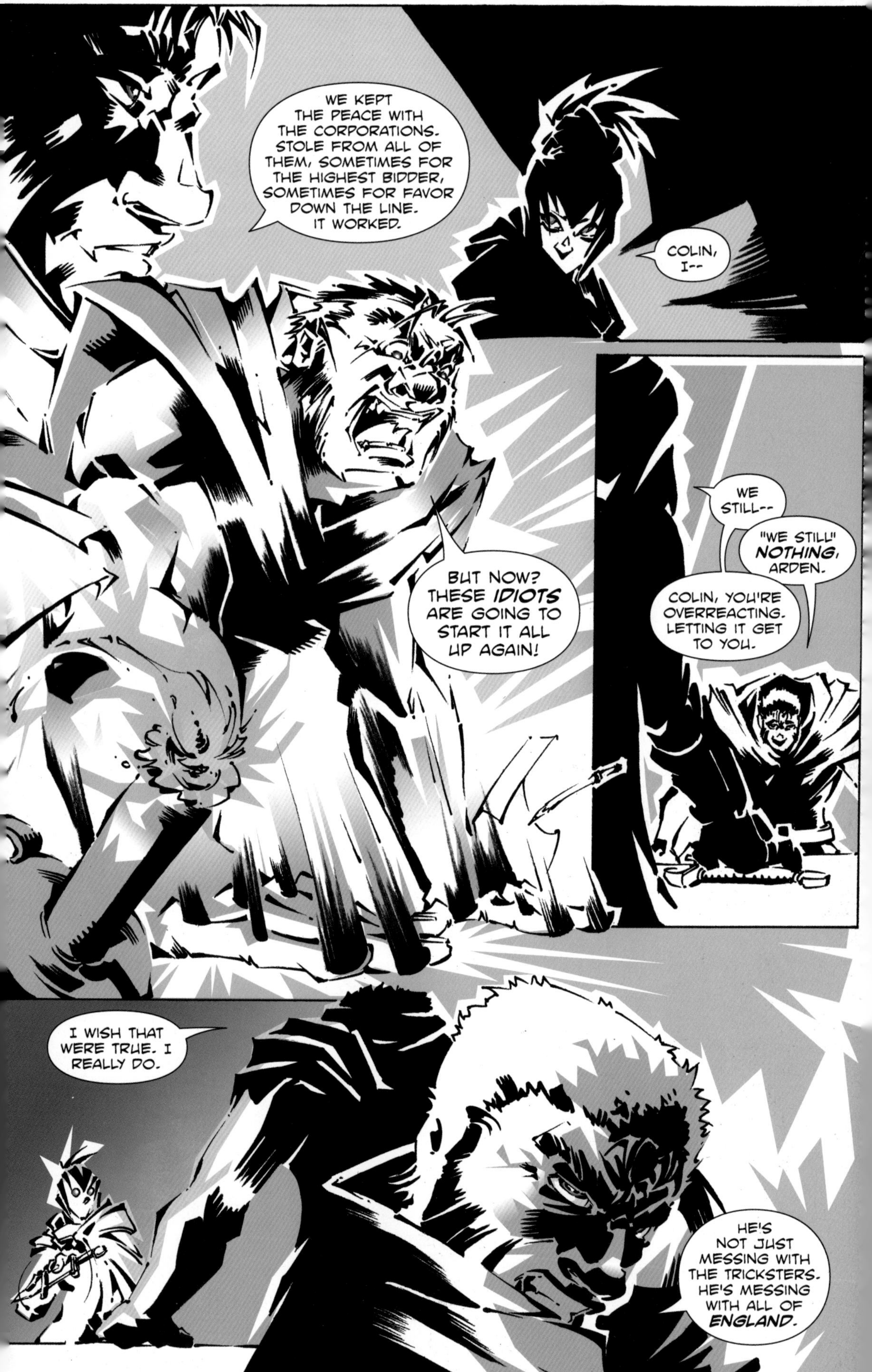
WE KEPT THE PEACE WITH THE CORPORATIONS. STOLE FROM ALL OF THEM, SOMETIMES FOR THE HIGHEST BIDDER, SOMETIMES FOR FAVOR DOWN THE LINE. IT WORKED.
COLIN, I--
BUT NOW? THESE *IDIOTS* ARE GOING TO START IT ALL UP AGAIN!
WE STILL--
"WE STILL" *NOTHING*, ARDEN.
COLIN, YOU'RE OVERREACTING. LETTING IT GET TO YOU.
I WISH THAT WERE TRUE. I REALLY DO.
HE'S NOT JUST MESSING WITH THE TRICKSTERS. HE'S MESSING WITH ALL OF *ENGLAND*.

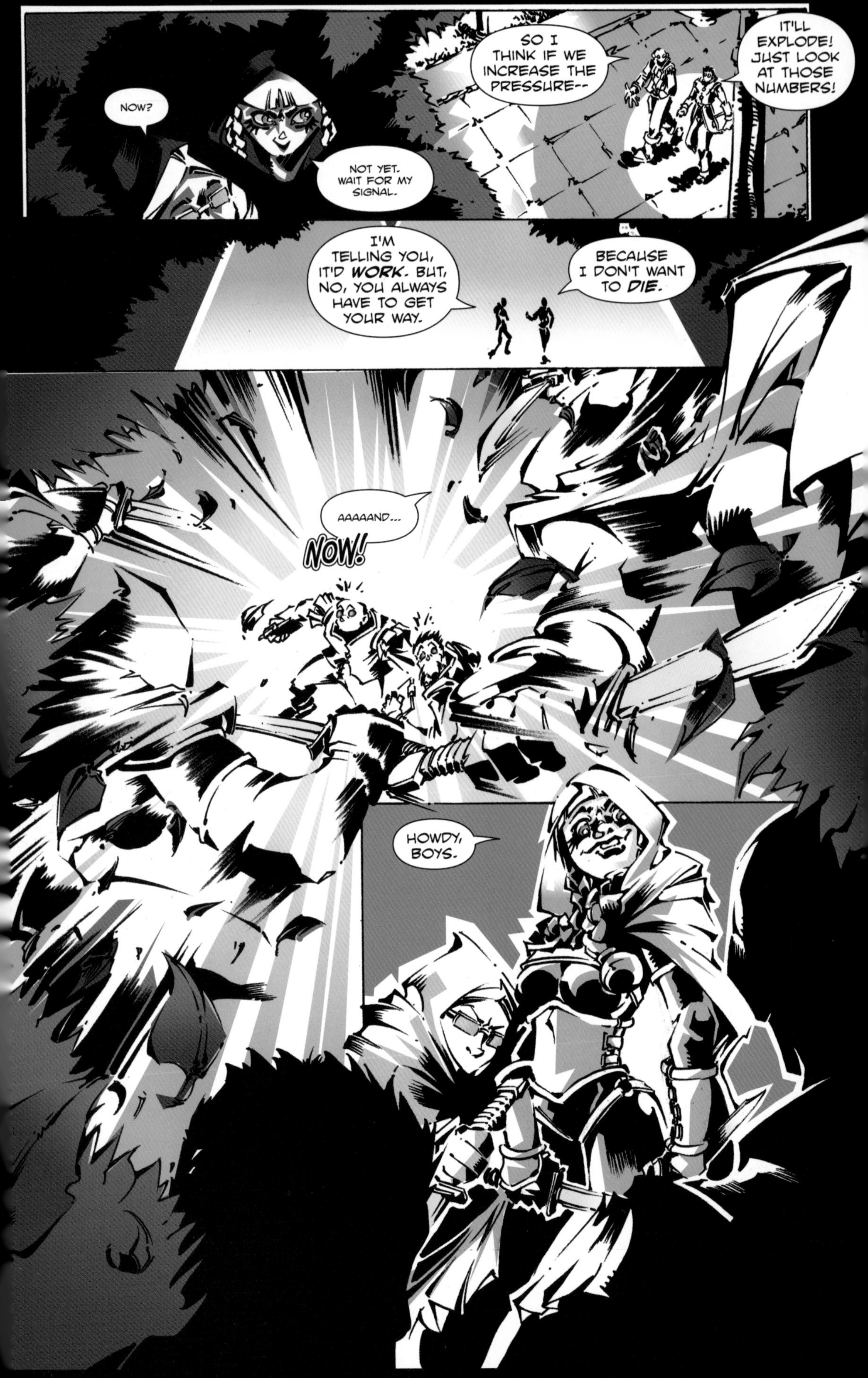
NOW?
NOT YET. WAIT FOR MY SIGNAL.
SO I THINK IF WE INCREASE THE PRESSURE--
IT'LL EXPLODE! JUST LOOK AT THOSE NUMBERS!
I'M TELLING YOU, IT'D WORK. BUT, NO, YOU ALWAYS HAVE TO GET YOUR WAY.
BECAUSE I DON'T WANT TO DIE.
AAAAAND...
NOW!
HOWDY, BOYS.

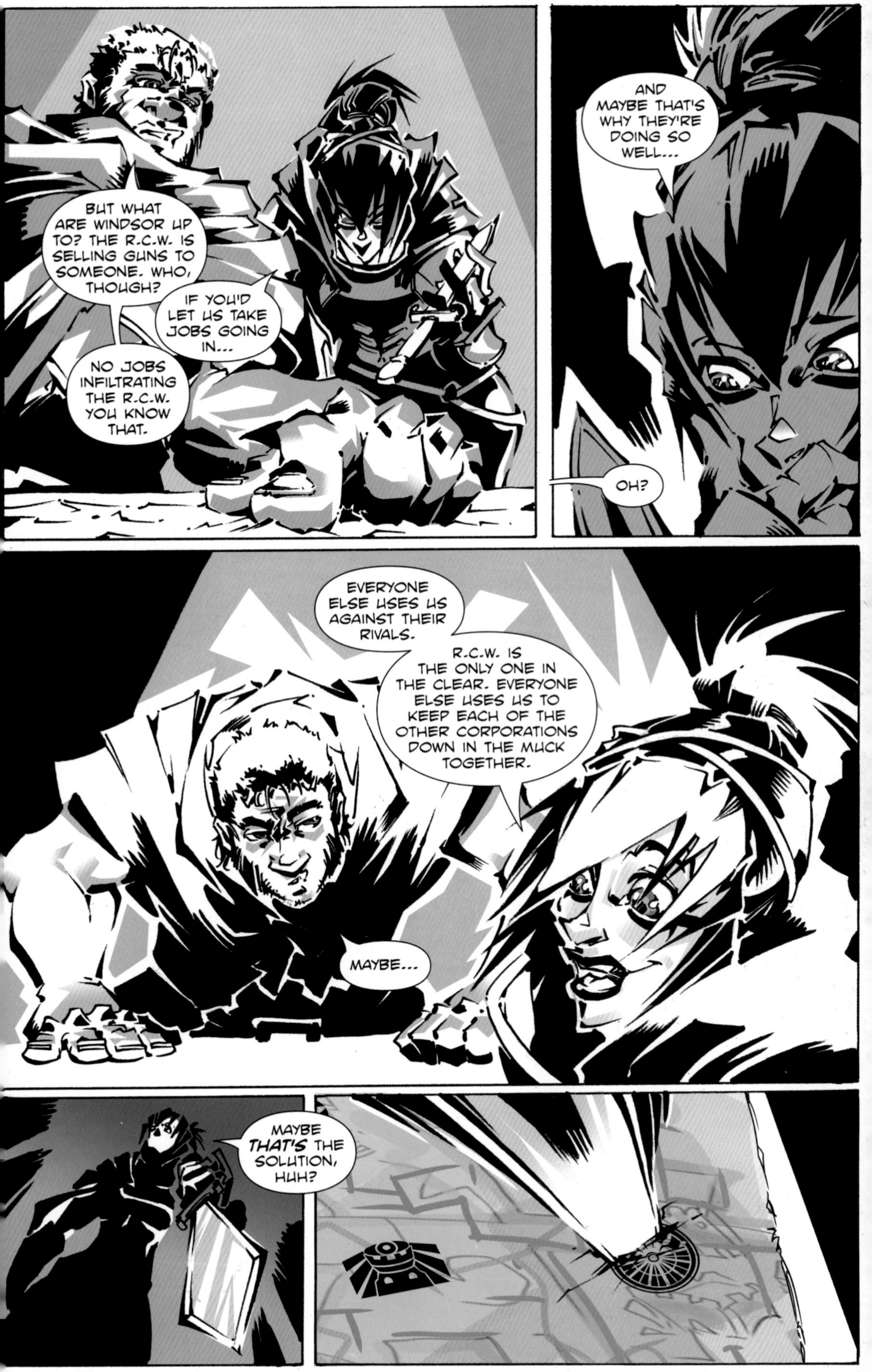
BUT WHAT ARE WINDSOR UP TO? THE R.C.W. IS SELLING GUNS TO SOMEONE. WHO, THOUGH?
IF YOU'D LET US TAKE JOBS GOING IN...
NO JOBS INFILTRATING THE R.C.W. YOU KNOW THAT.
AND MAYBE THAT'S WHY THEY'RE DOING SO WELL...
OH?
EVERYONE ELSE USES US AGAINST THEIR RIVALS.
R.C.W. IS THE ONLY ONE IN THE CLEAR. EVERYONE ELSE USES US TO KEEP EACH OF THE OTHER CORPORATIONS DOWN IN THE MUCK TOGETHER.
MAYBE...
MAYBE THAT'S THE SOLUTION, HUH?

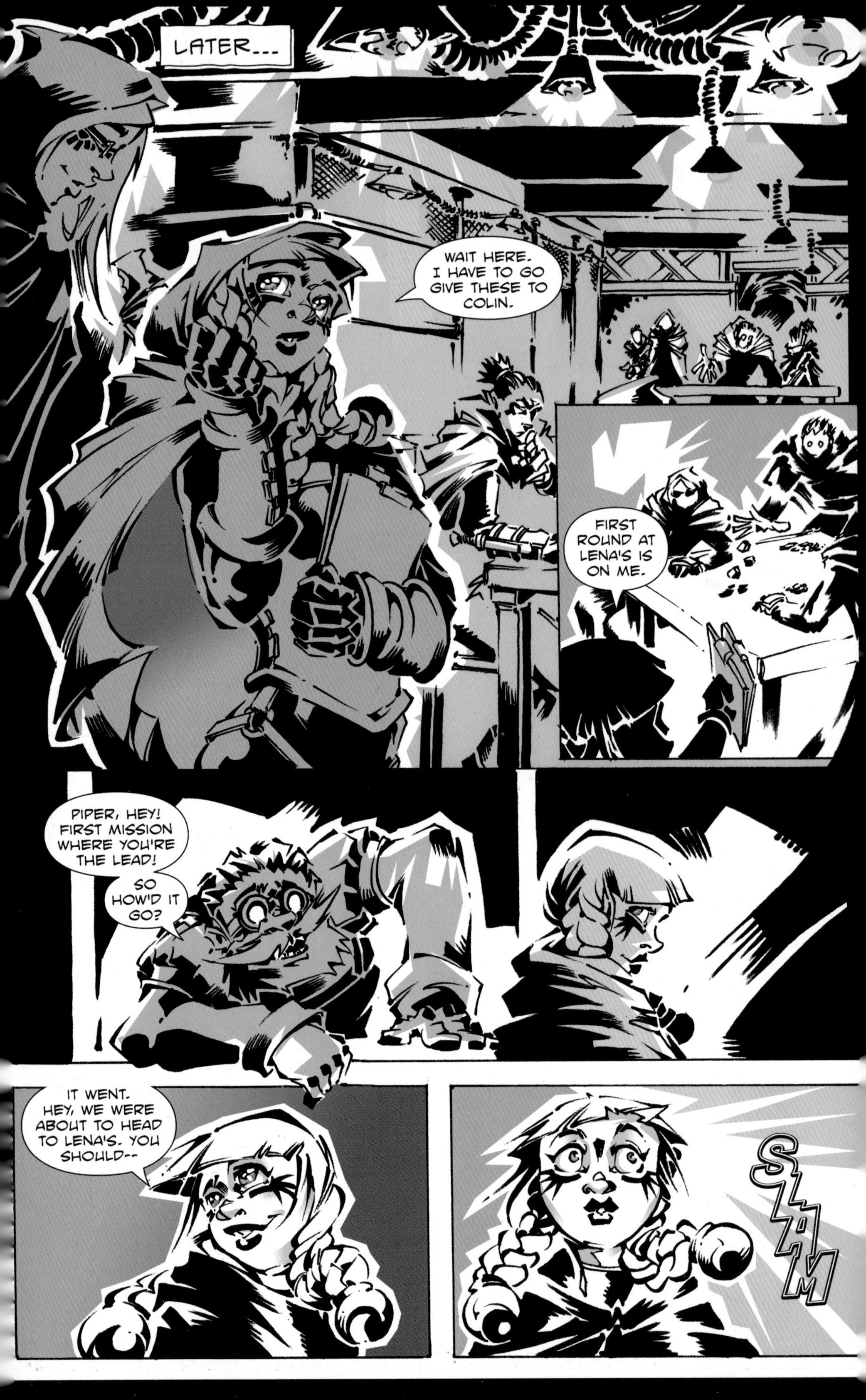

LATER...
WAIT HERE. I HAVE TO GO GIVE THESE TO COLIN.
FIRST ROUND AT LENA'S IS ON ME.
PIPER, HEY! FIRST MISSION WHERE YOU'RE THE LEAD!
SO HOW'D IT GO?
IT WENT. HEY, WE WERE ABOUT TO HEAD TO LENA'S. YOU SHOULD--
SLAM

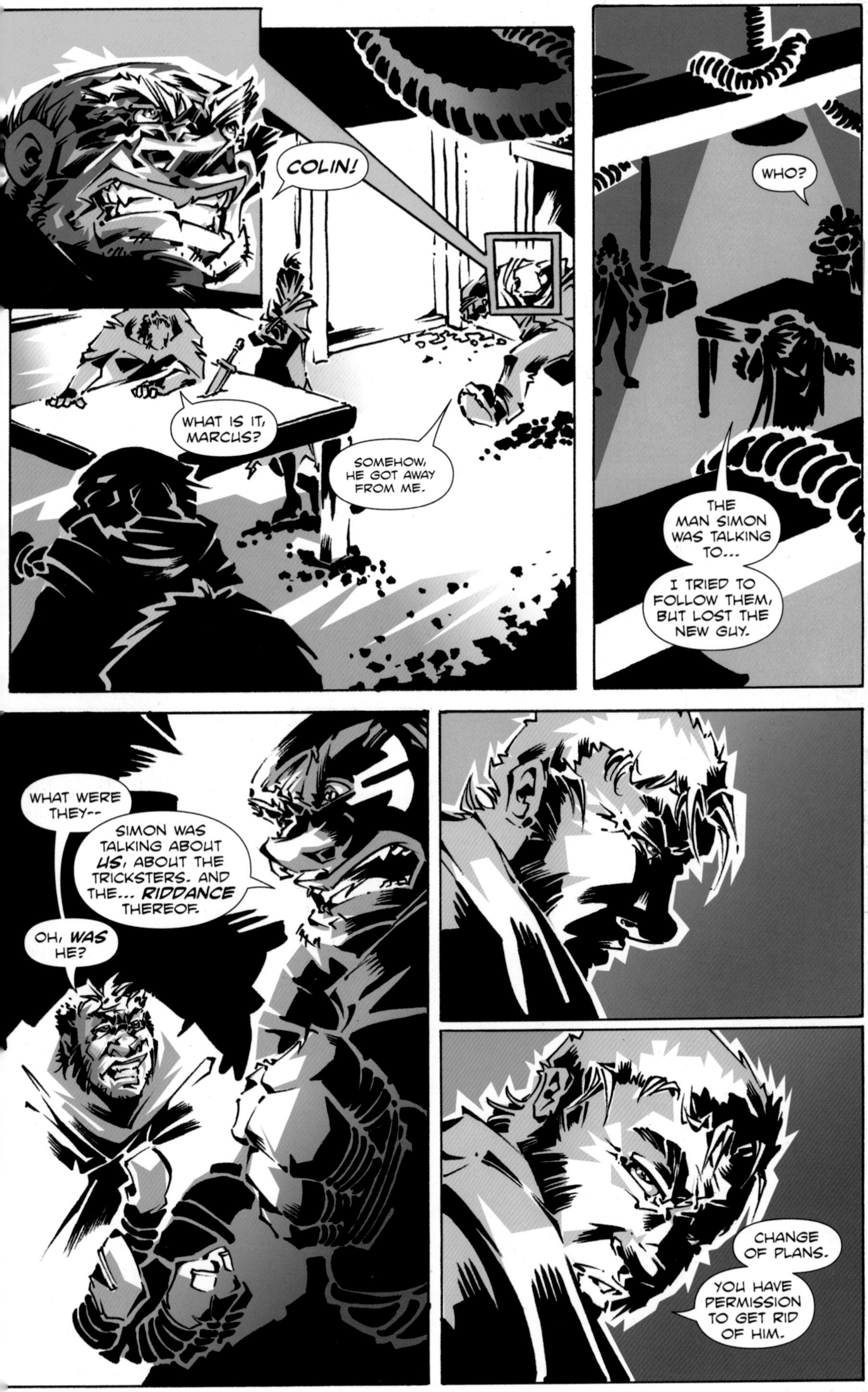
COLIN!
WHAT IS IT, MARCUS?
SOMEHOW, HE GOT AWAY FROM ME.
WHO?
THE MAN SIMON WAS TALKING TO...
I TRIED TO FOLLOW THEM, BUT LOST THE NEW GUY.
WHAT WERE THEY--
SIMON WAS TALKING ABOUT *US*, ABOUT THE TRICKSTERS. AND THE... *RIDDANCE* THEREOF.
OH, *WAS* HE?
CHANGE OF PLANS.
YOU HAVE PERMISSION TO GET RID OF HIM.

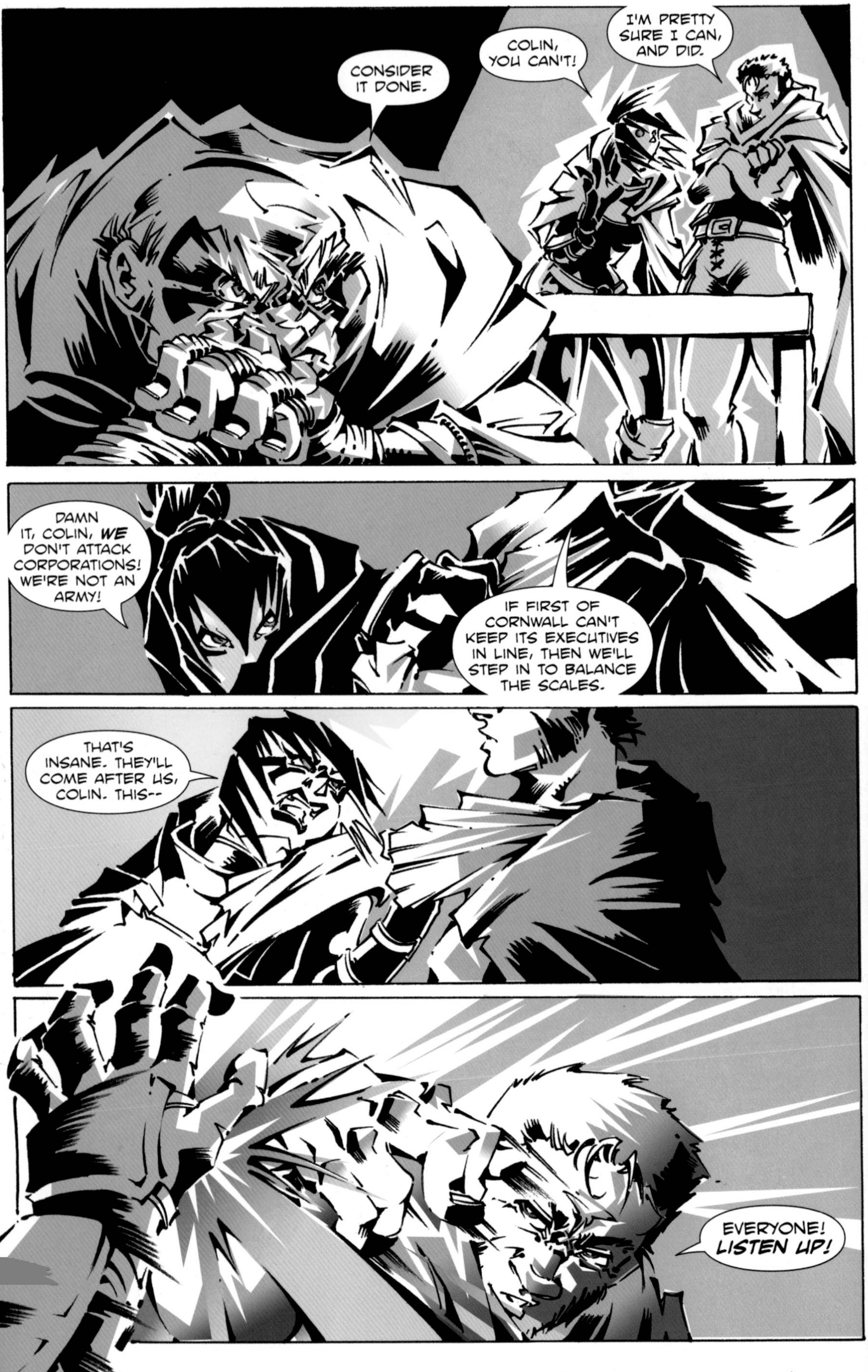
CONSIDER IT DONE.
COLIN, YOU CAN'T!
I'M PRETTY SURE I CAN, AND DID.
DAMN IT, COLIN, **WE** DON'T ATTACK CORPORATIONS! WE'RE NOT AN ARMY!
IF FIRST OF CORNWALL CAN'T KEEP ITS EXECUTIVES IN LINE, THEN WE'LL STEP IN TO BALANCE THE SCALES.
THAT'S INSANE. THEY'LL COME AFTER US, COLIN. THIS--
EVERYONE! ***LISTEN UP!***

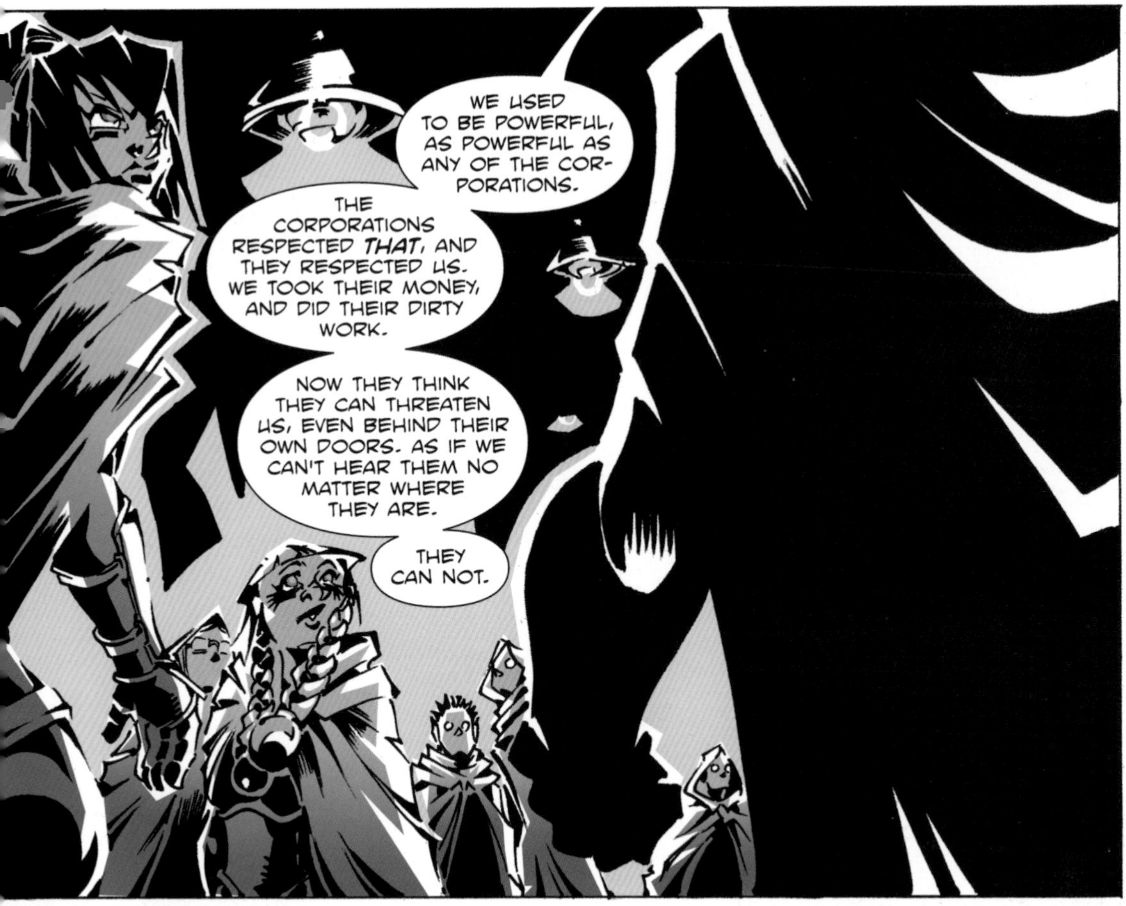
WE USED TO BE POWERFUL, AS POWERFUL AS ANY OF THE COR-PORATIONS.
THE CORPORATIONS RESPECTED *THAT*, AND THEY RESPECTED US. WE TOOK THEIR MONEY, AND DID THEIR DIRTY WORK.
NOW THEY THINK THEY CAN THREATEN US, EVEN BEHIND THEIR OWN DOORS. AS IF WE CAN'T HEAR THEM NO MATTER WHERE THEY ARE.
THEY CAN NOT.

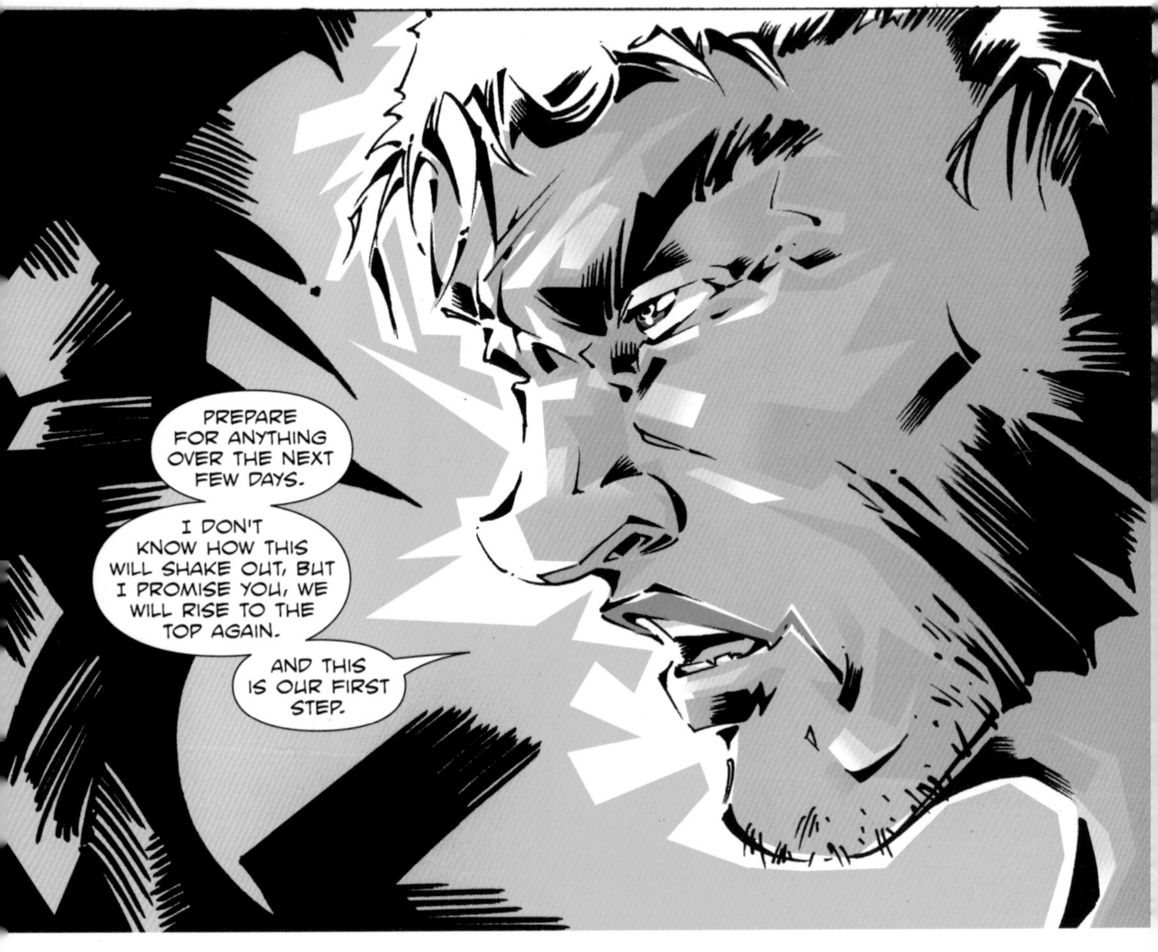
PREPARE FOR ANYTHING OVER THE NEXT FEW DAYS.
I DON'T KNOW HOW THIS WILL SHAKE OUT, BUT I PROMISE YOU, WE WILL RISE TO THE TOP AGAIN.
AND THIS IS OUR FIRST STEP.

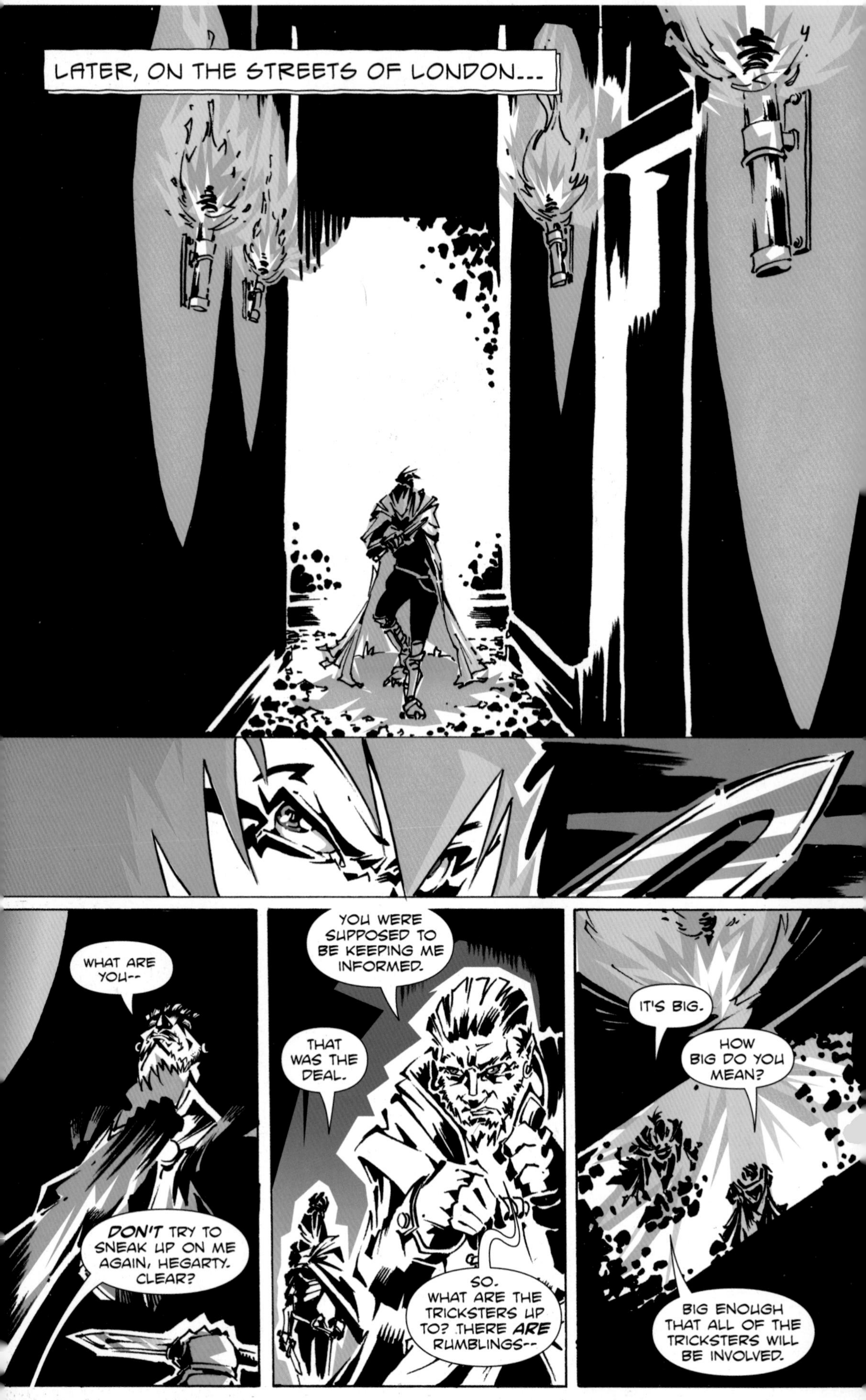

LATER, ON THE STREETS OF LONDON...
WHAT ARE YOU--
DON'T TRY TO SNEAK UP ON ME AGAIN, HEGARTY. CLEAR?
YOU WERE SUPPOSED TO BE KEEPING ME INFORMED.
THAT WAS THE DEAL.
SO. WHAT ARE THE TRICKSTERS UP TO? THERE ARE RUMBLINGS--
IT'S BIG.
HOW BIG DO YOU MEAN?
BIG ENOUGH THAT ALL OF THE TRICKSTERS WILL BE INVOLVED.

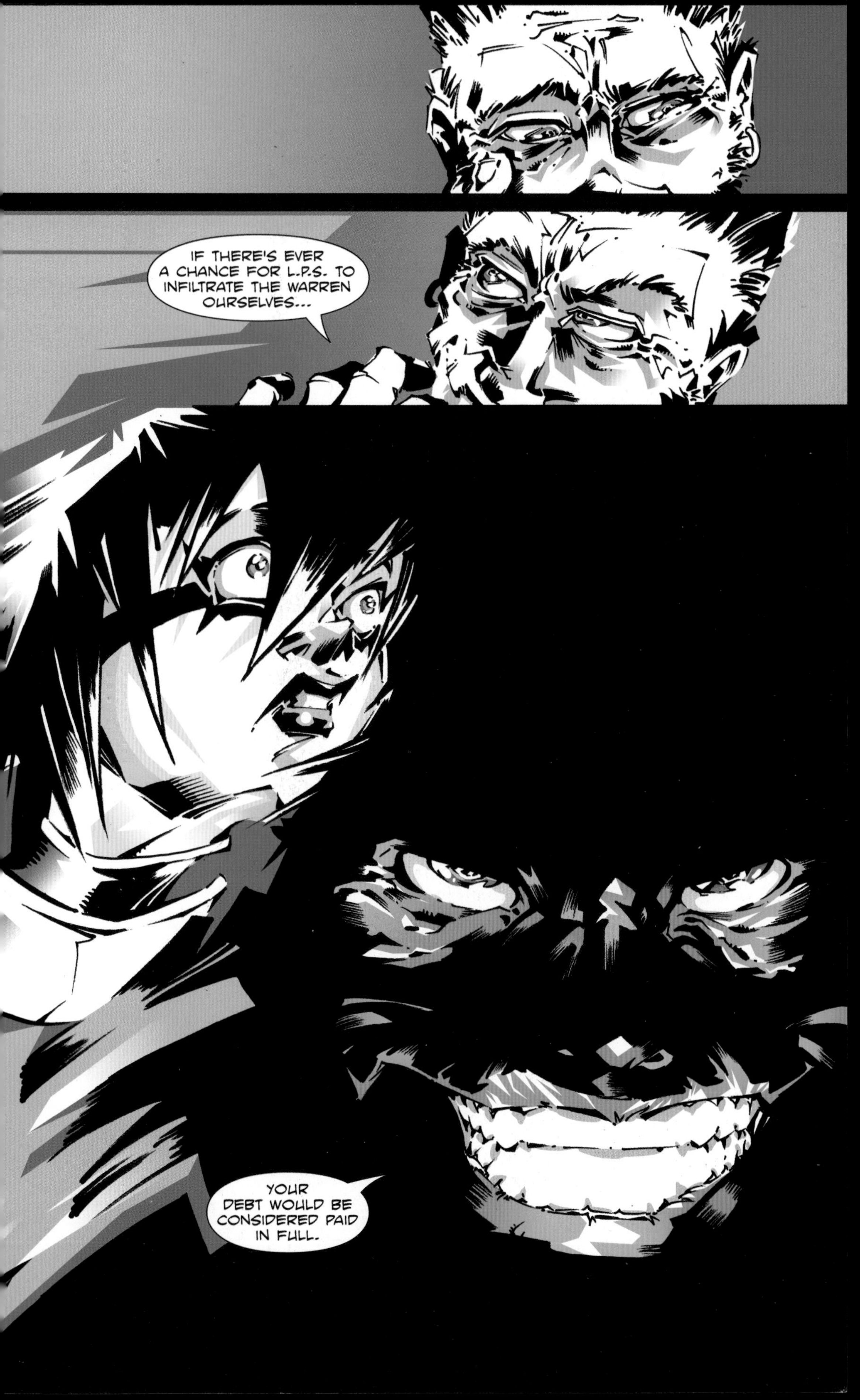
IF THERE'S EVER A CHANCE FOR L.P.S. TO INFILTRATE THE WARREN OURSELVES...
YOUR DEBT WOULD BE CONSIDERED PAID IN FULL.

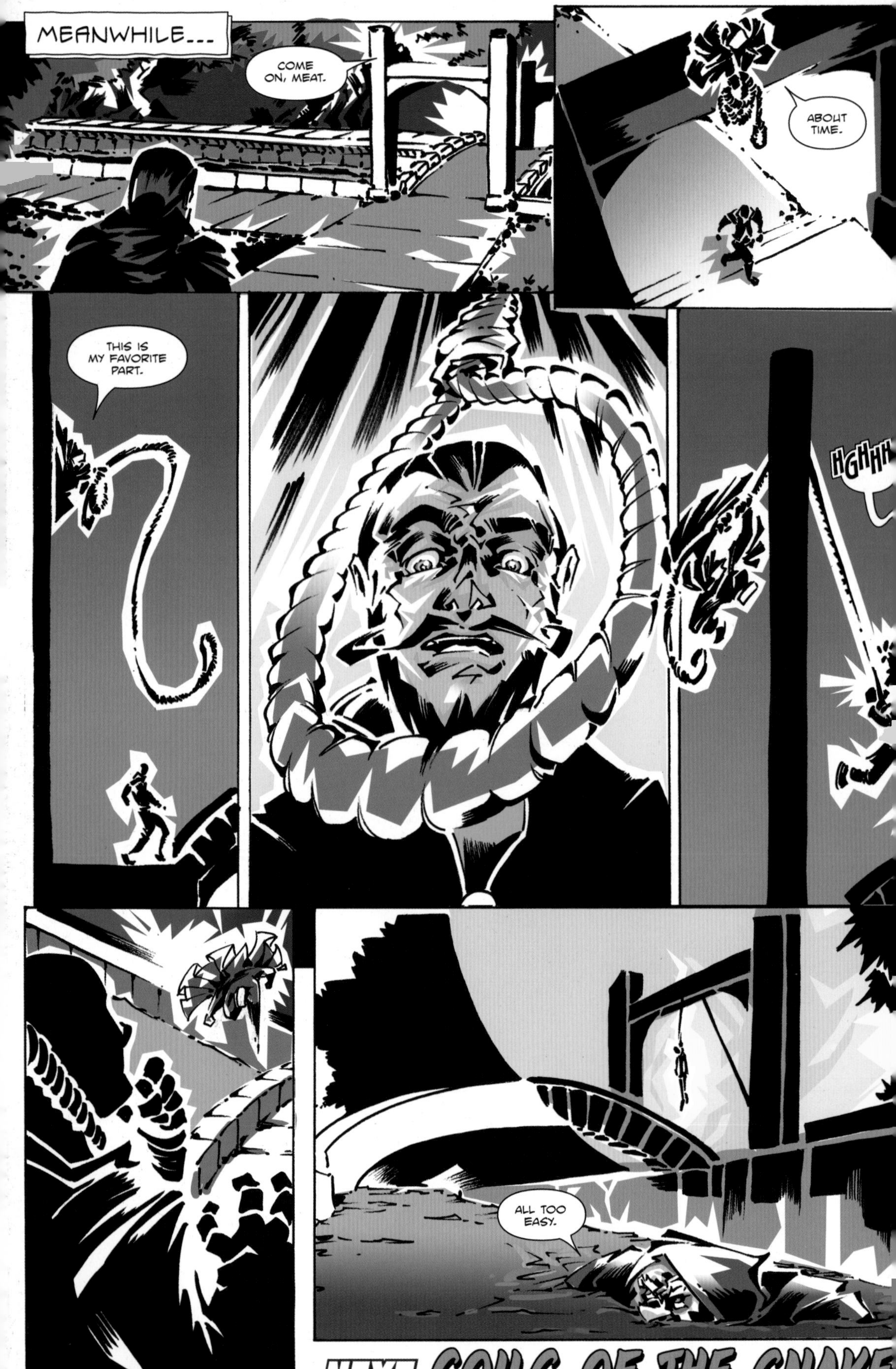
MEANWHILE...
COME ON, MEAT.
ABOUT TIME.
THIS IS MY FAVORITE PART.
HGHHH
ALL TOO EASY.
NEXT: COILS OF THE SNAKE

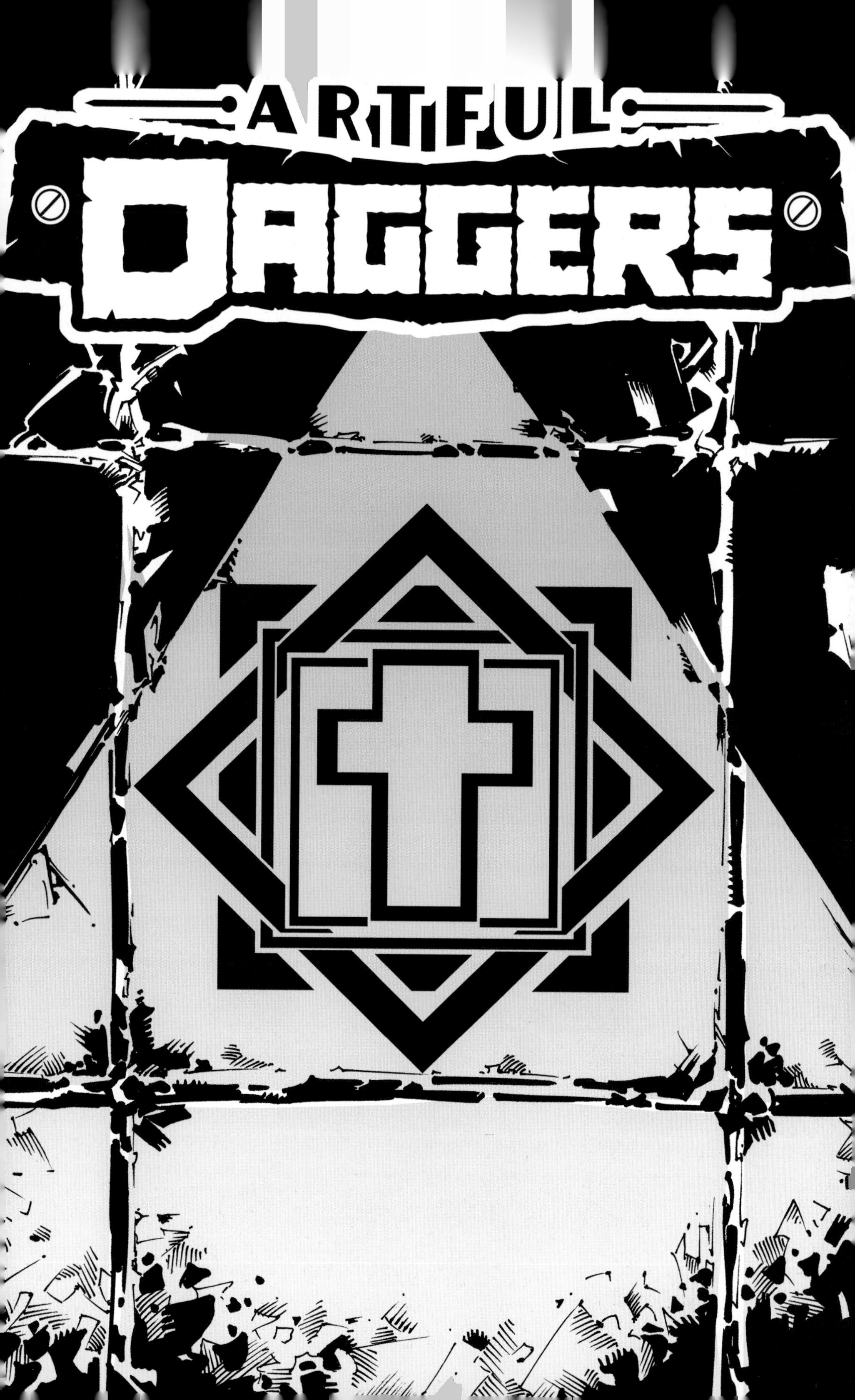
ARTFUL
DAGGERS

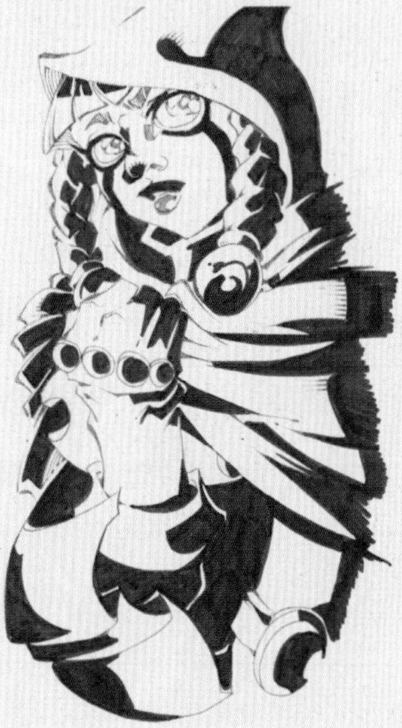
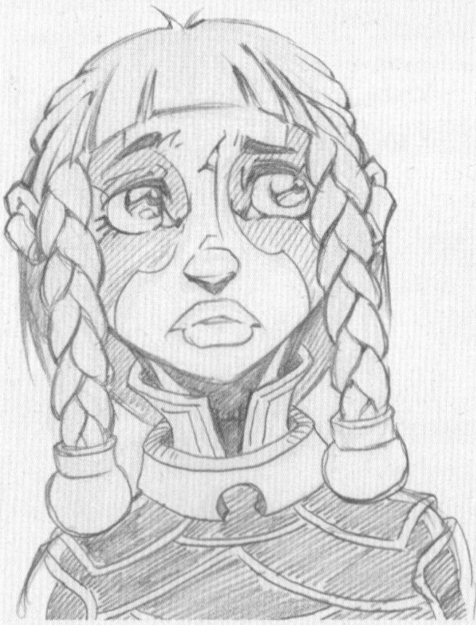
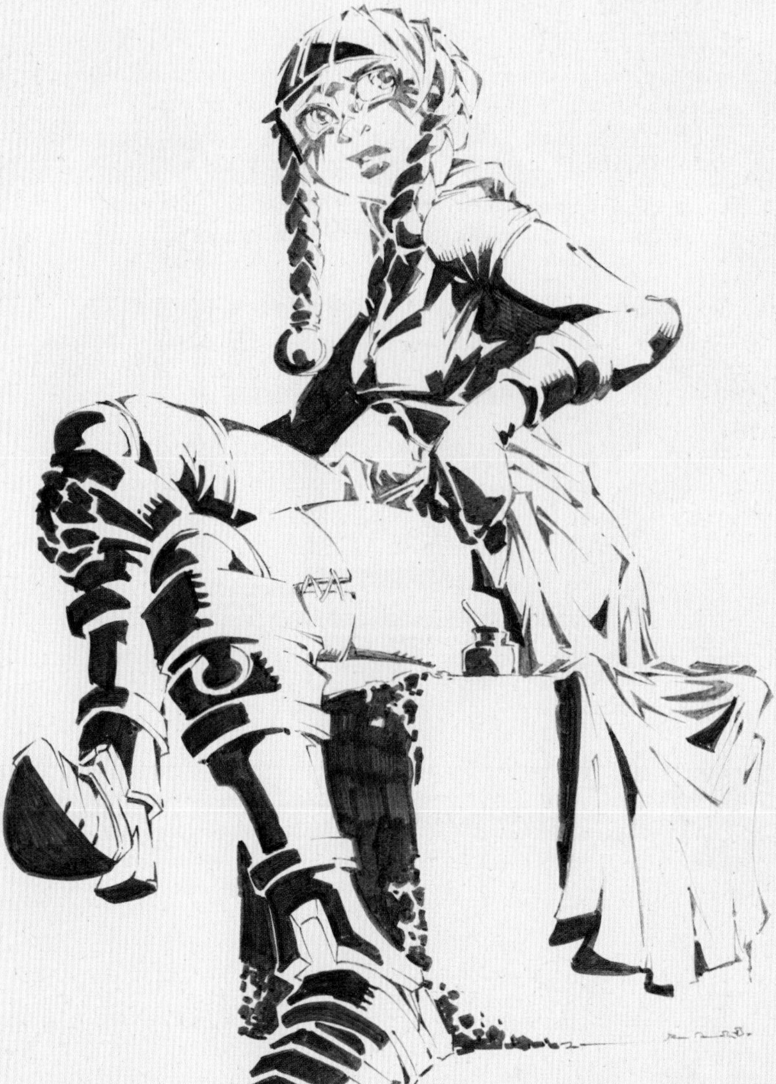

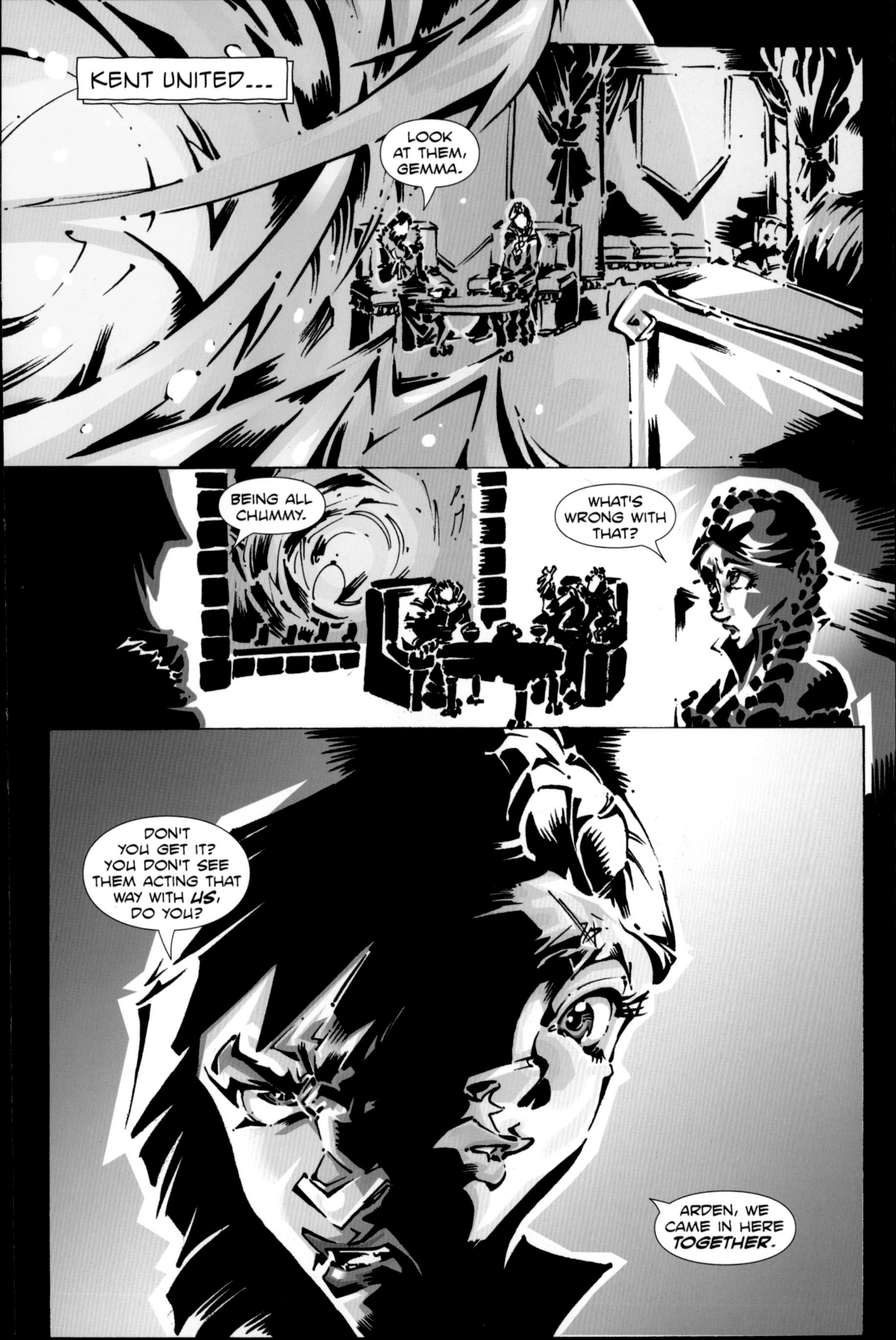
KENT UNITED...
LOOK AT THEM, GEMMA.
BEING ALL CHUMMY.
WHAT'S WRONG WITH THAT?
DON'T YOU GET IT? YOU DON'T SEE THEM ACTING THAT WAY WITH *US*, DO YOU?
ARDEN, WE CAME IN HERE *TOGETHER*.

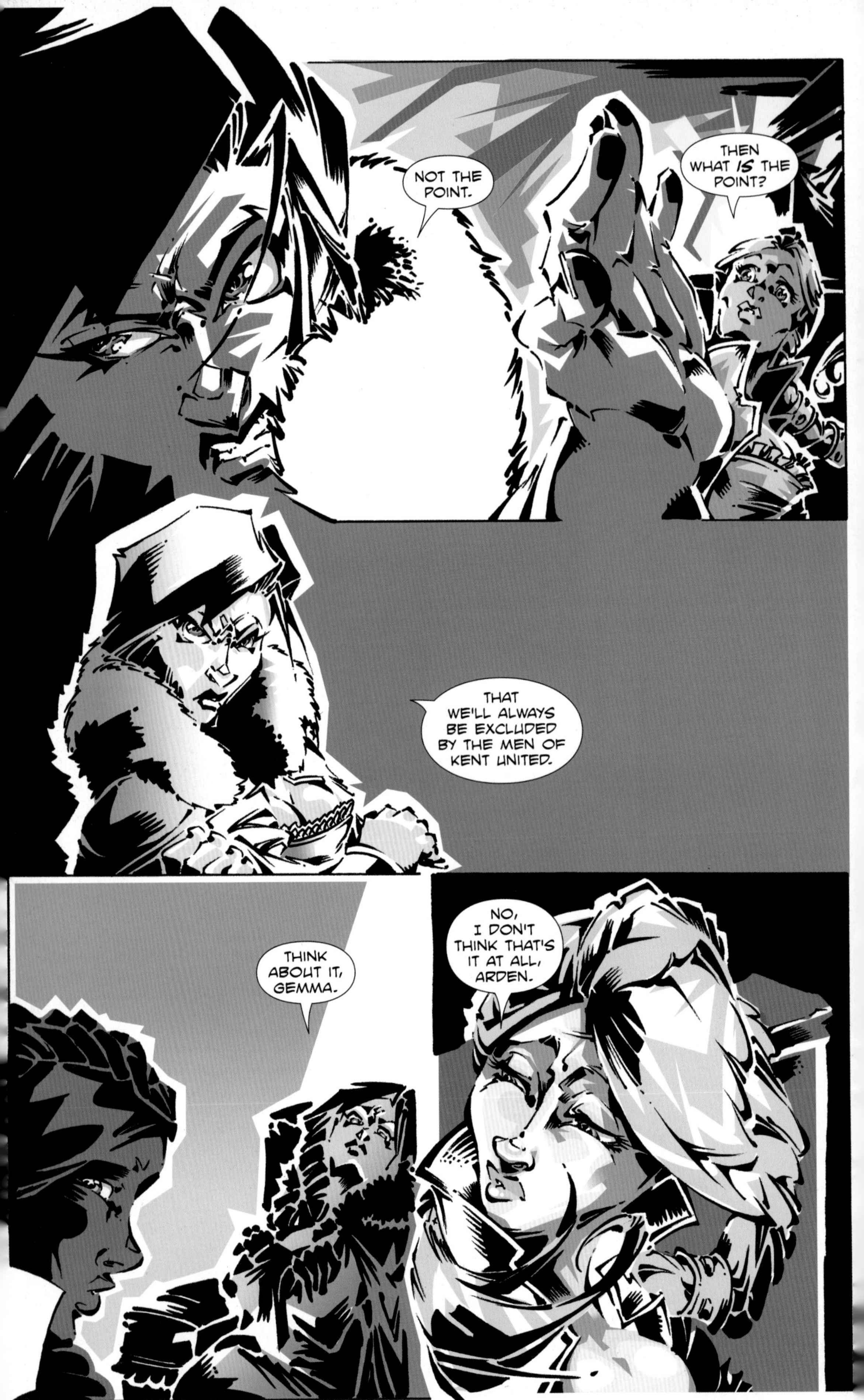
NOT THE POINT.
THEN WHAT IS THE POINT?
THAT WE'LL ALWAYS BE EXCLUDED BY THE MEN OF KENT UNITED.
THINK ABOUT IT, GEMMA.
NO, I DON'T THINK THAT'S IT AT ALL, ARDEN.

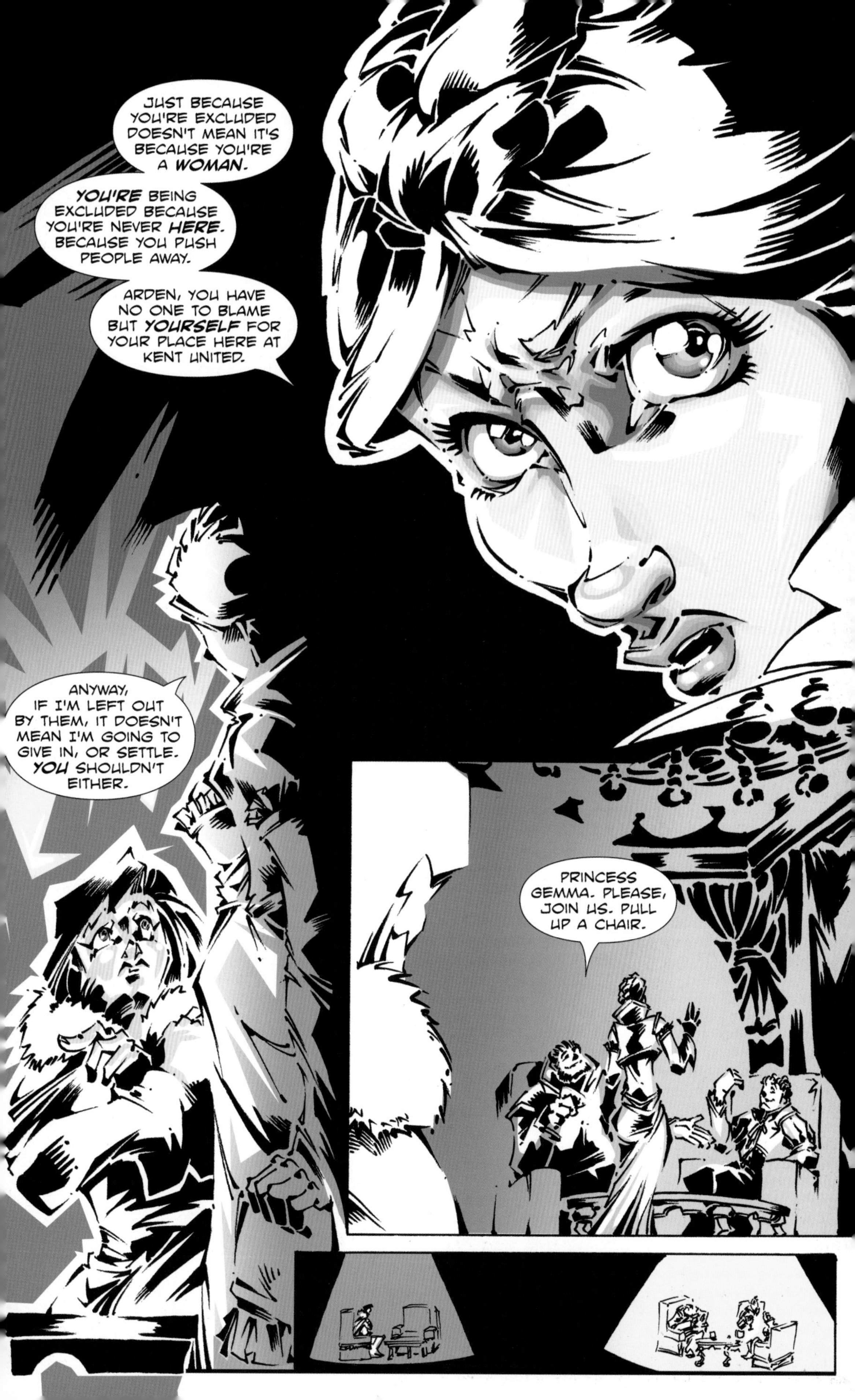

JUST BECAUSE YOU'RE EXCLUDED DOESN'T MEAN IT'S BECAUSE YOU'RE A WOMAN.
YOU'RE BEING EXCLUDED BECAUSE YOU'RE NEVER HERE. BECAUSE YOU PUSH PEOPLE AWAY.
ARDEN, YOU HAVE NO ONE TO BLAME BUT YOURSELF FOR YOUR PLACE HERE AT KENT UNITED.
ANYWAY, IF I'M LEFT OUT BY THEM, IT DOESN'T MEAN I'M GOING TO GIVE IN, OR SETTLE. YOU SHOULDN'T EITHER.
PRINCESS GEMMA. PLEASE, JOIN US. PULL UP A CHAIR.

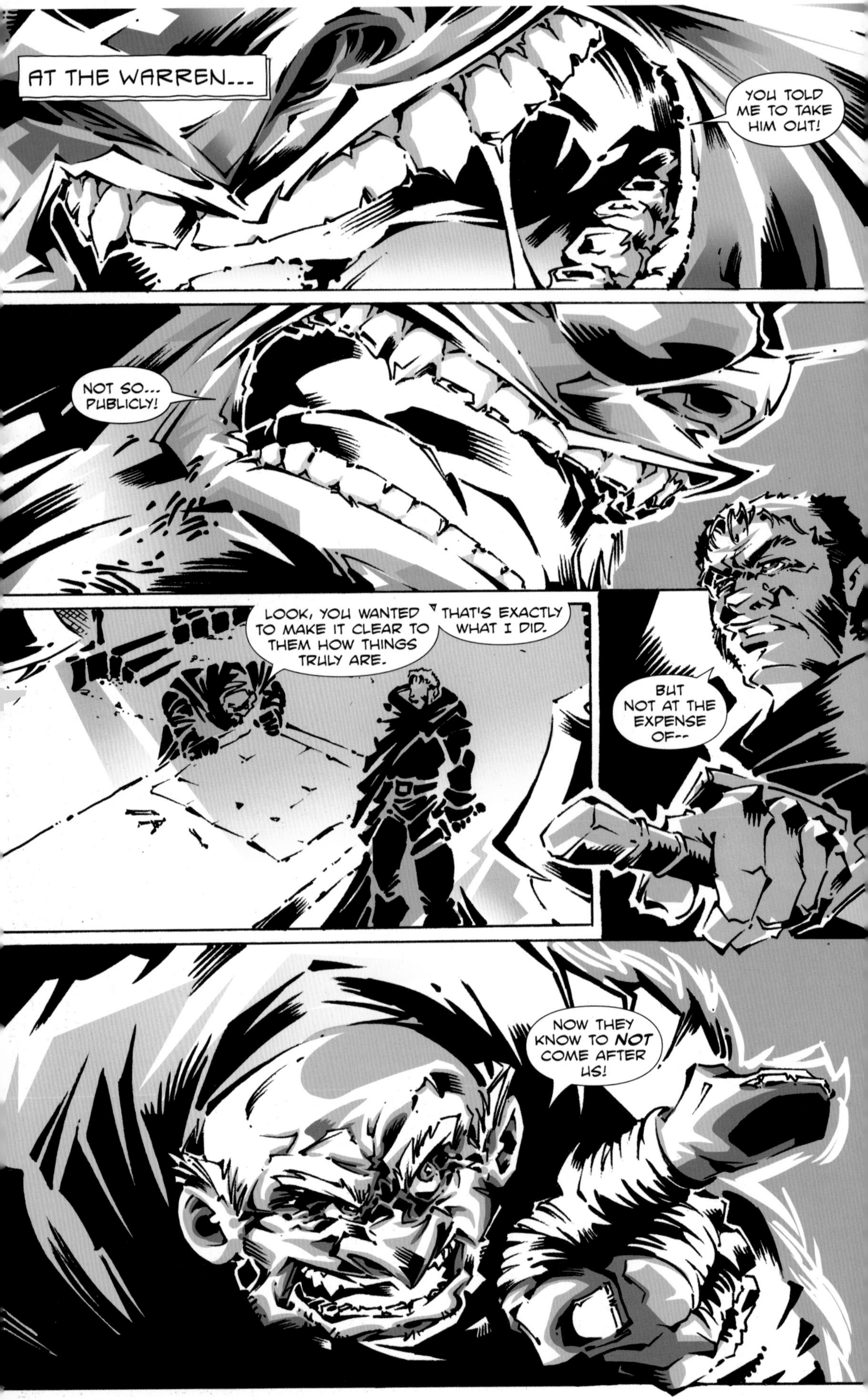
AT THE WARREN...
YOU TOLD ME TO TAKE HIM OUT!
NOT SO... PUBLICLY!
LOOK, YOU WANTED TO MAKE IT CLEAR TO THEM HOW THINGS TRULY ARE.
THAT'S EXACTLY WHAT I DID.
BUT NOT AT THE EXPENSE OF--
NOW THEY KNOW TO NOT COME AFTER US!

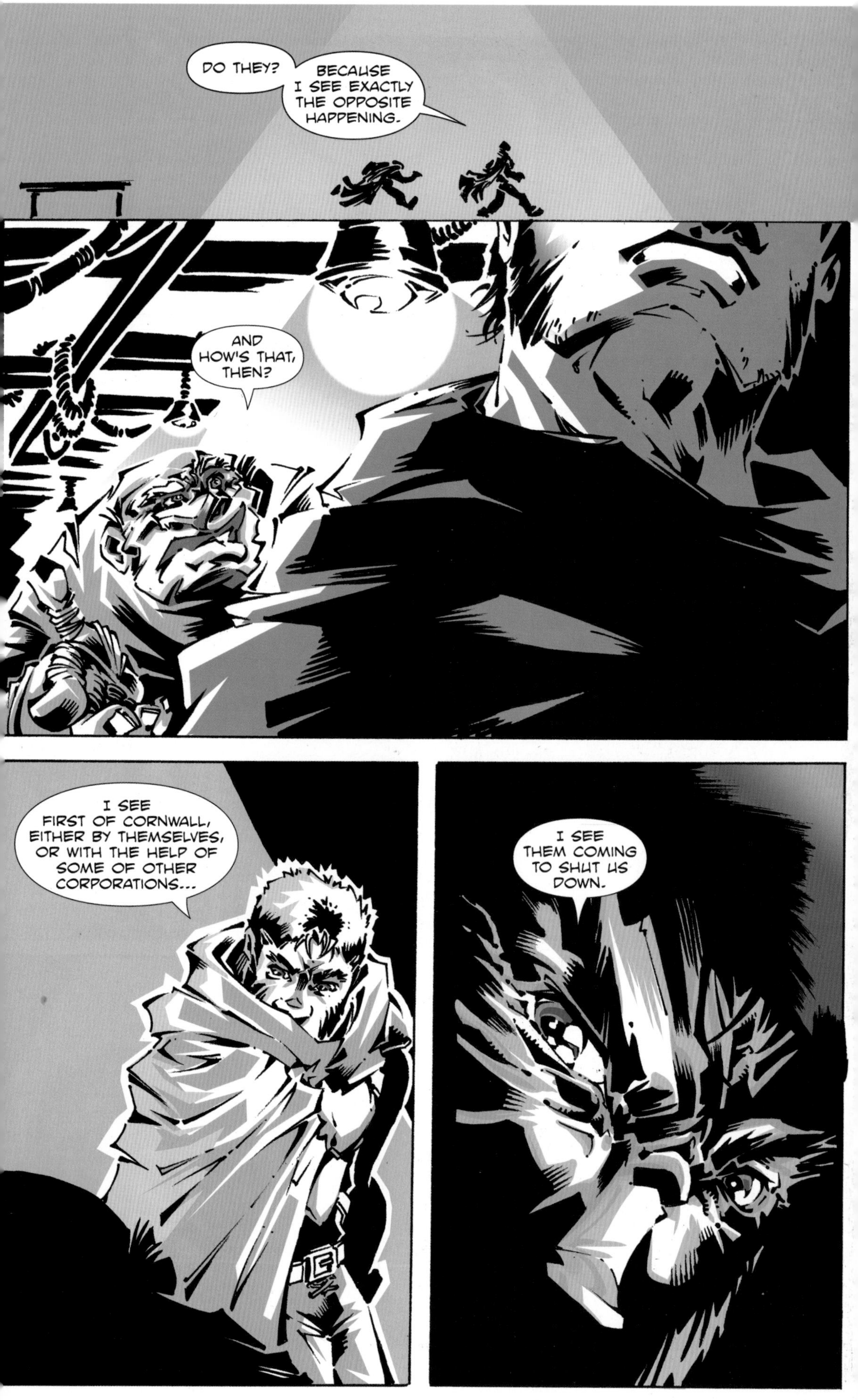
DO THEY?
BECAUSE I SEE EXACTLY THE OPPOSITE HAPPENING.
AND HOW'S THAT, THEN?
I SEE FIRST OF CORNWALL, EITHER BY THEMSELVES, OR WITH THE HELP OF SOME OF OTHER CORPORATIONS...
I SEE THEM COMING TO SHUT US DOWN.

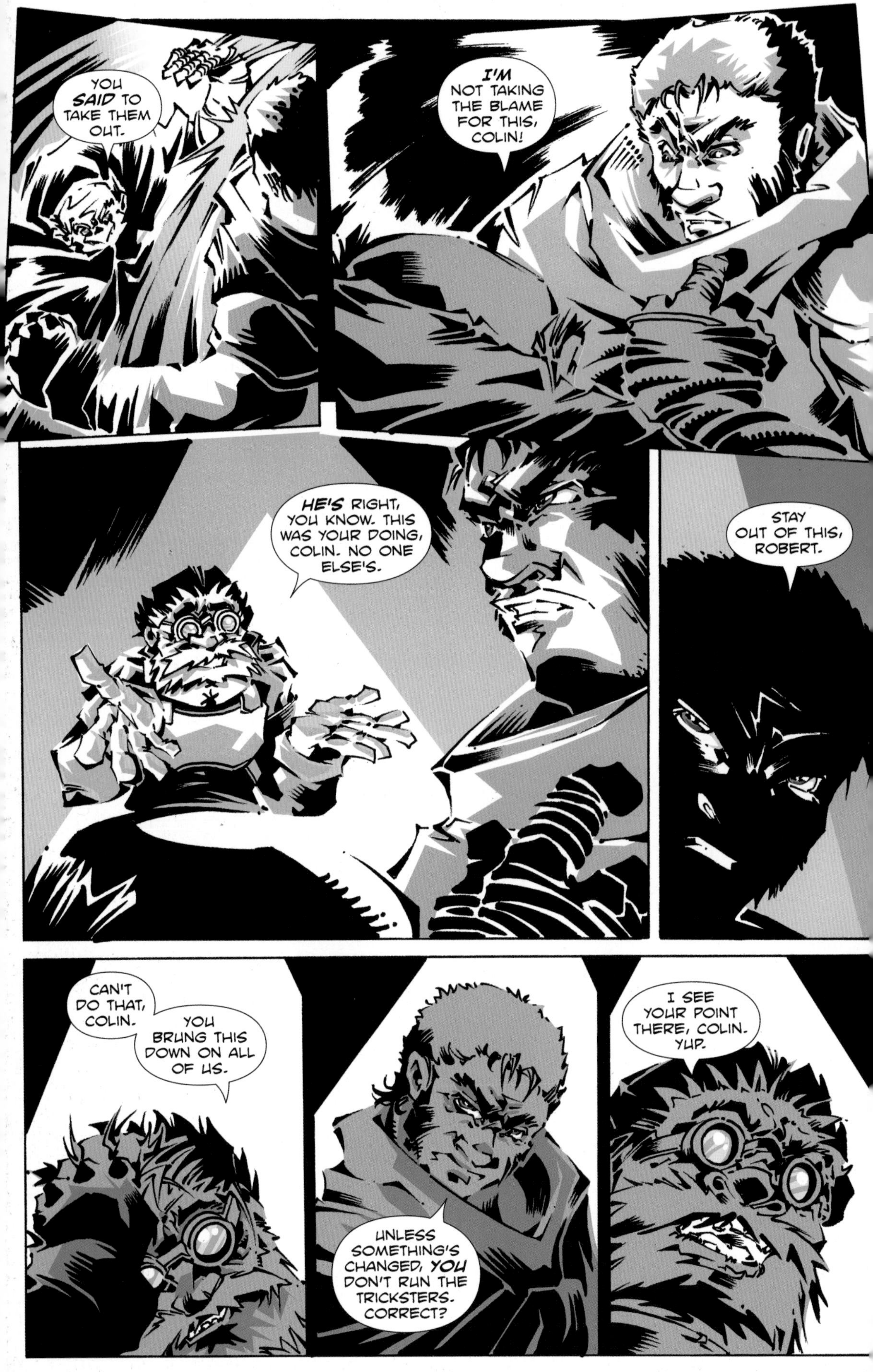

YOU SAID TO TAKE THEM OUT.
I'M NOT TAKING THE BLAME FOR THIS, COLIN!
HE'S RIGHT, YOU KNOW. THIS WAS YOUR DOING, COLIN. NO ONE ELSE'S.
STAY OUT OF THIS, ROBERT.
CAN'T DO THAT, COLIN.
YOU BRUNG THIS DOWN ON ALL OF US.
UNLESS SOMETHING'S CHANGED, YOU DON'T RUN THE TRICKSTERS. CORRECT?
I SEE YOUR POINT THERE, COLIN. YUP.

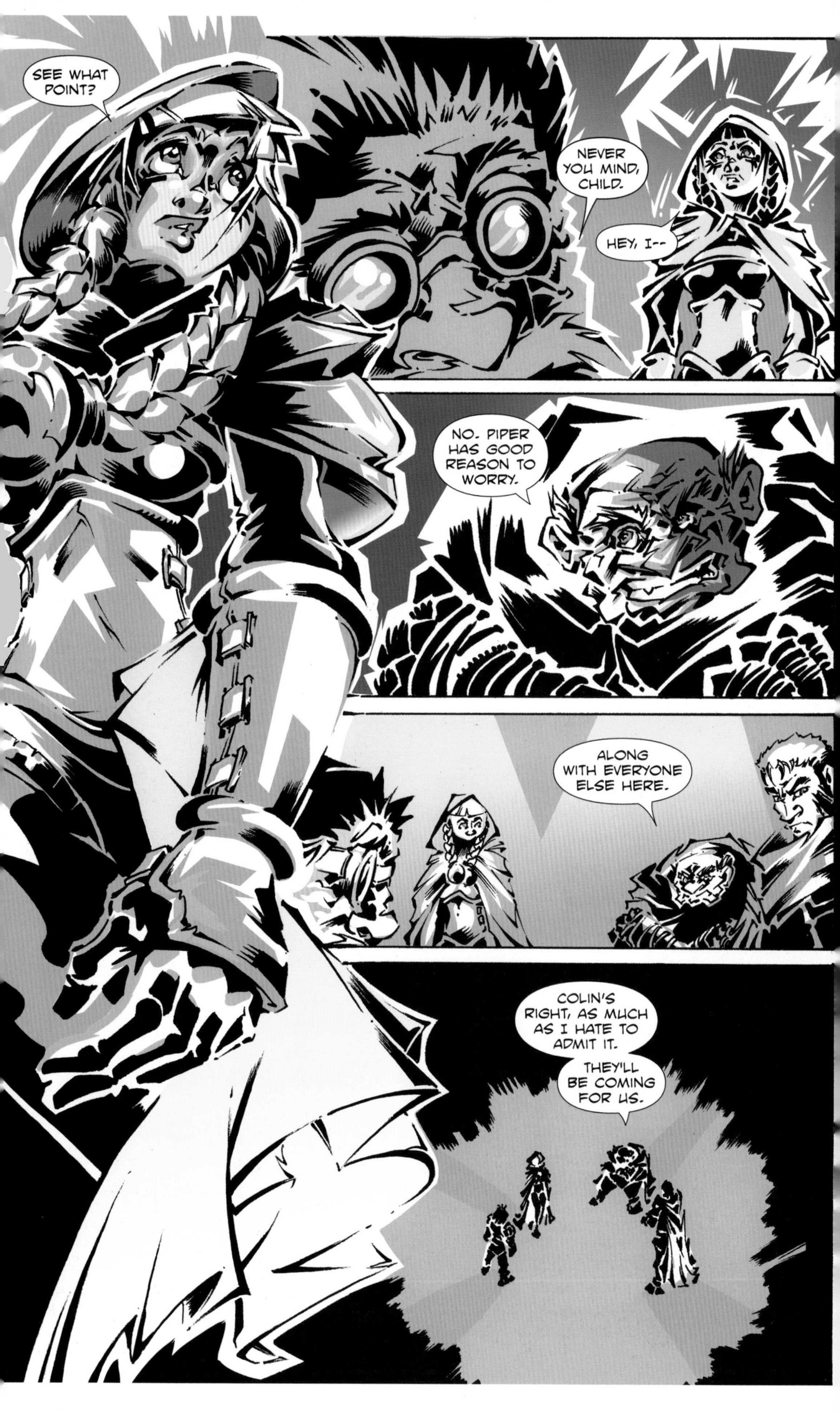
SEE WHAT POINT?
NEVER YOU MIND, CHILD.
HEY, I--
NO. PIPER HAS GOOD REASON TO WORRY.
ALONG WITH EVERYONE ELSE HERE.
COLIN'S RIGHT, AS MUCH AS I HATE TO ADMIT IT.
THEY'LL BE COMING FOR US.

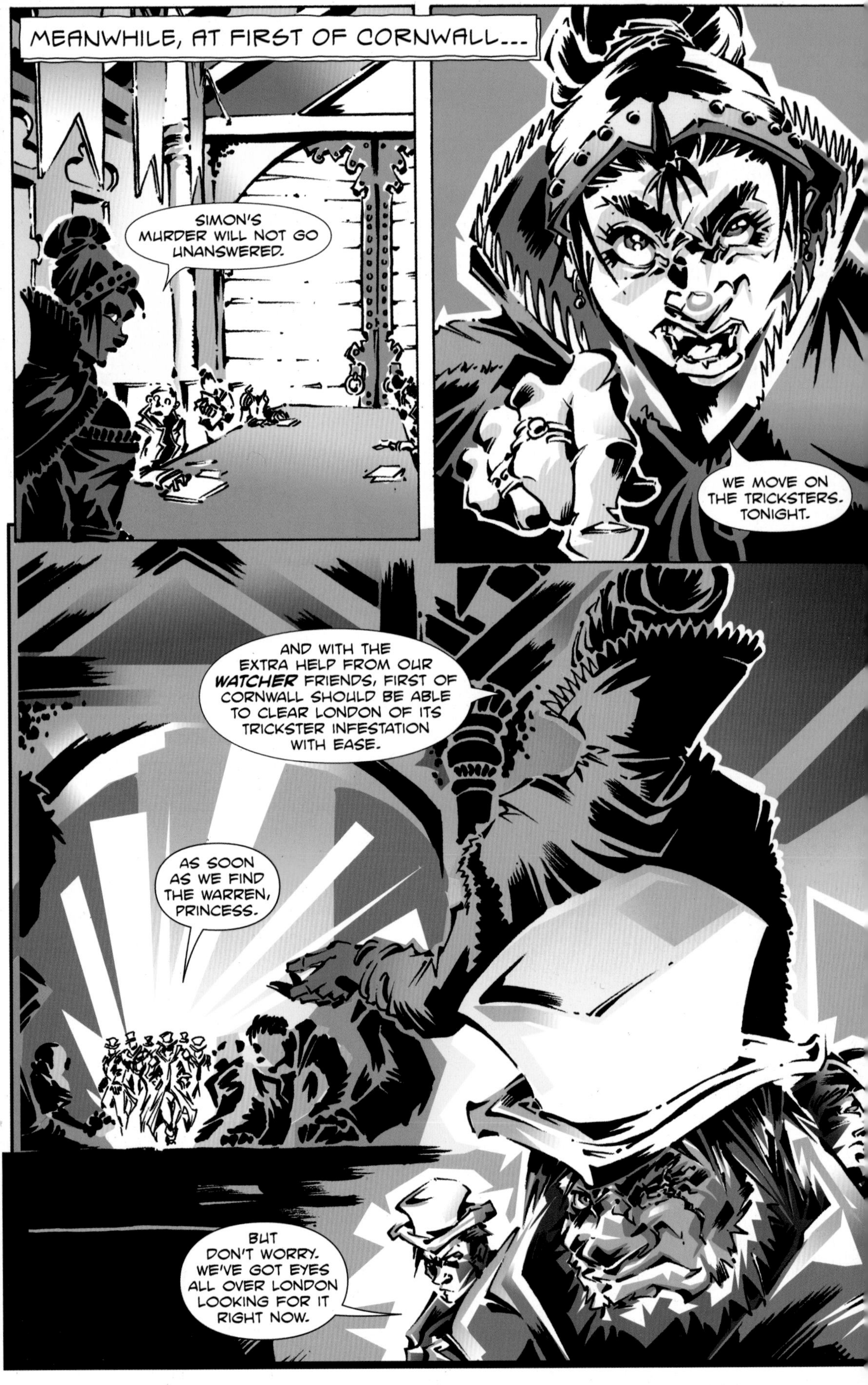
MEANWHILE, AT FIRST OF CORNWALL...
SIMON'S MURDER WILL NOT GO UNANSWERED.
WE MOVE ON THE TRICKSTERS. TONIGHT.
AND WITH THE EXTRA HELP FROM OUR WATCHER FRIENDS, FIRST OF CORNWALL SHOULD BE ABLE TO CLEAR LONDON OF ITS TRICKSTER INFESTATION WITH EASE.
AS SOON AS WE FIND THE WARREN, PRINCESS.
BUT DON'T WORRY. WE'VE GOT EYES ALL OVER LONDON LOOKING FOR IT RIGHT NOW.

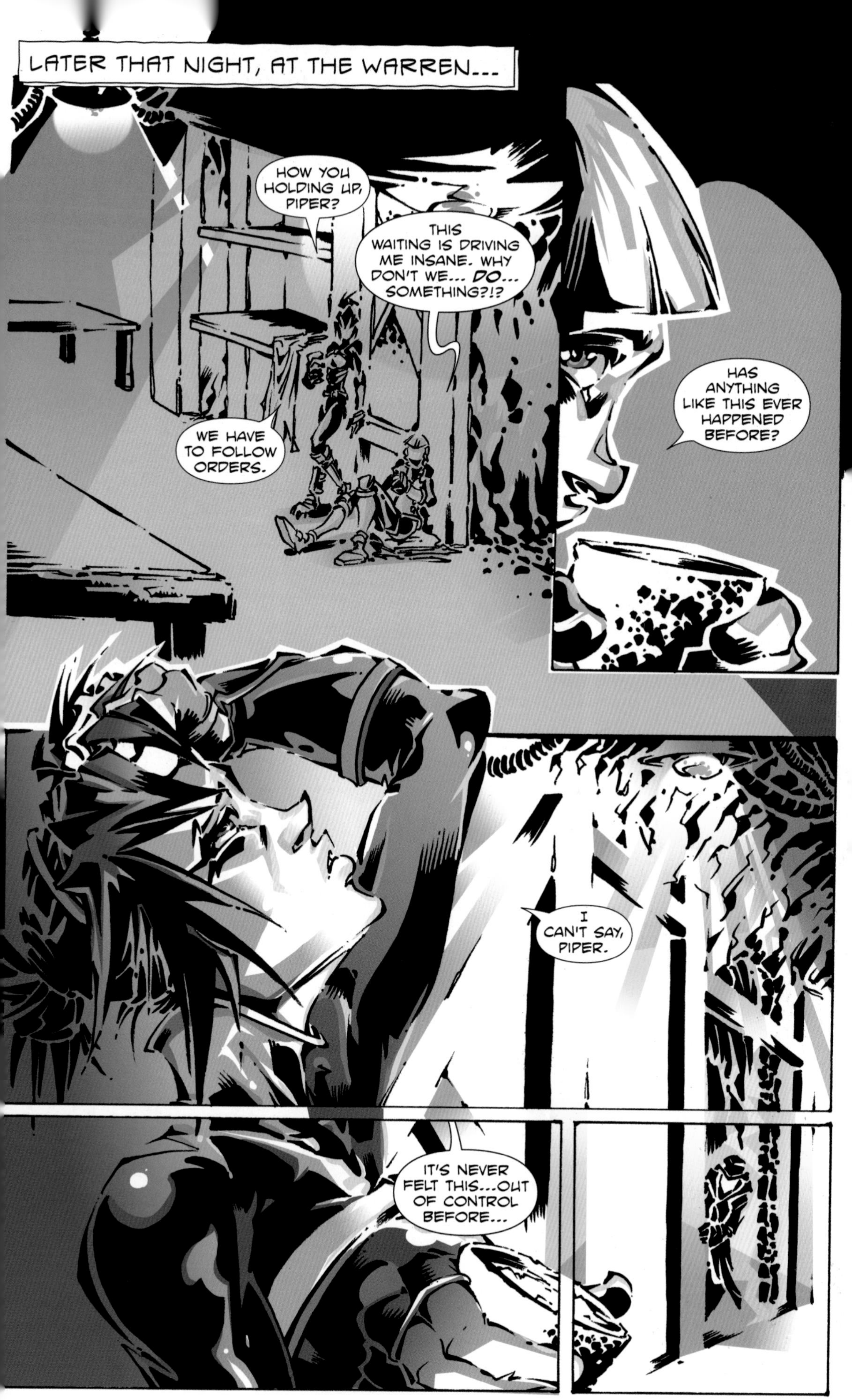
LATER THAT NIGHT, AT THE WARREN...
HOW YOU HOLDING UP, PIPER?
THIS WAITING IS DRIVING ME INSANE. WHY DON'T WE... DO... SOMETHING?!?
WE HAVE TO FOLLOW ORDERS.
HAS ANYTHING LIKE THIS EVER HAPPENED BEFORE?
I CAN'T SAY, PIPER.
IT'S NEVER FELT THIS...OUT OF CONTROL BEFORE...

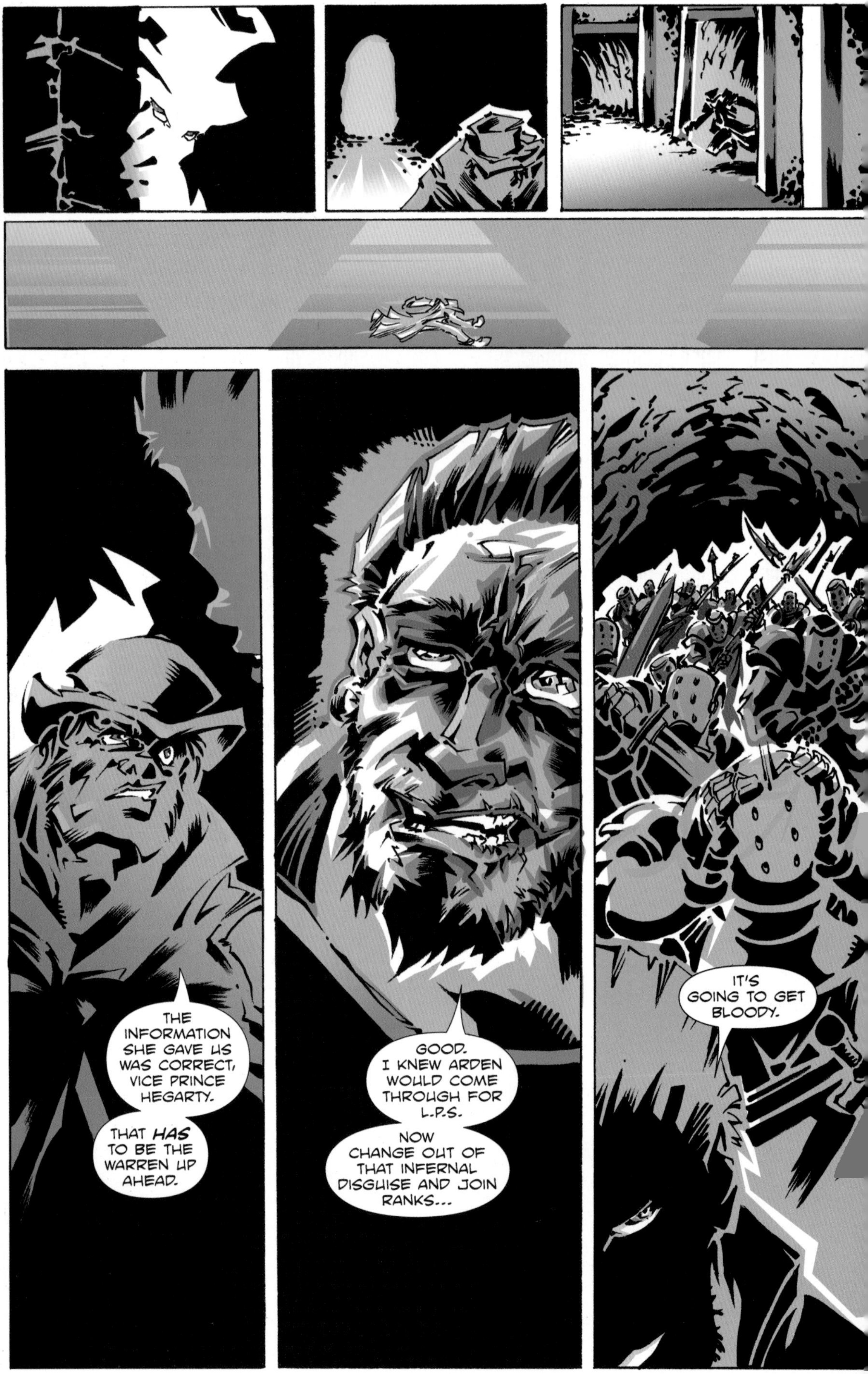
THE INFORMATION SHE GAVE US WAS CORRECT, VICE PRINCE HEGARTY.
THAT HAS TO BE THE WARREN UP AHEAD.
GOOD. I KNEW ARDEN WOULD COME THROUGH FOR L.P.S.
NOW CHANGE OUT OF THAT INFERNAL DISGUISE AND JOIN RANKS...
IT'S GOING TO GET BLOODY.

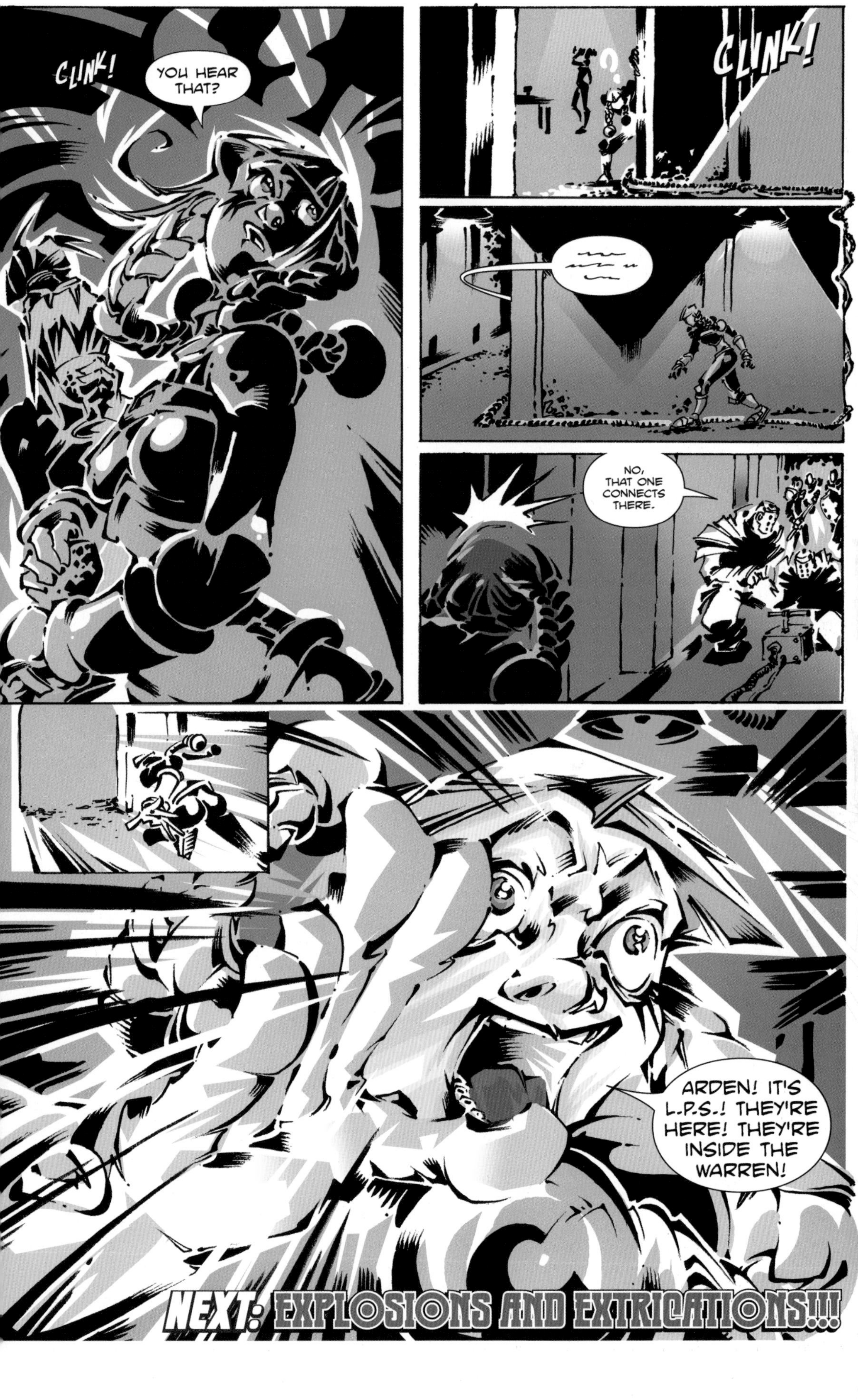
CLINK!
YOU HEAR THAT?
CLINK!
NO, THAT ONE CONNECTS THERE.
ARDEN! IT'S L.P.S.! THEY'RE HERE! THEY'RE INSIDE THE WARREN!
NEXT: EXPLOSIONS AND EXTRICATIONS!!!

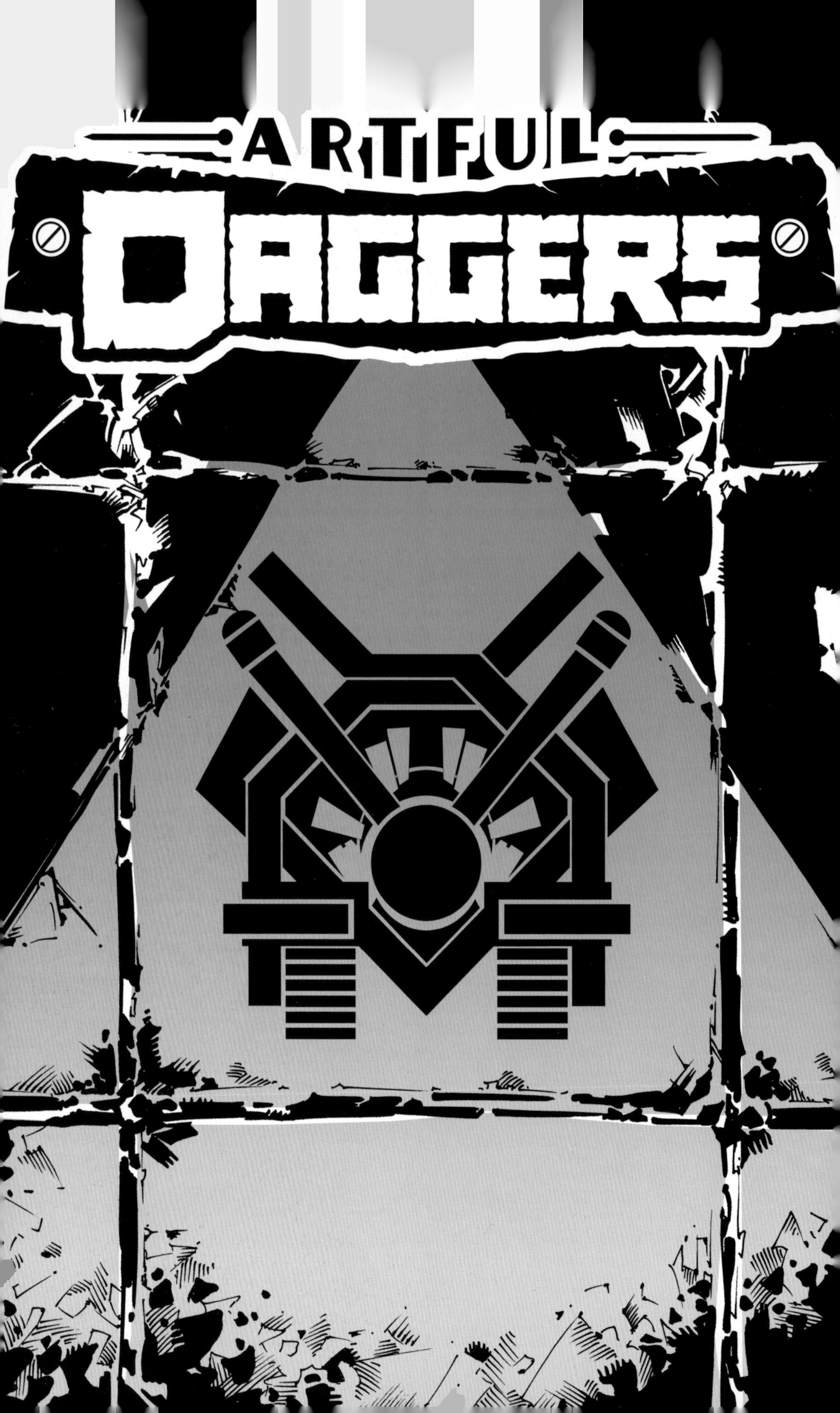
ARTFUL
DAGGERS

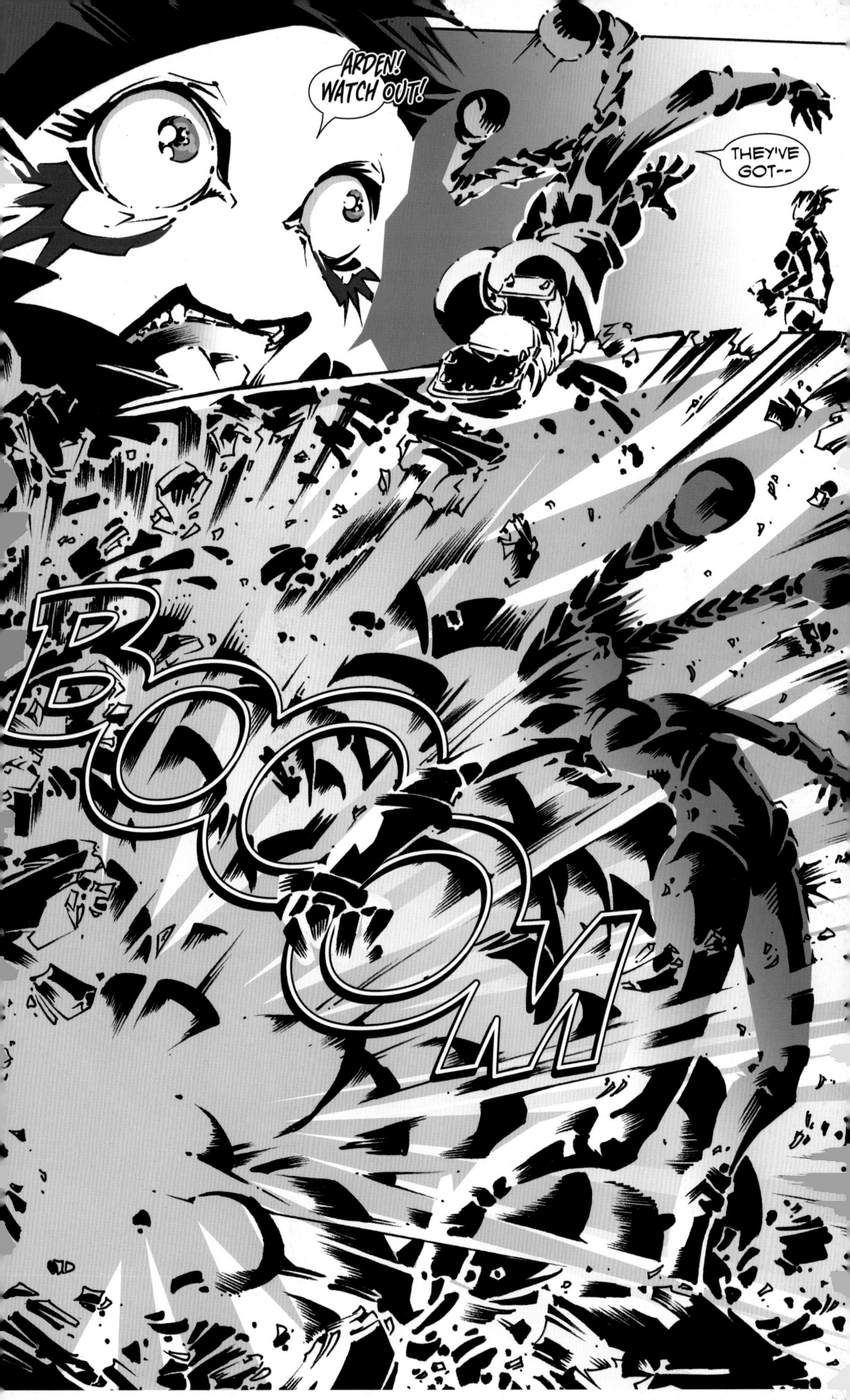
ARDEN! WATCH OUT!
THEY'VE GOT--
BOOOM

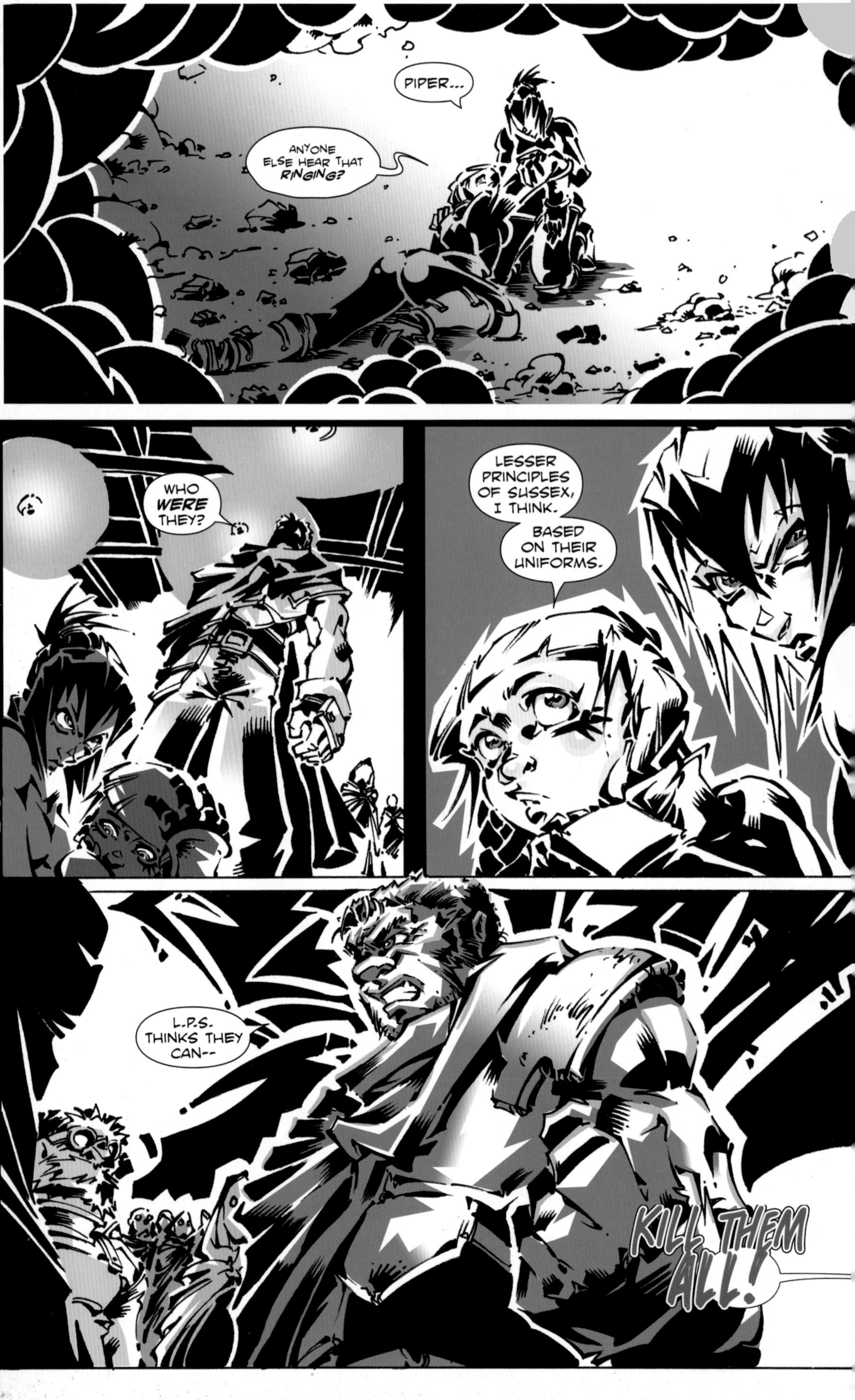
PIPER...
ANYONE ELSE HEAR THAT RINGING?
WHO WERE THEY?
LESSER PRINCIPLES OF SUSSEX, I THINK.
BASED ON THEIR UNIFORMS.
L.P.S. THINKS THEY CAN--
KILL THEM ALL!

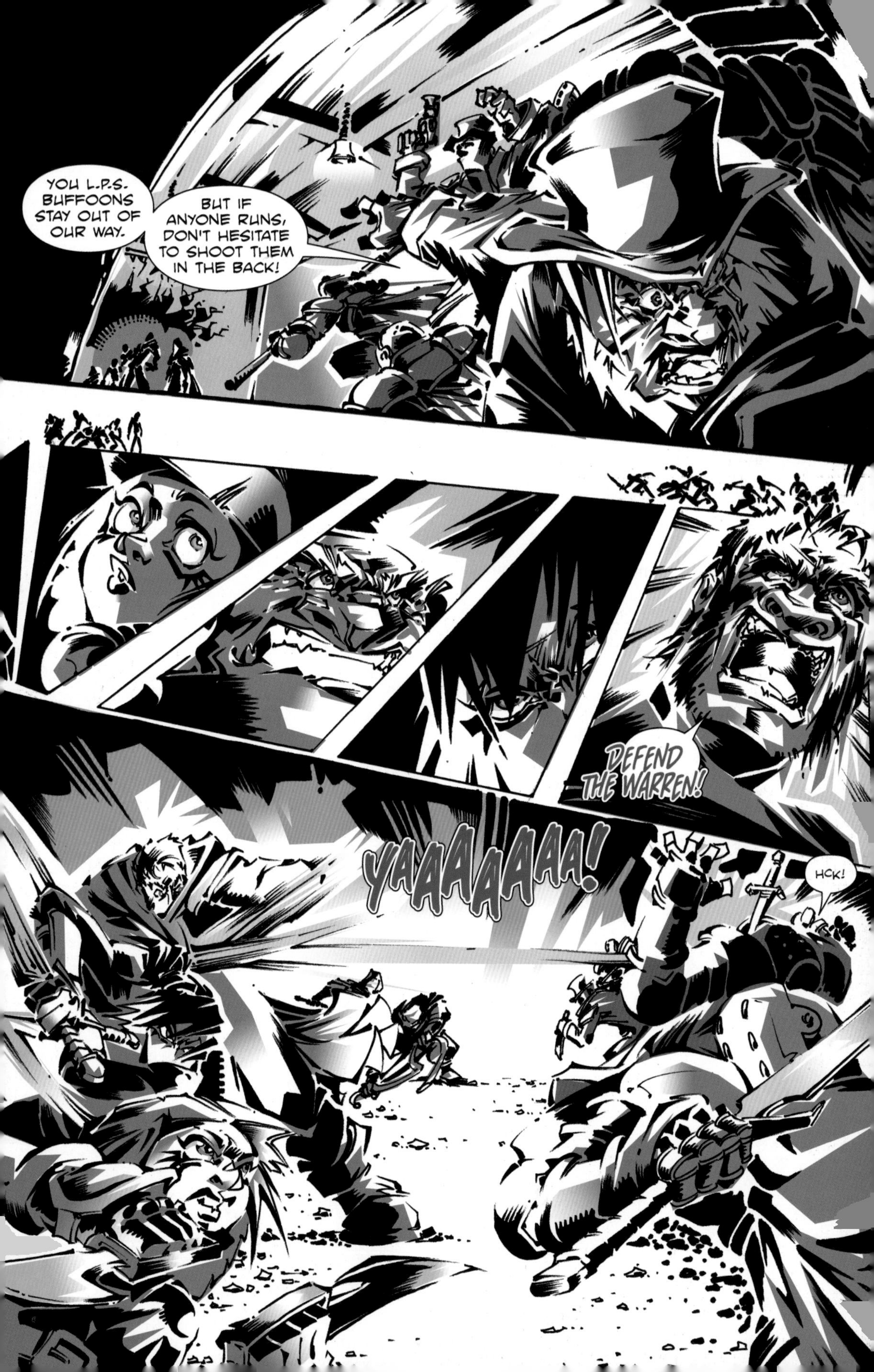
YOU L.P.S. BUFFOONS STAY OUT OF OUR WAY.
BUT IF ANYONE RUNS, DON'T HESITATE TO SHOOT THEM IN THE BACK!
DEFEND THE WARREN!
YAAAAAAAA!
HCK!

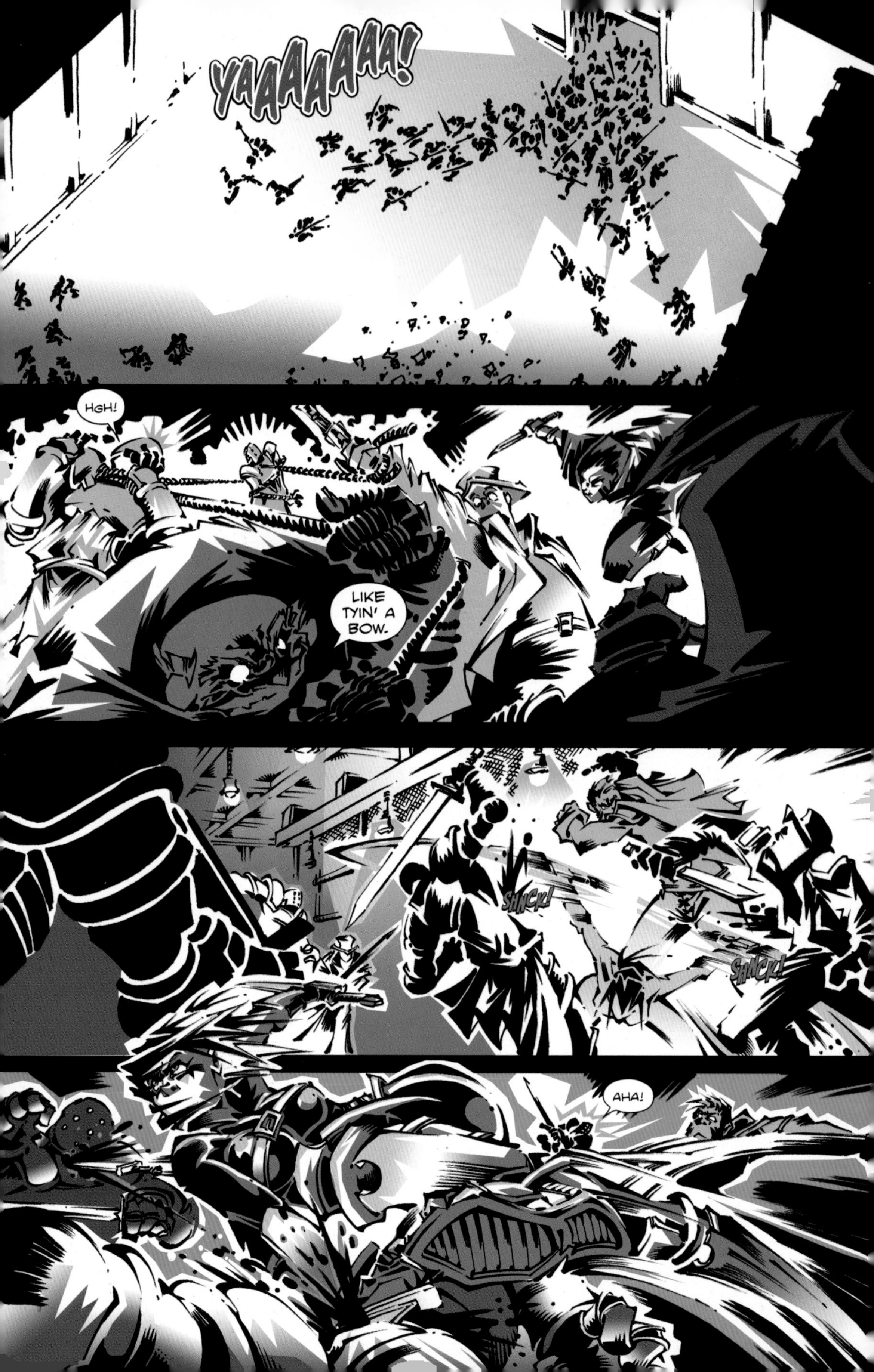
YAAAAAAA!
HGH!
LIKE TYIN' A BOW.
SHNCK!
SHNCK!
AHA!

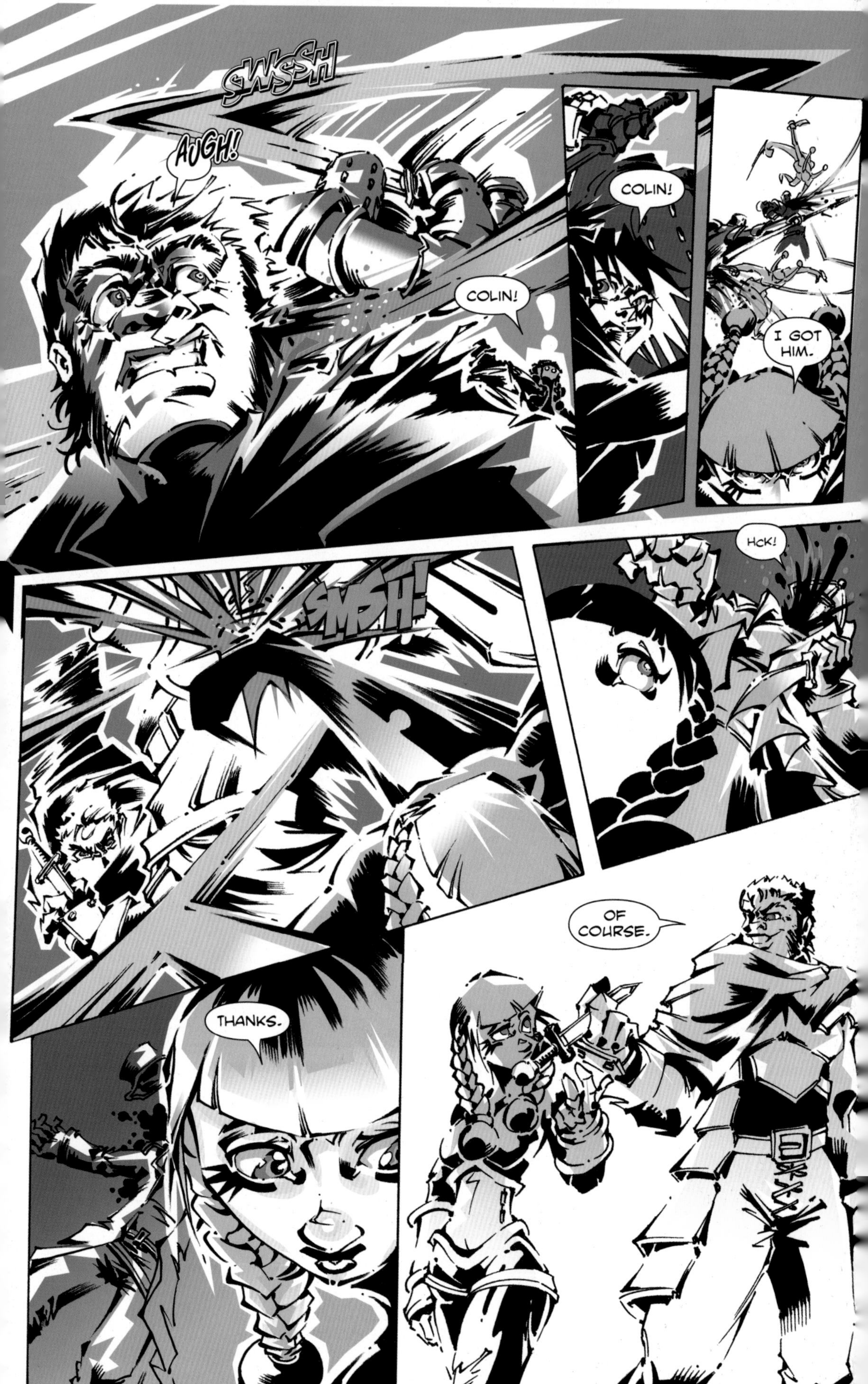
SWSSH
AUGH!
COLIN!
COLIN!
I GOT HIM.
SMSH!
HCK!
OF COURSE.
THANKS.

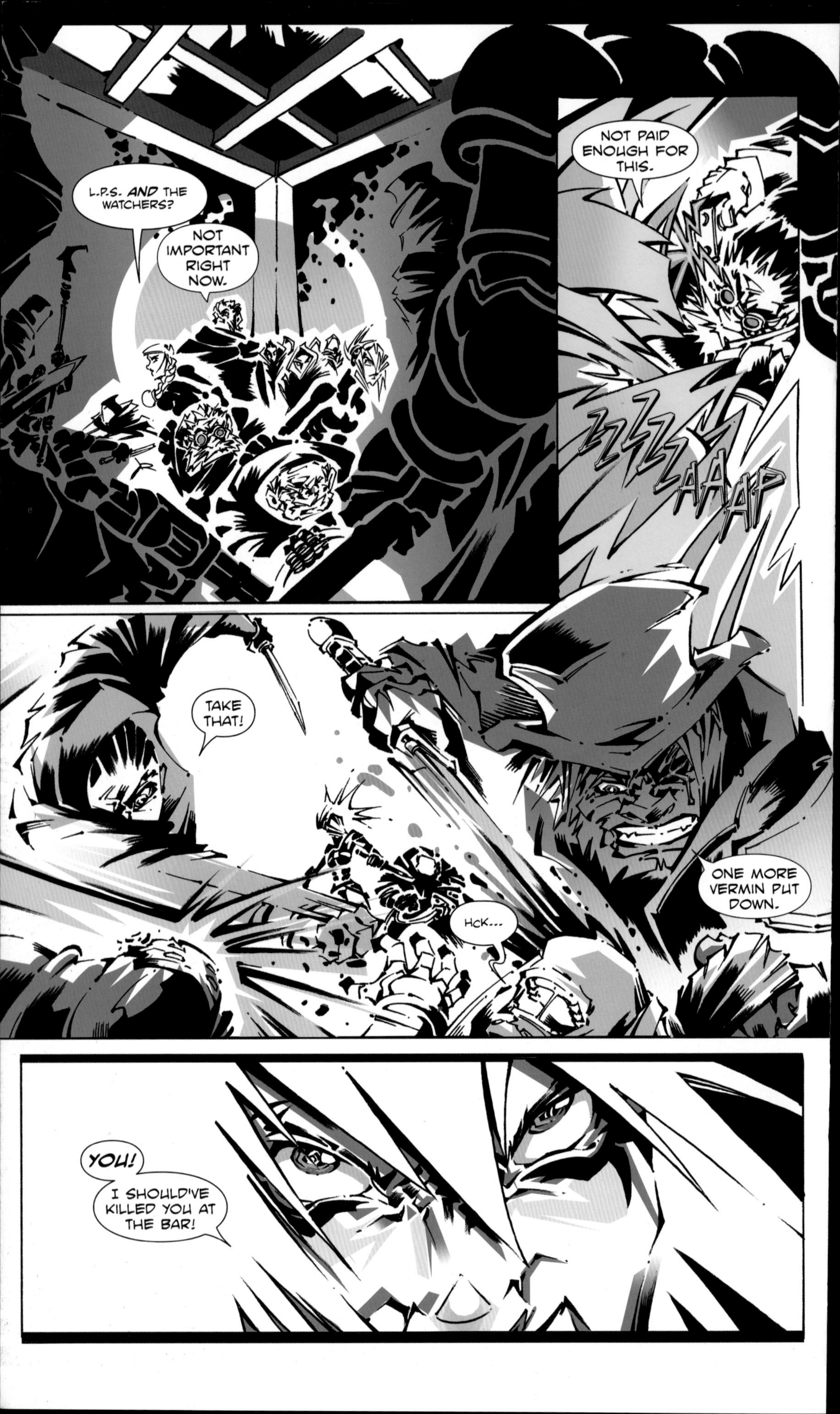
L.P.S. AND THE WATCHERS?
NOT IMPORTANT RIGHT NOW.
NOT PAID ENOUGH FOR THIS.
ZZZZZAAAAP
TAKE THAT!
ONE MORE VERMIN PUT DOWN.
HCK...
YOU!
I SHOULD'VE KILLED YOU AT THE BAR!

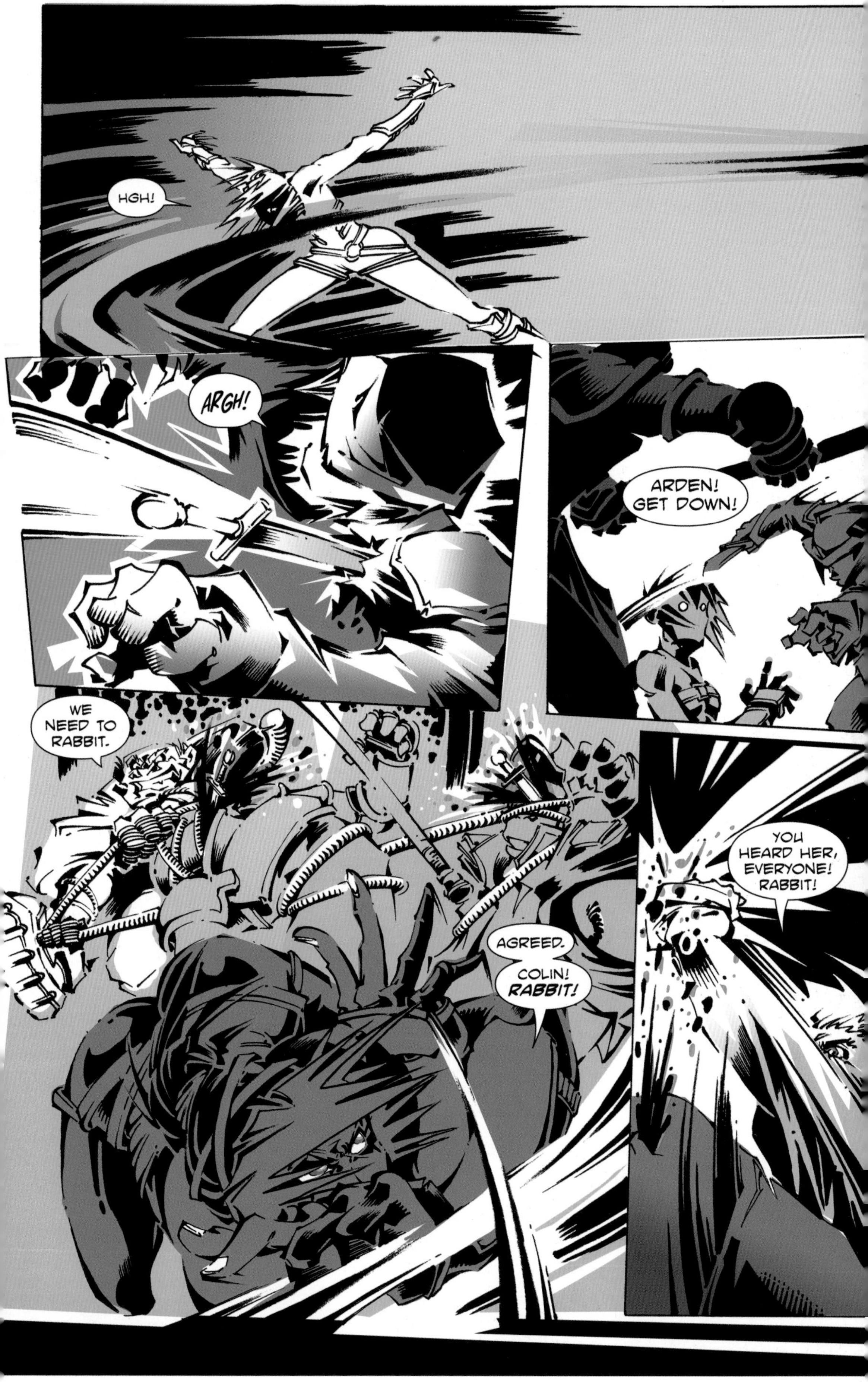
HGH!
ARGH!
ARDEN! GET DOWN!
WE NEED TO RABBIT.
AGREED.
COLIN! RABBIT!
YOU HEARD HER, EVERYONE! RABBIT!

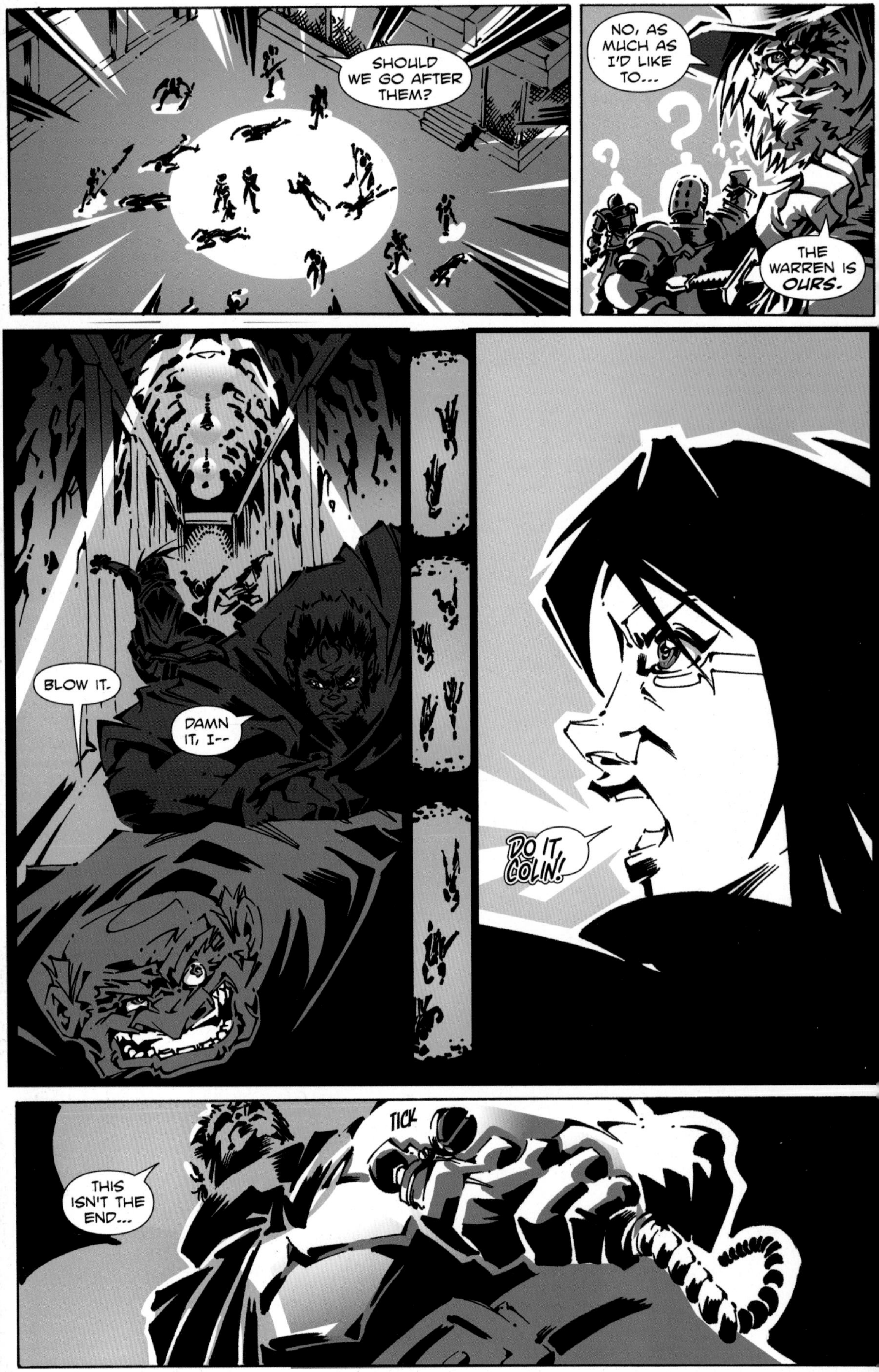
SHOULD WE GO AFTER THEM?
NO, AS MUCH AS I'D LIKE TO...
THE WARREN IS OURS.
BLOW IT.
DAMN IT, I--
DO IT COLIN!
TICK
THIS ISN'T THE END...

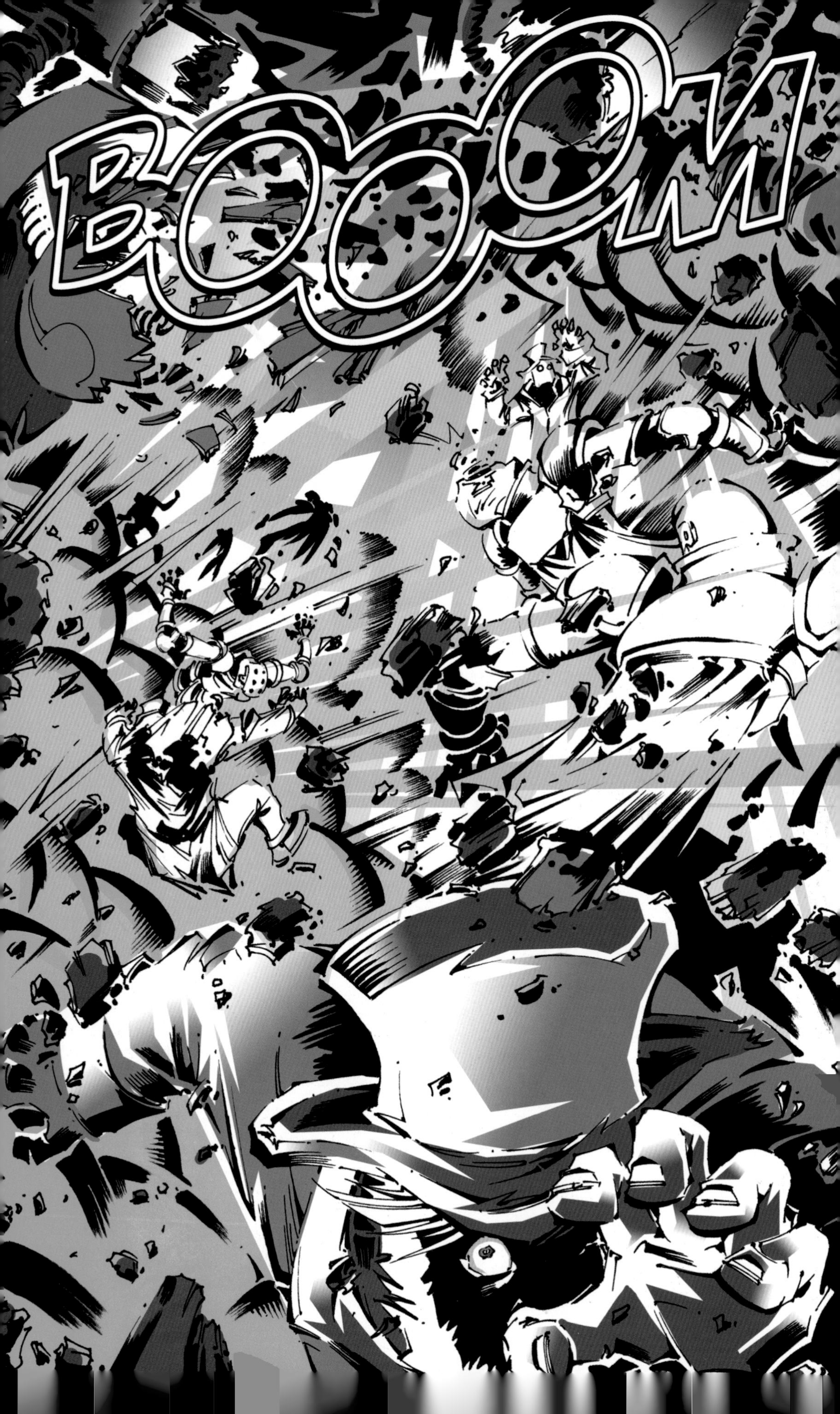
BOOOM

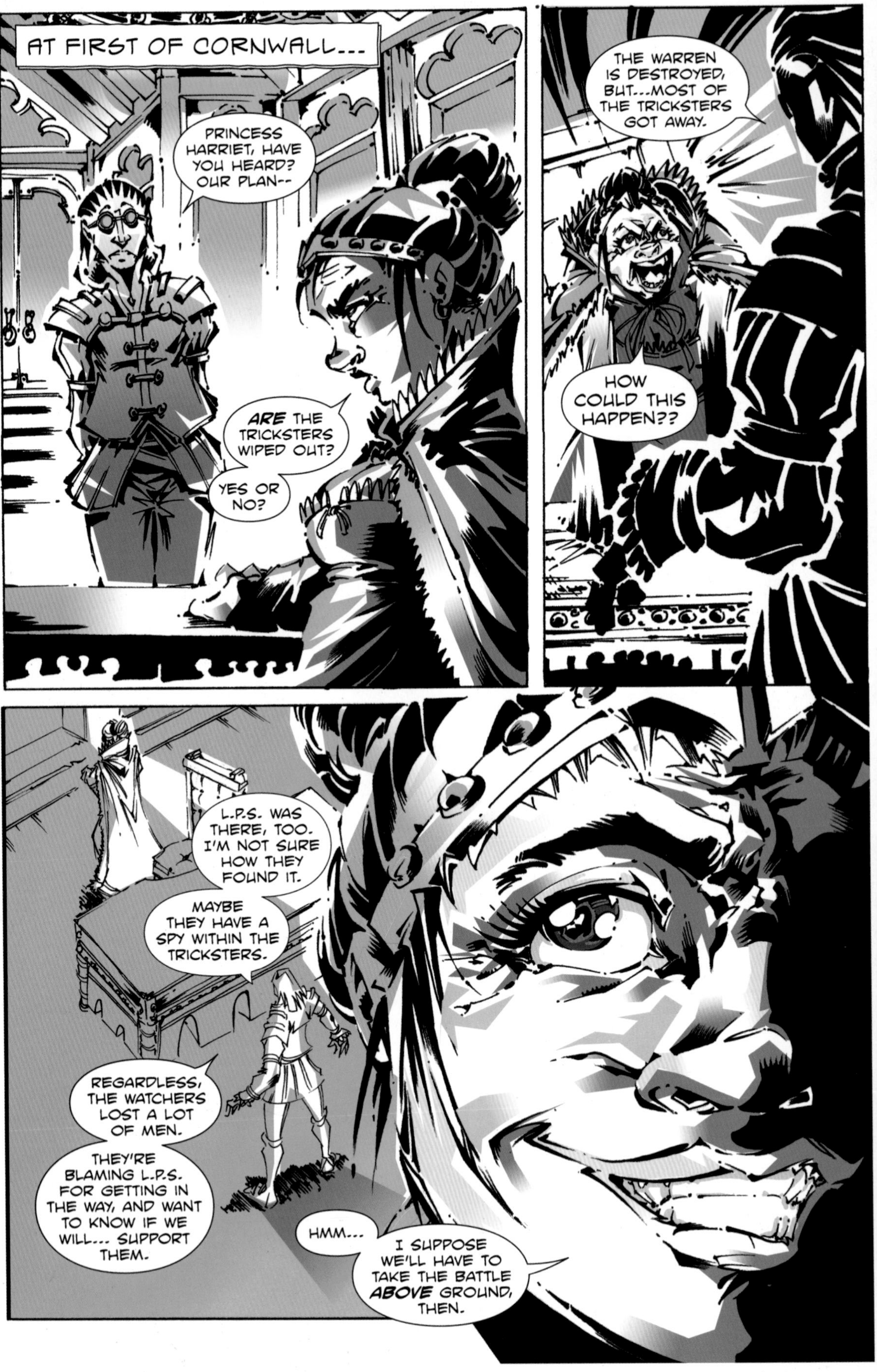
AT FIRST OF CORNWALL...
PRINCESS HARRIET, HAVE YOU HEARD? OUR PLAN--
ARE THE TRICKSTERS WIPED OUT?
YES OR NO?
THE WARREN IS DESTROYED, BUT...MOST OF THE TRICKSTERS GOT AWAY.
HOW COULD THIS HAPPEN??
L.P.S. WAS THERE, TOO. I'M NOT SURE HOW THEY FOUND IT.
MAYBE THEY HAVE A SPY WITHIN THE TRICKSTERS.
REGARDLESS, THE WATCHERS LOST A LOT OF MEN.
THEY'RE BLAMING L.P.S. FOR GETTING IN THE WAY, AND WANT TO KNOW IF WE WILL... SUPPORT THEM.
HMM...
I SUPPOSE WE'LL HAVE TO TAKE THE BATTLE ABOVE GROUND, THEN.

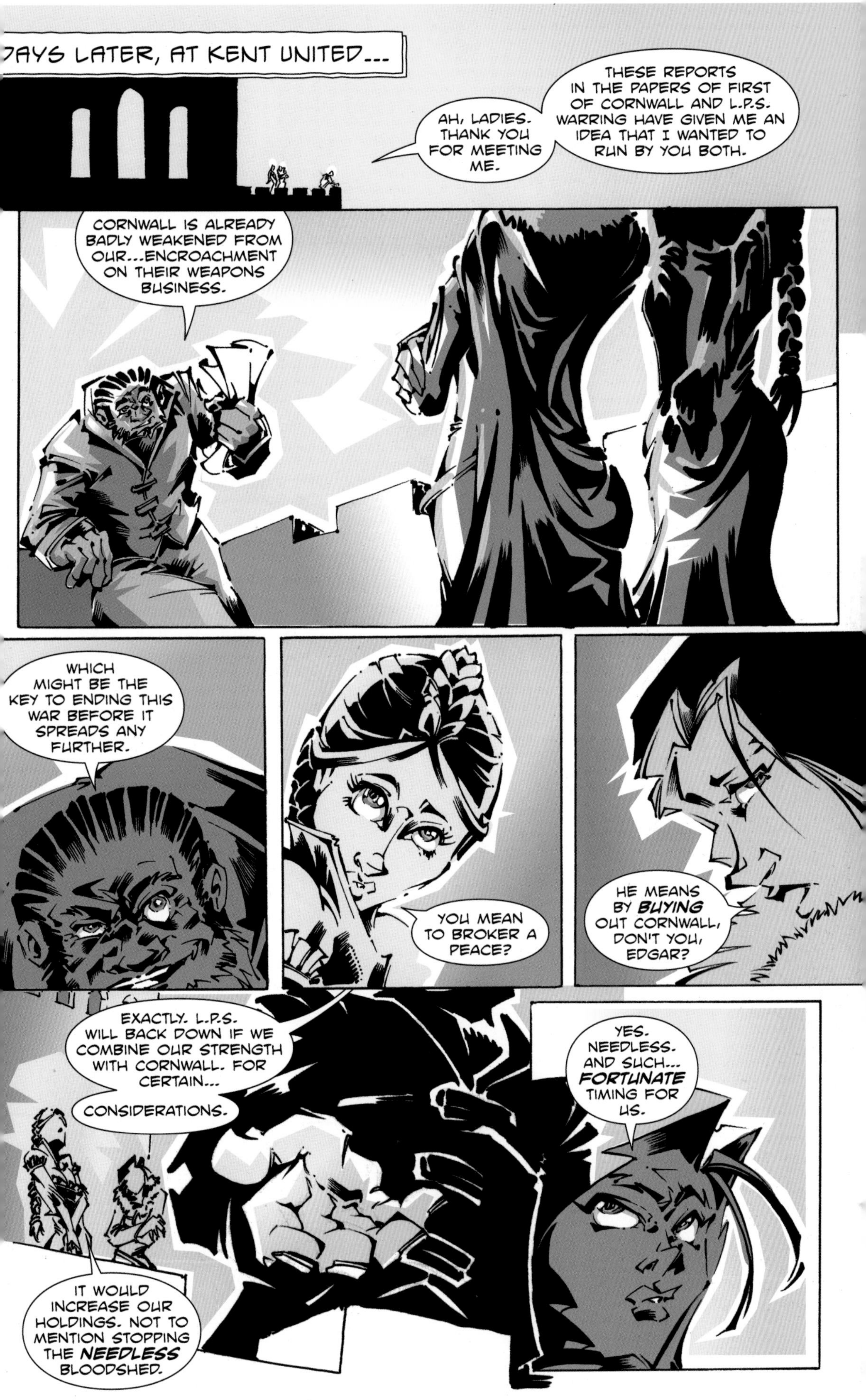
DAYS LATER, AT KENT UNITED...
AH, LADIES. THANK YOU FOR MEETING ME.
THESE REPORTS IN THE PAPERS OF FIRST OF CORNWALL AND L.P.S. WARRING HAVE GIVEN ME AN IDEA THAT I WANTED TO RUN BY YOU BOTH.
CORNWALL IS ALREADY BADLY WEAKENED FROM OUR...ENCROACHMENT ON THEIR WEAPONS BUSINESS.
WHICH MIGHT BE THE KEY TO ENDING THIS WAR BEFORE IT SPREADS ANY FURTHER.
YOU MEAN TO BROKER A PEACE?
HE MEANS BY **BUYING** OUT CORNWALL, DON'T YOU, EDGAR?
EXACTLY. L.P.S. WILL BACK DOWN IF WE COMBINE OUR STRENGTH WITH CORNWALL. FOR CERTAIN...
CONSIDERATIONS.
IT WOULD INCREASE OUR HOLDINGS. NOT TO MENTION STOPPING THE **NEEDLESS** BLOODSHED.
YES. NEEDLESS. AND SUCH... **FORTUNATE** TIMING FOR US.

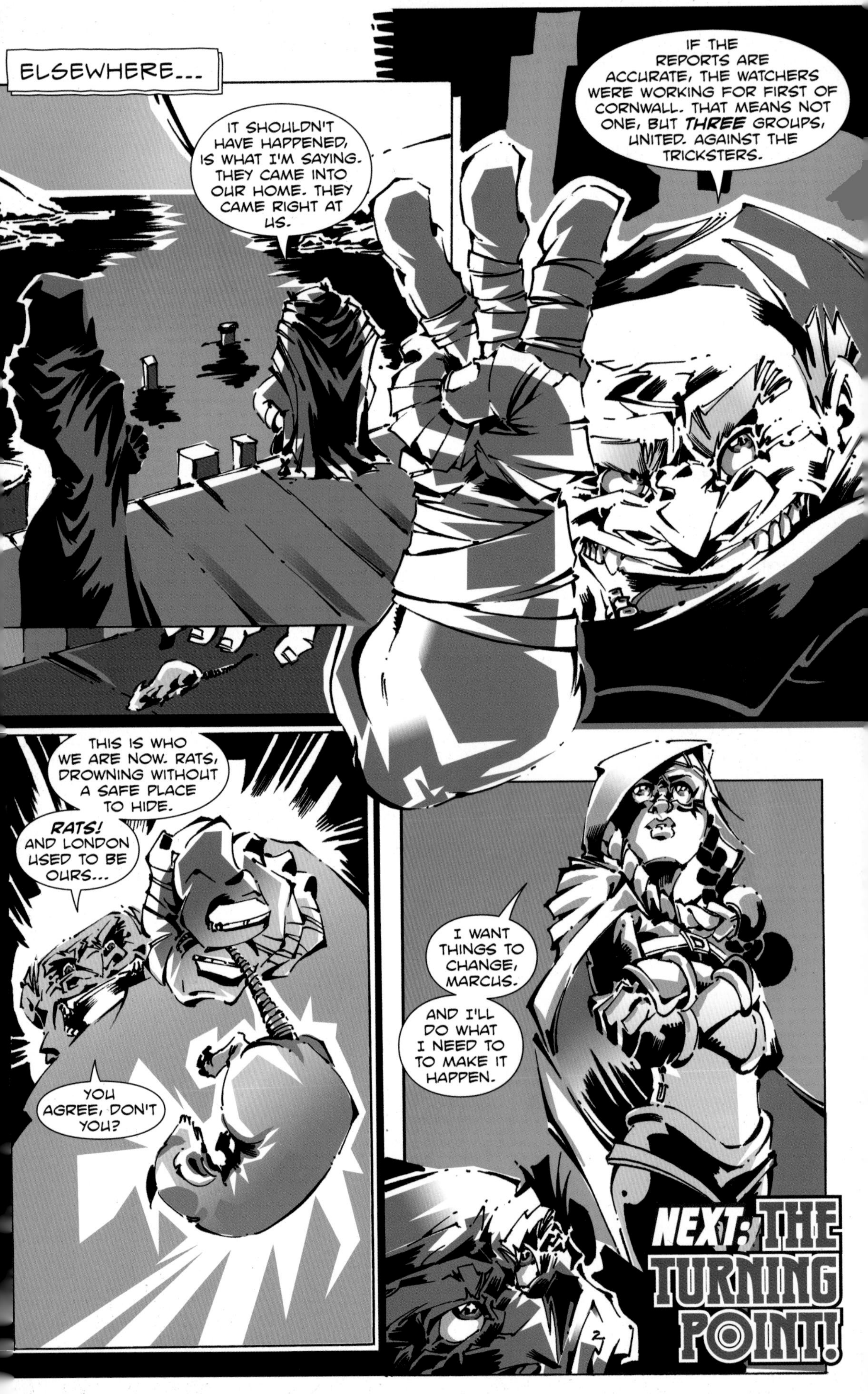
ELSEWHERE...
IT SHOULDN'T HAVE HAPPENED, IS WHAT I'M SAYING. THEY CAME INTO OUR HOME. THEY CAME RIGHT AT US.
IF THE REPORTS ARE ACCURATE, THE WATCHERS WERE WORKING FOR FIRST OF CORNWALL. THAT MEANS NOT ONE, BUT *THREE* GROUPS, UNITED. AGAINST THE TRICKSTERS.
THIS IS WHO WE ARE NOW. RATS, DROWNING WITHOUT A SAFE PLACE TO HIDE.
RATS! AND LONDON USED TO BE OURS...
YOU AGREE, DON'T YOU?
I WANT THINGS TO CHANGE, MARCUS.
AND I'LL DO WHAT I NEED TO TO MAKE IT HAPPEN.
NEXT: THE TURNING POINT!

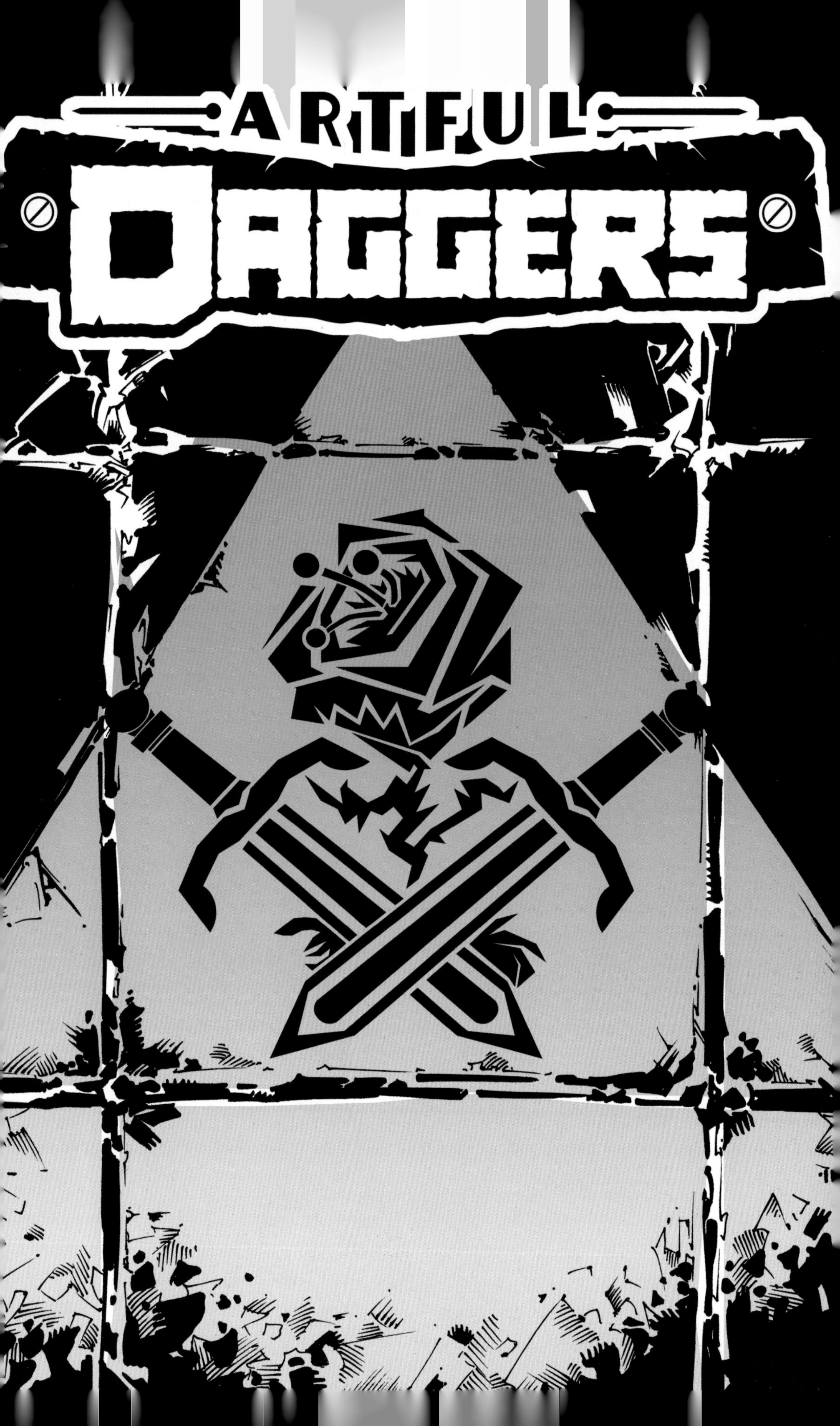
ARTFUL
DAGGERS

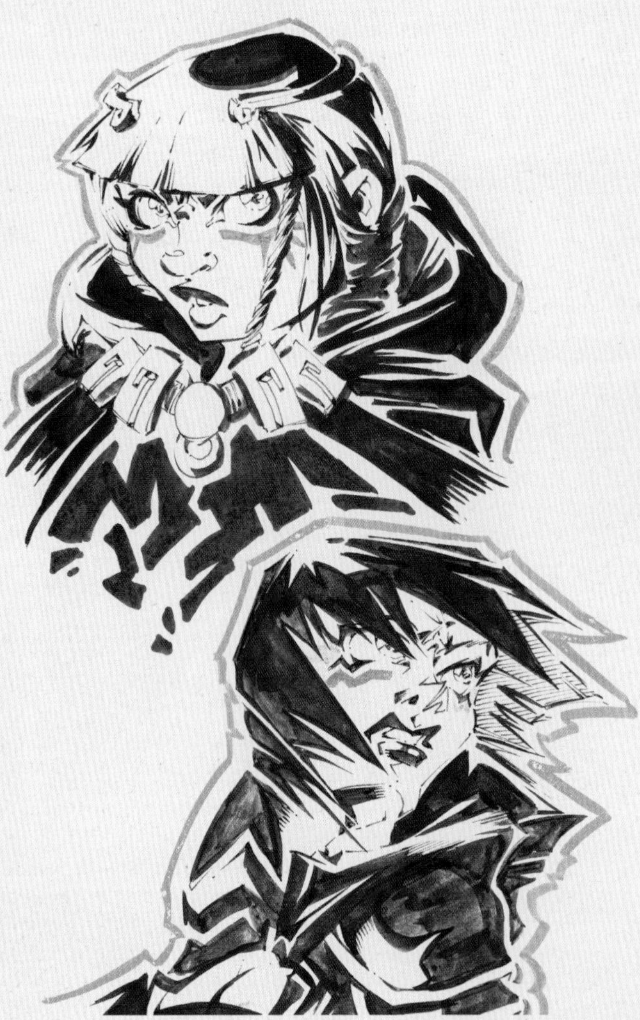

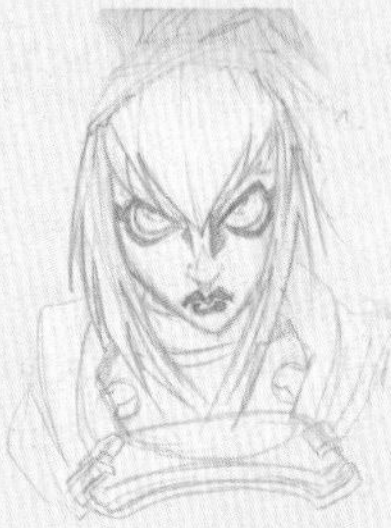

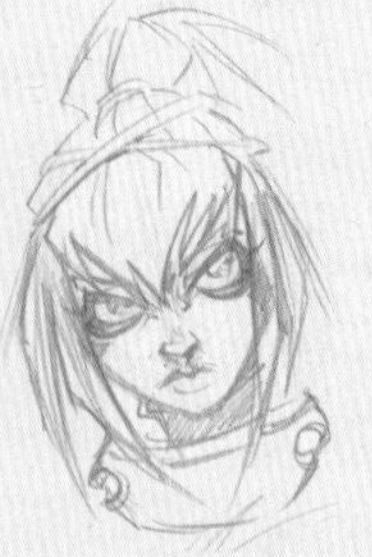

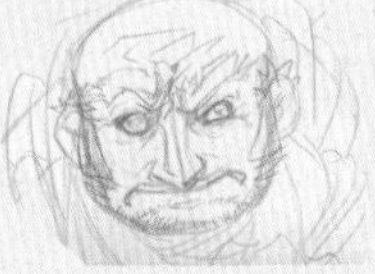

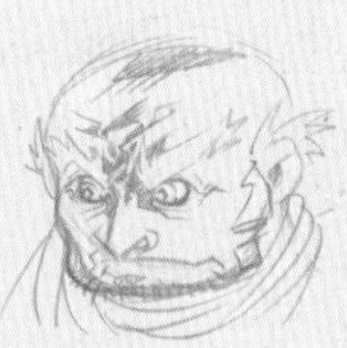

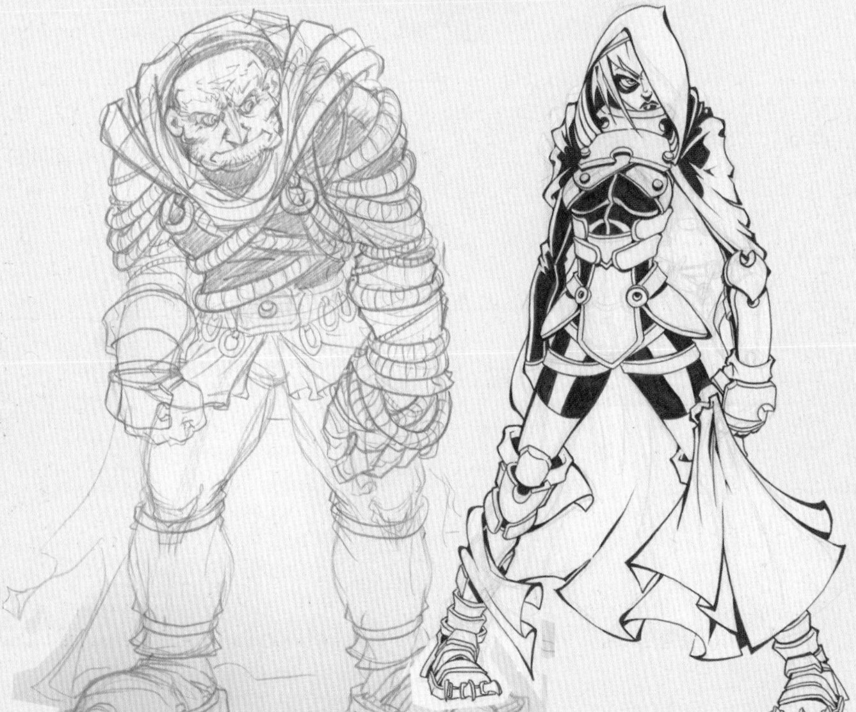

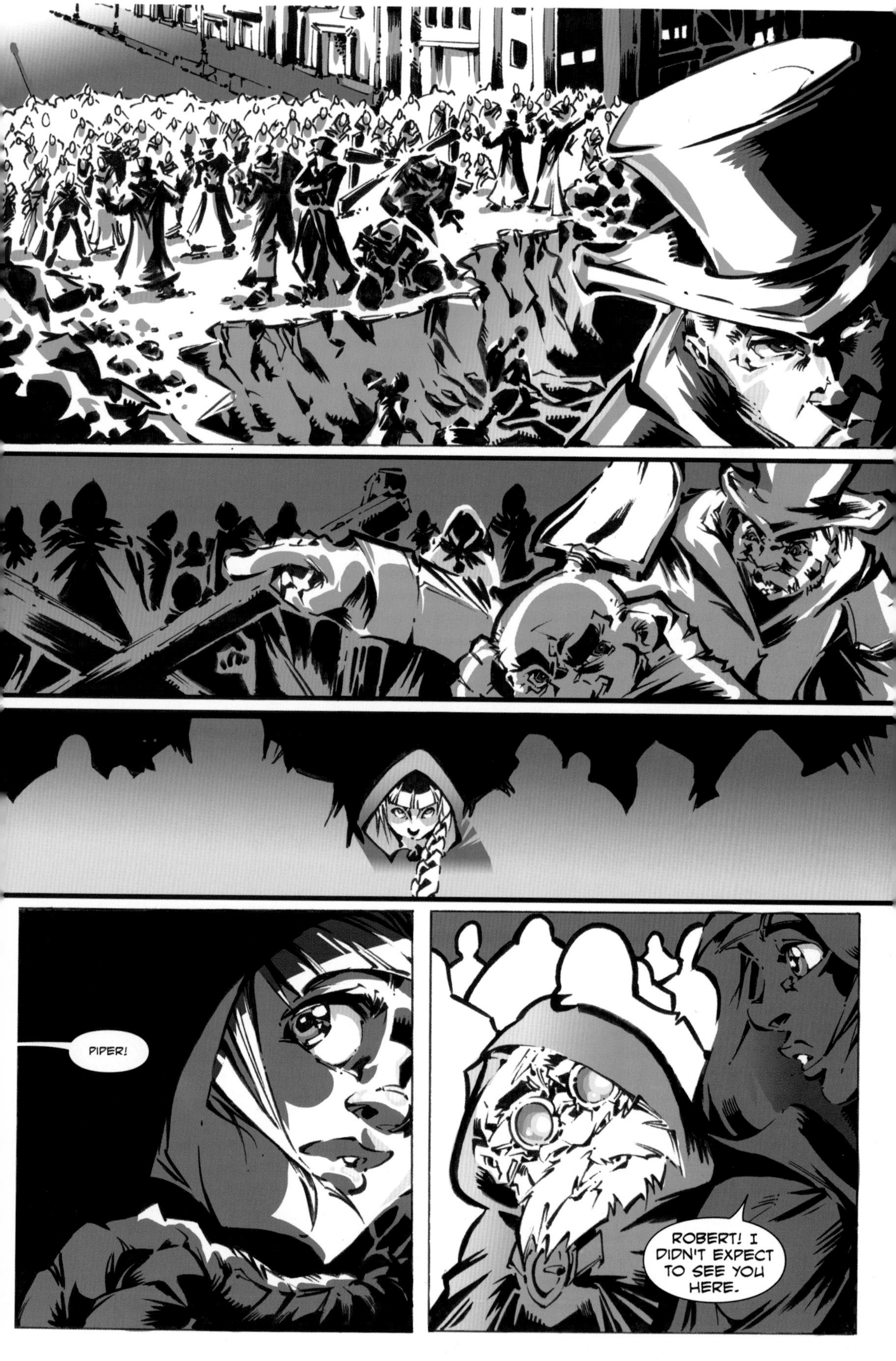
PIPER!
ROBERT! I DIDN'T EXPECT TO SEE YOU HERE.

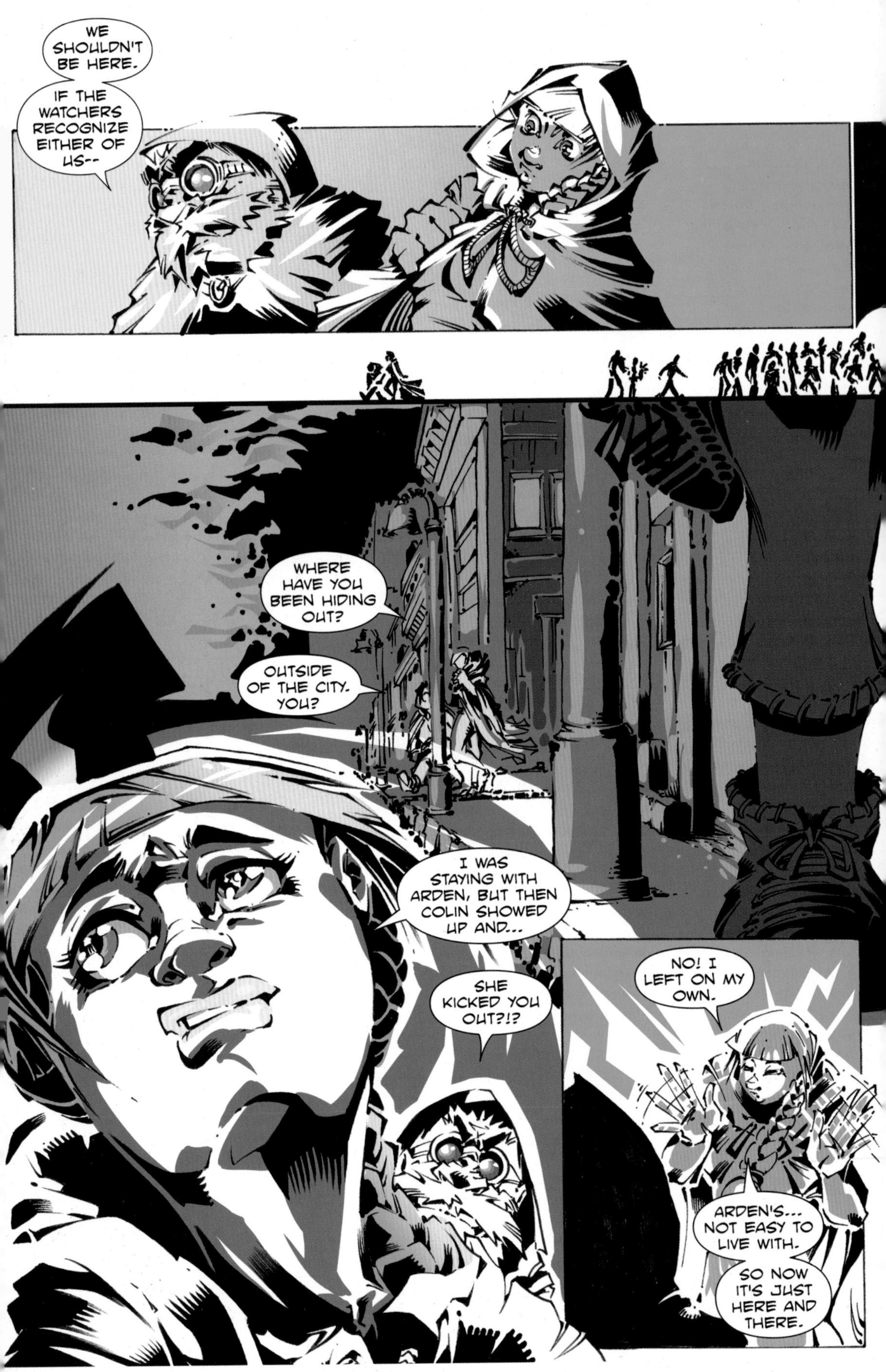

WE SHOULDN'T BE HERE.
IF THE WATCHERS RECOGNIZE EITHER OF US--
WHERE HAVE YOU BEEN HIDING OUT?
OUTSIDE OF THE CITY. YOU?
I WAS STAYING WITH ARDEN, BUT THEN COLIN SHOWED UP AND...
SHE KICKED YOU OUT?!?
NO! I LEFT ON MY OWN.
ARDEN'S... NOT EASY TO LIVE WITH.
SO NOW IT'S JUST HERE AND THERE.

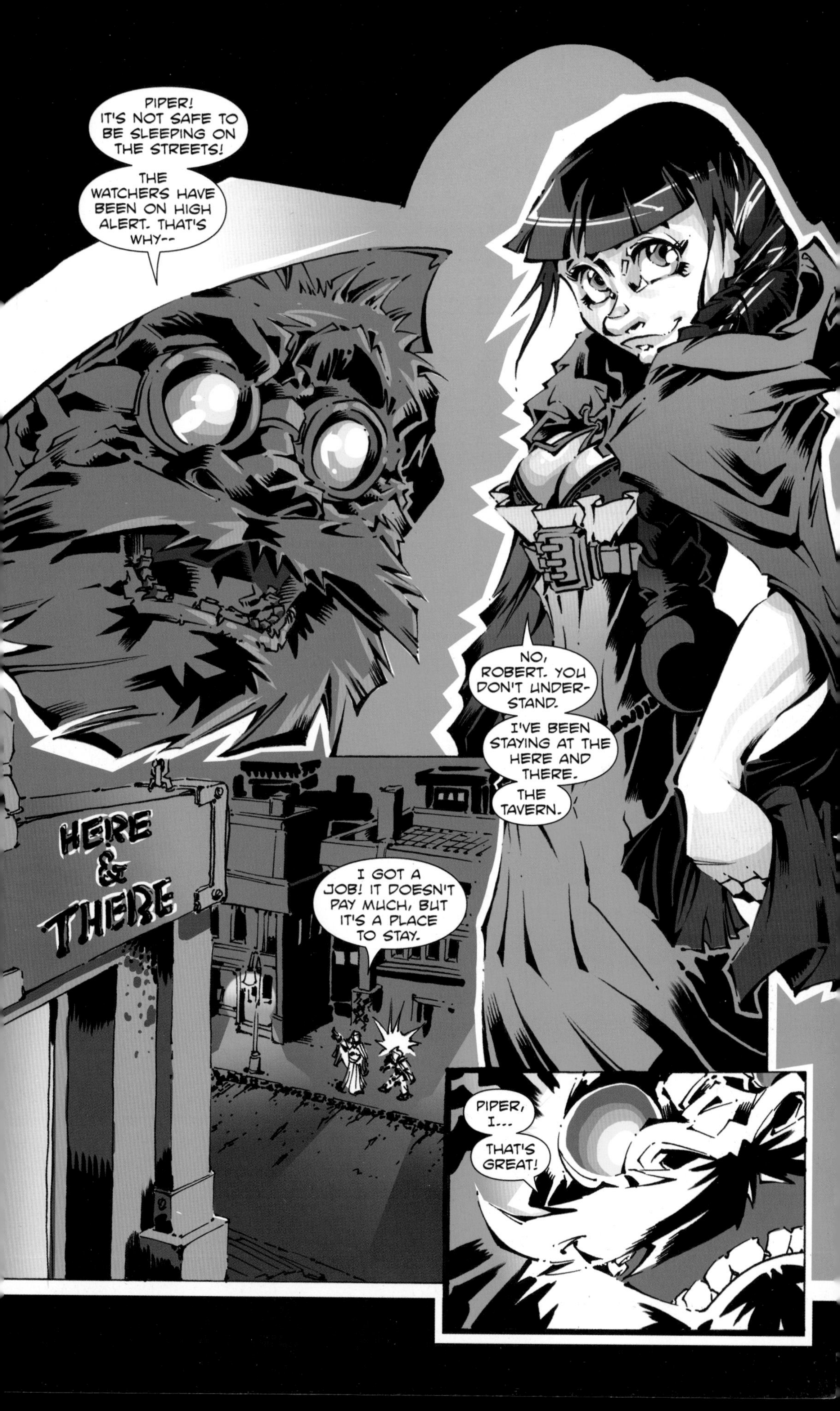
PIPER! IT'S NOT SAFE TO BE SLEEPING ON THE STREETS!
THE WATCHERS HAVE BEEN ON HIGH ALERT. THAT'S WHY--
NO, ROBERT. YOU DON'T UNDER-STAND.
I'VE BEEN STAYING AT THE HERE AND THERE.
THE TAVERN.
HERE & THERE
I GOT A JOB! IT DOESN'T PAY MUCH, BUT IT'S A PLACE TO STAY.
PIPER, I...
THAT'S GREAT!

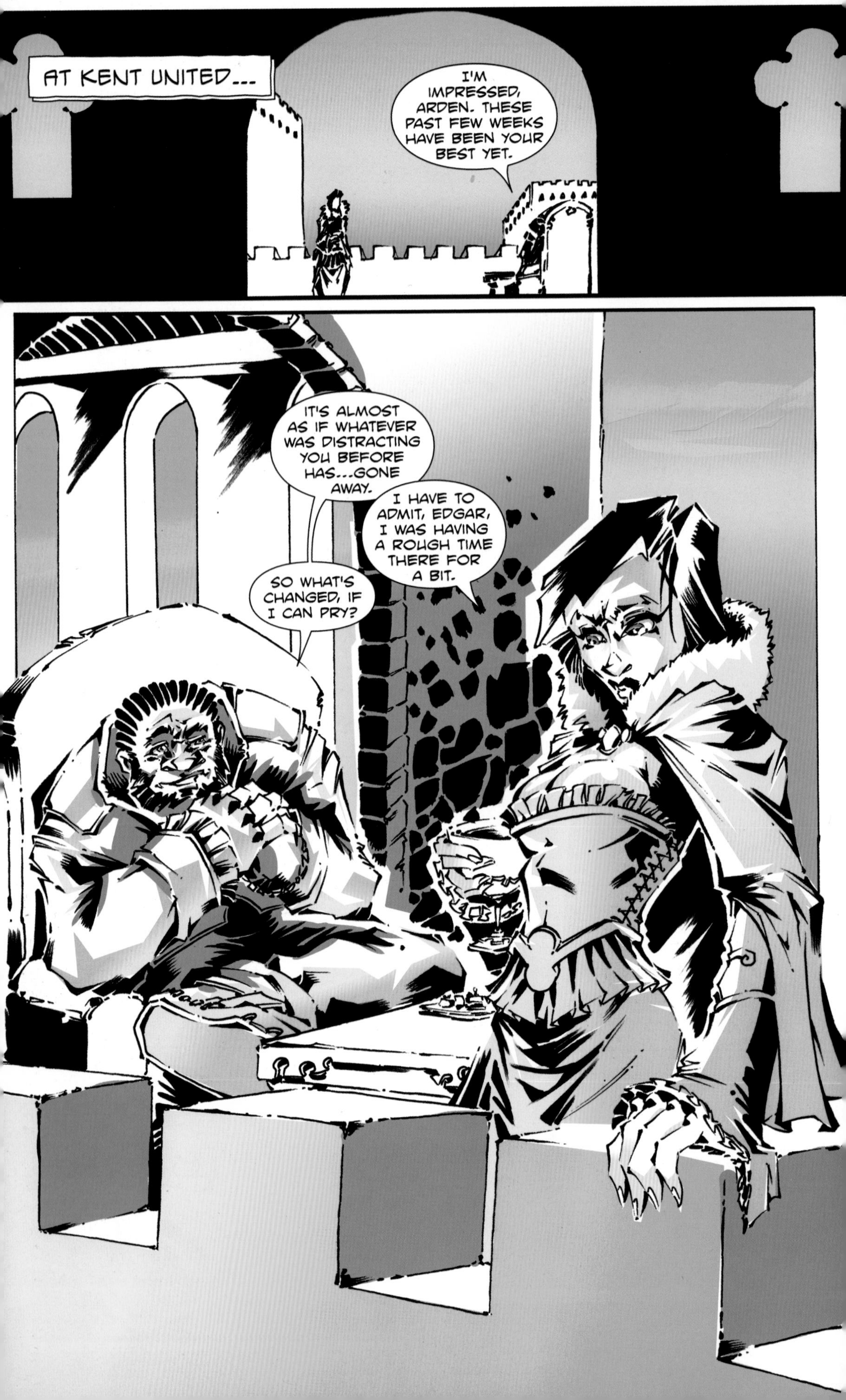
AT KENT UNITED...
I'M IMPRESSED, ARDEN. THESE PAST FEW WEEKS HAVE BEEN YOUR BEST YET.
IT'S ALMOST AS IF WHATEVER WAS DISTRACTING YOU BEFORE HAS...GONE AWAY.
I HAVE TO ADMIT, EDGAR, I WAS HAVING A ROUGH TIME THERE FOR A BIT.
SO WHAT'S CHANGED, IF I CAN PRY?

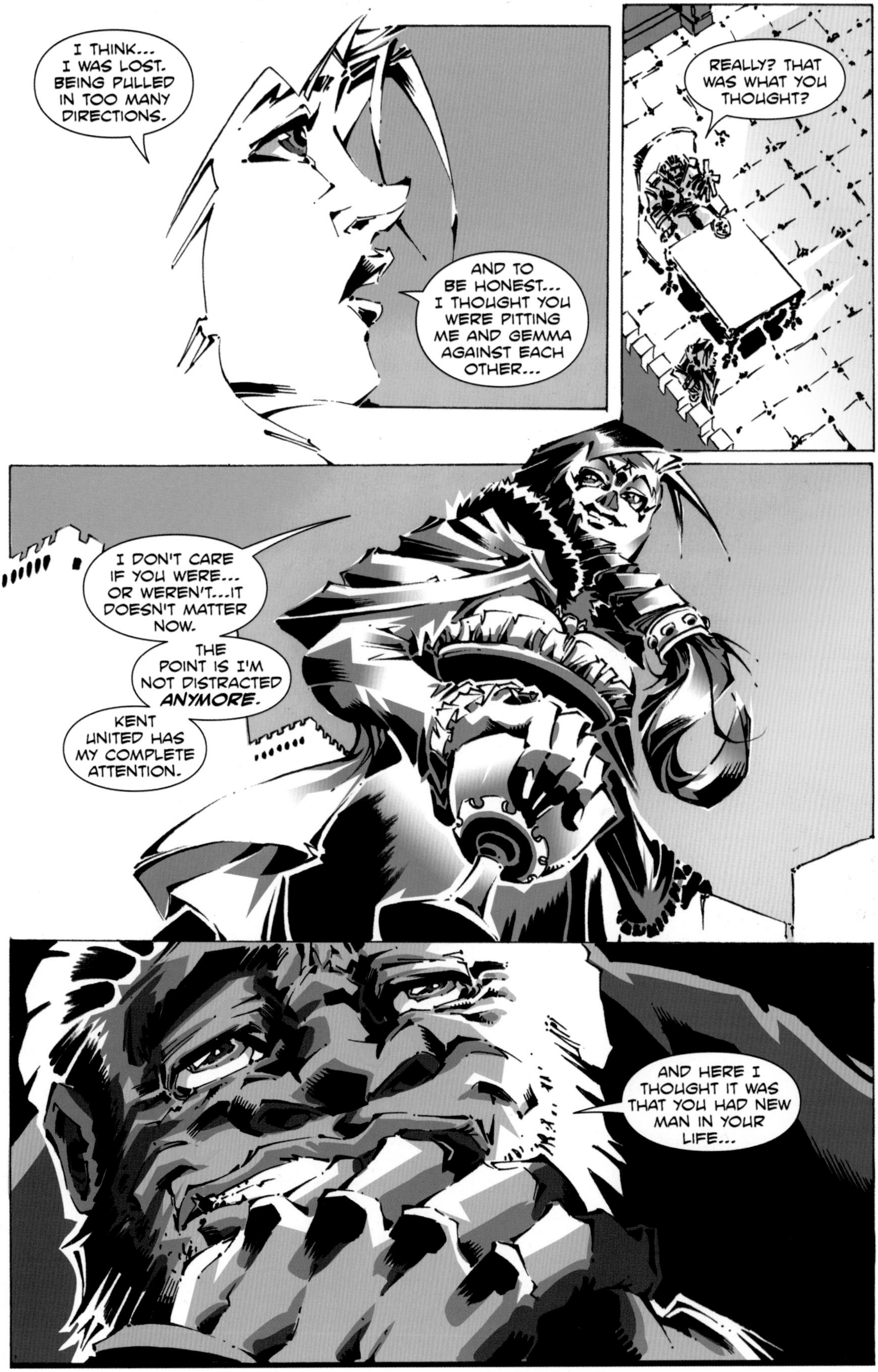
I THINK... I WAS LOST. BEING PULLED IN TOO MANY DIRECTIONS.
AND TO BE HONEST... I THOUGHT YOU WERE PITTING ME AND GEMMA AGAINST EACH OTHER...
REALLY? THAT WAS WHAT YOU THOUGHT?
I DON'T CARE IF YOU WERE... OR WEREN'T...IT DOESN'T MATTER NOW.
THE POINT IS I'M NOT DISTRACTED ANYMORE.
KENT UNITED HAS MY COMPLETE ATTENTION.
AND HERE I THOUGHT IT WAS THAT YOU HAD NEW MAN IN YOUR LIFE...

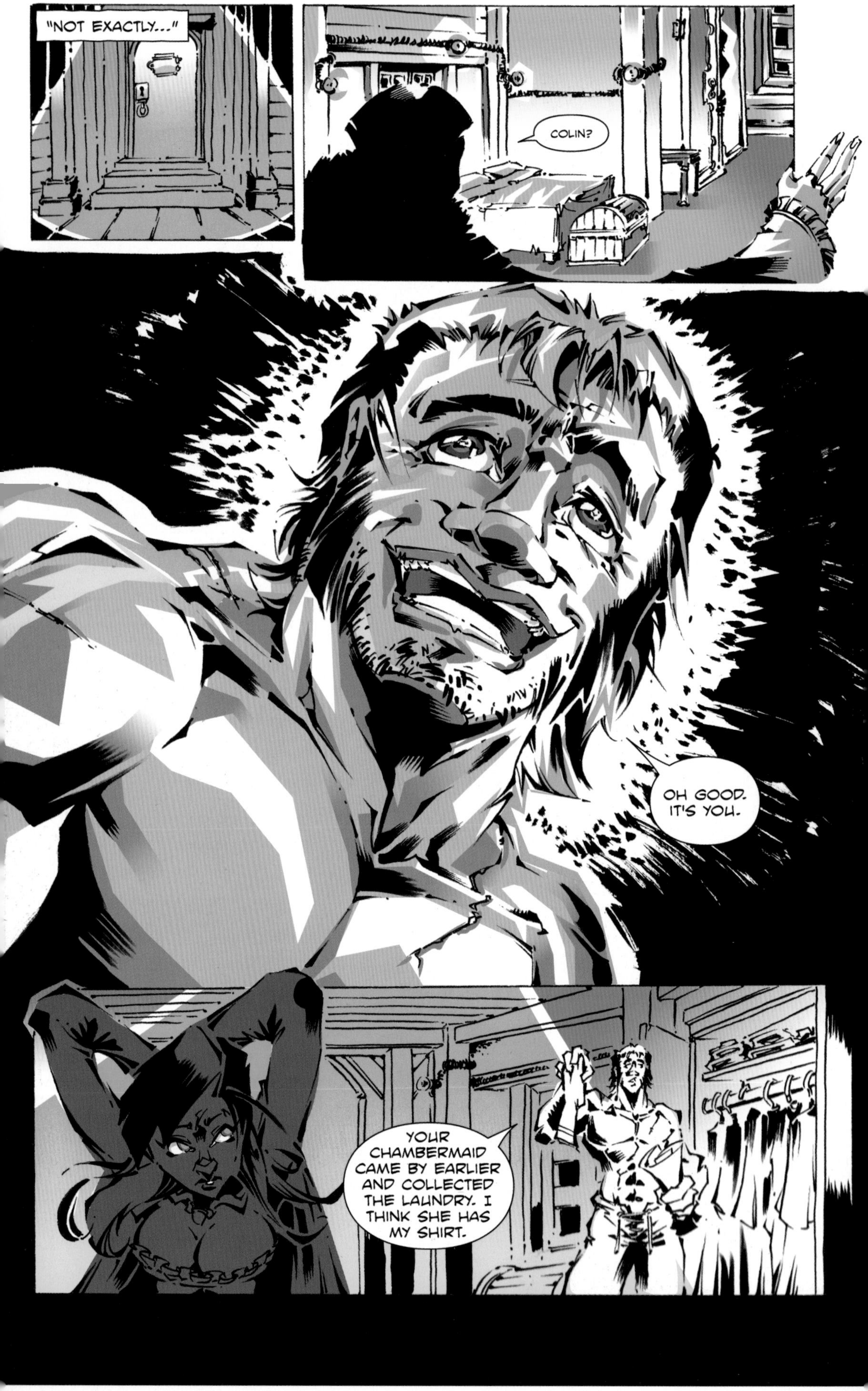
"NOT EXACTLY..."
COLIN?
OH GOOD. IT'S YOU.
YOUR CHAMBERMAID CAME BY EARLIER AND COLLECTED THE LAUNDRY. I THINK SHE HAS MY SHIRT.

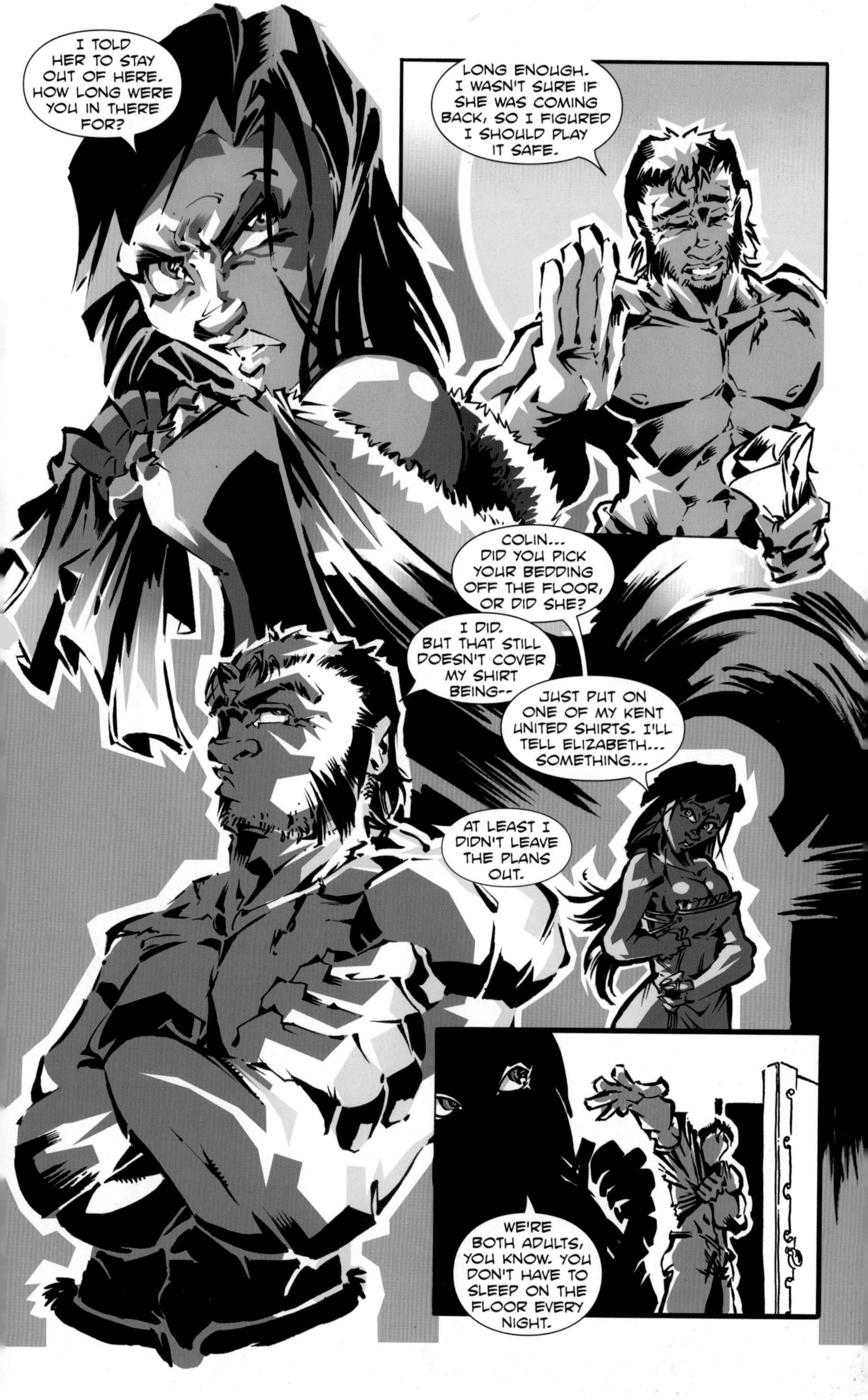
I TOLD HER TO STAY OUT OF HERE. HOW LONG WERE YOU IN THERE FOR?
LONG ENOUGH. I WASN'T SURE IF SHE WAS COMING BACK, SO I FIGURED I SHOULD PLAY IT SAFE.
COLIN... DID YOU PICK YOUR BEDDING OFF THE FLOOR, OR DID SHE?
I DID. BUT THAT STILL DOESN'T COVER MY SHIRT BEING--
JUST PUT ON ONE OF MY KENT UNITED SHIRTS. I'LL TELL ELIZABETH... SOMETHING...
AT LEAST I DIDN'T LEAVE THE PLANS OUT.
WE'RE BOTH ADULTS, YOU KNOW. YOU DON'T HAVE TO SLEEP ON THE FLOOR EVERY NIGHT.

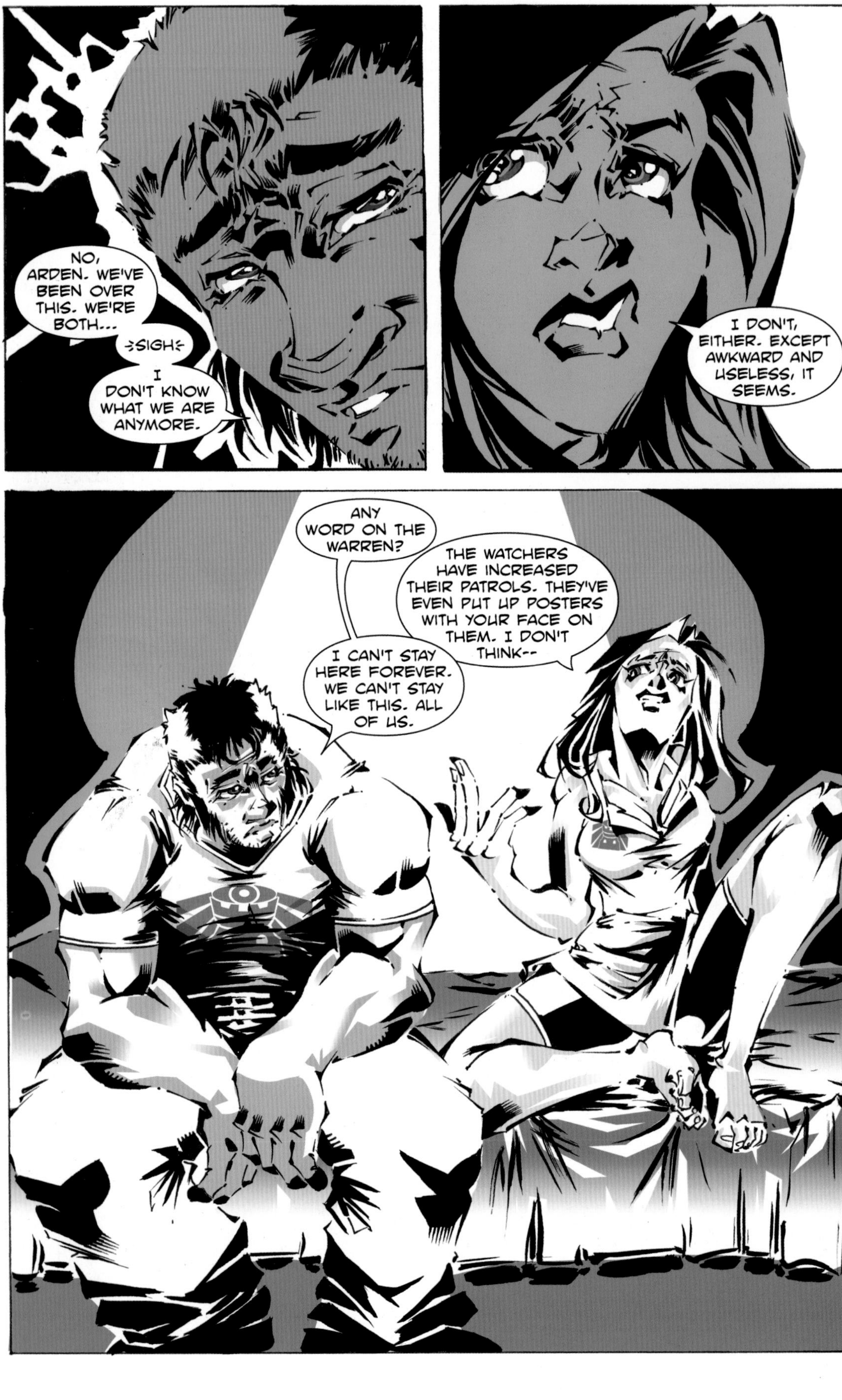
NO, ARDEN. WE'VE BEEN OVER THIS. WE'RE BOTH...
SIGH
I DON'T KNOW WHAT WE ARE ANYMORE.
I DON'T, EITHER. EXCEPT AWKWARD AND USELESS, IT SEEMS.
ANY WORD ON THE WARREN?
THE WATCHERS HAVE INCREASED THEIR PATROLS. THEY'VE EVEN PUT UP POSTERS WITH YOUR FACE ON THEM. I DON'T THINK--
I CAN'T STAY HERE FOREVER. WE CAN'T STAY LIKE THIS. ALL OF US.

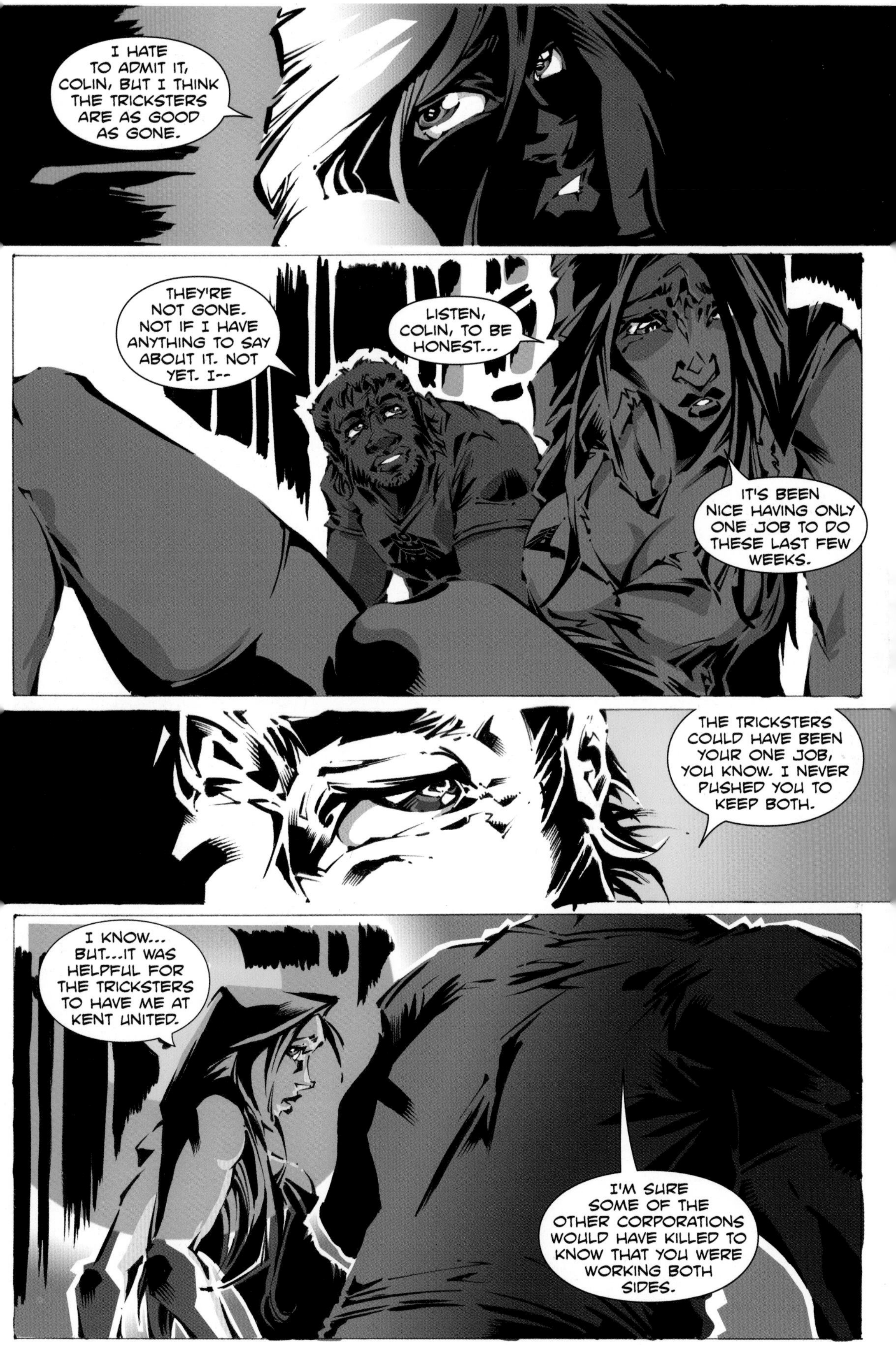
I HATE TO ADMIT IT, COLIN, BUT I THINK THE TRICKSTERS ARE AS GOOD AS GONE.
THEY'RE NOT GONE. NOT IF I HAVE ANYTHING TO SAY ABOUT IT. NOT YET. I--
LISTEN, COLIN, TO BE HONEST...
IT'S BEEN NICE HAVING ONLY ONE JOB TO DO THESE LAST FEW WEEKS.
THE TRICKSTERS COULD HAVE BEEN YOUR ONE JOB, YOU KNOW. I NEVER PUSHED YOU TO KEEP BOTH.
I KNOW... BUT...IT WAS HELPFUL FOR THE TRICKSTERS TO HAVE ME AT KENT UNITED.
I'M SURE SOME OF THE OTHER CORPORATIONS WOULD HAVE KILLED TO KNOW THAT YOU WERE WORKING BOTH SIDES.

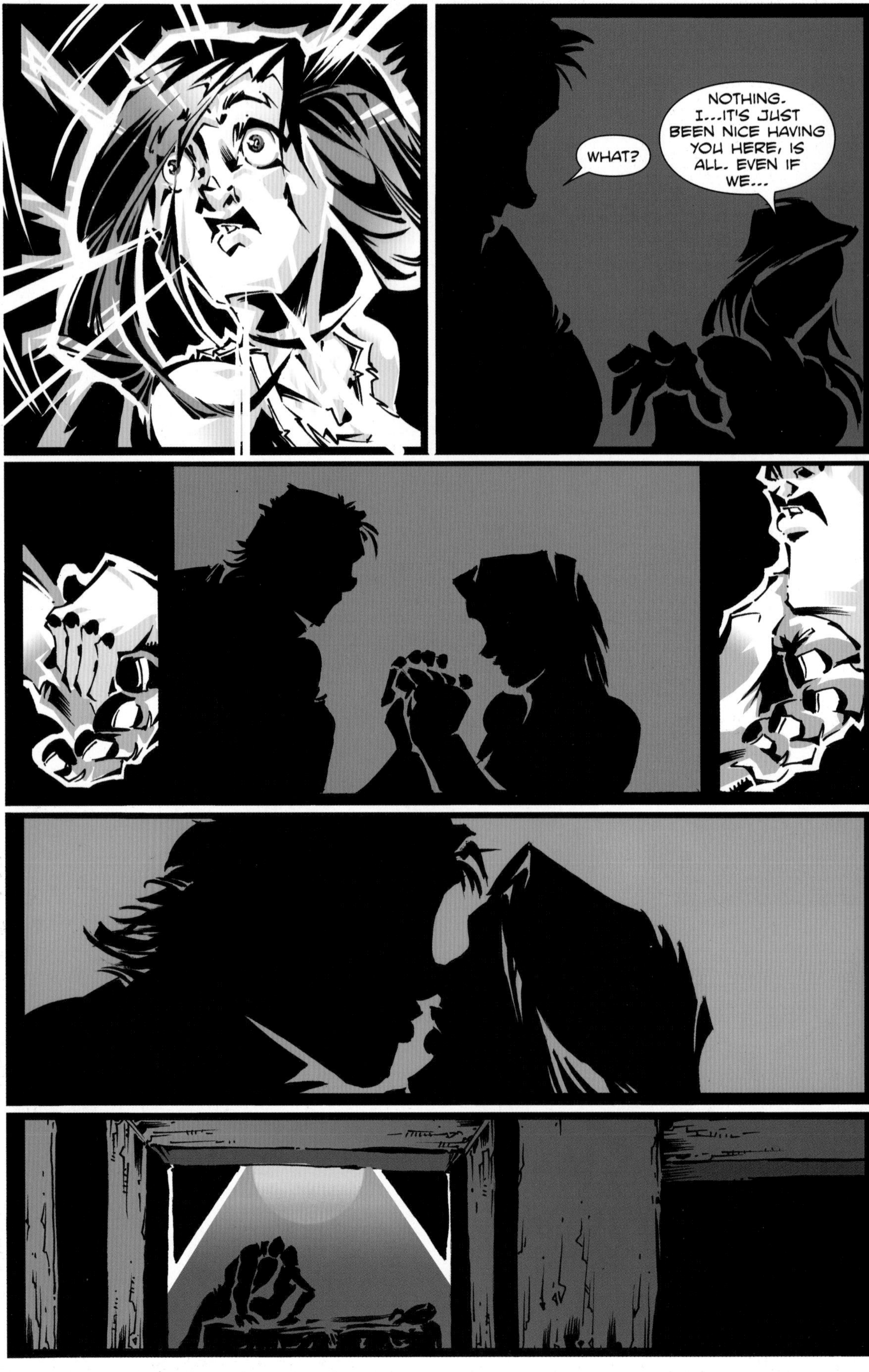
WHAT?
NOTHING. I...IT'S JUST BEEN NICE HAVING YOU HERE, IS ALL. EVEN IF WE...

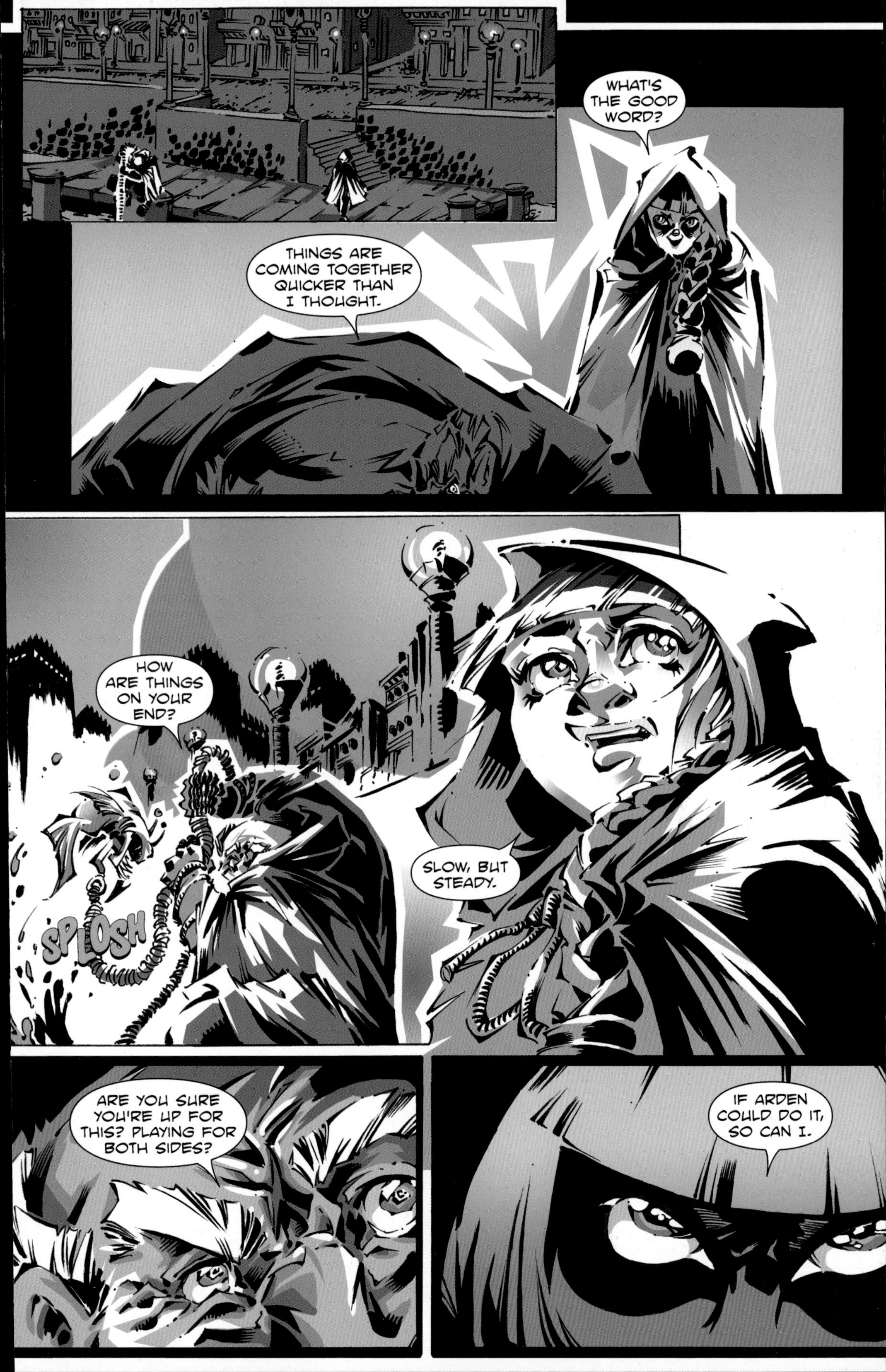
WHAT'S THE GOOD WORD?
THINGS ARE COMING TOGETHER QUICKER THAN I THOUGHT.
HOW ARE THINGS ON YOUR END?
SPLOSH
SLOW, BUT STEADY.
ARE YOU SURE YOU'RE UP FOR THIS? PLAYING FOR BOTH SIDES?
IF ARDEN COULD DO IT, SO CAN I.

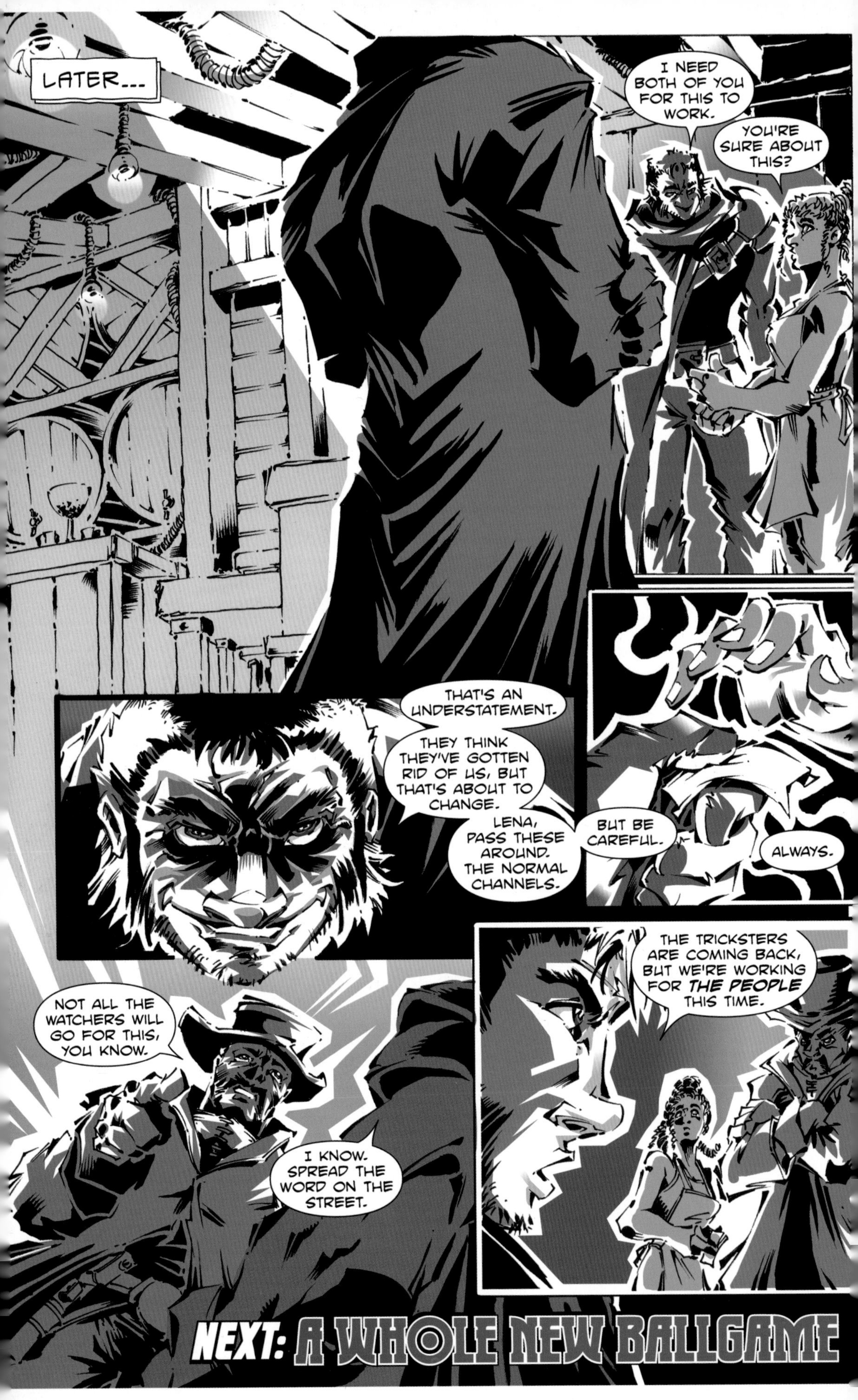
LATER...
I NEED BOTH OF YOU FOR THIS TO WORK.
YOU'RE SURE ABOUT THIS?
THAT'S AN UNDERSTATEMENT.
THEY THINK THEY'VE GOTTEN RID OF US, BUT THAT'S ABOUT TO CHANGE.
LENA, PASS THESE AROUND. THE NORMAL CHANNELS.
BUT BE CAREFUL.
ALWAYS.
NOT ALL THE WATCHERS WILL GO FOR THIS, YOU KNOW.
I KNOW. SPREAD THE WORD ON THE STREET.
THE TRICKSTERS ARE COMING BACK, BUT WE'RE WORKING FOR THE PEOPLE THIS TIME.
NEXT: A WHOLE NEW BALLGAME

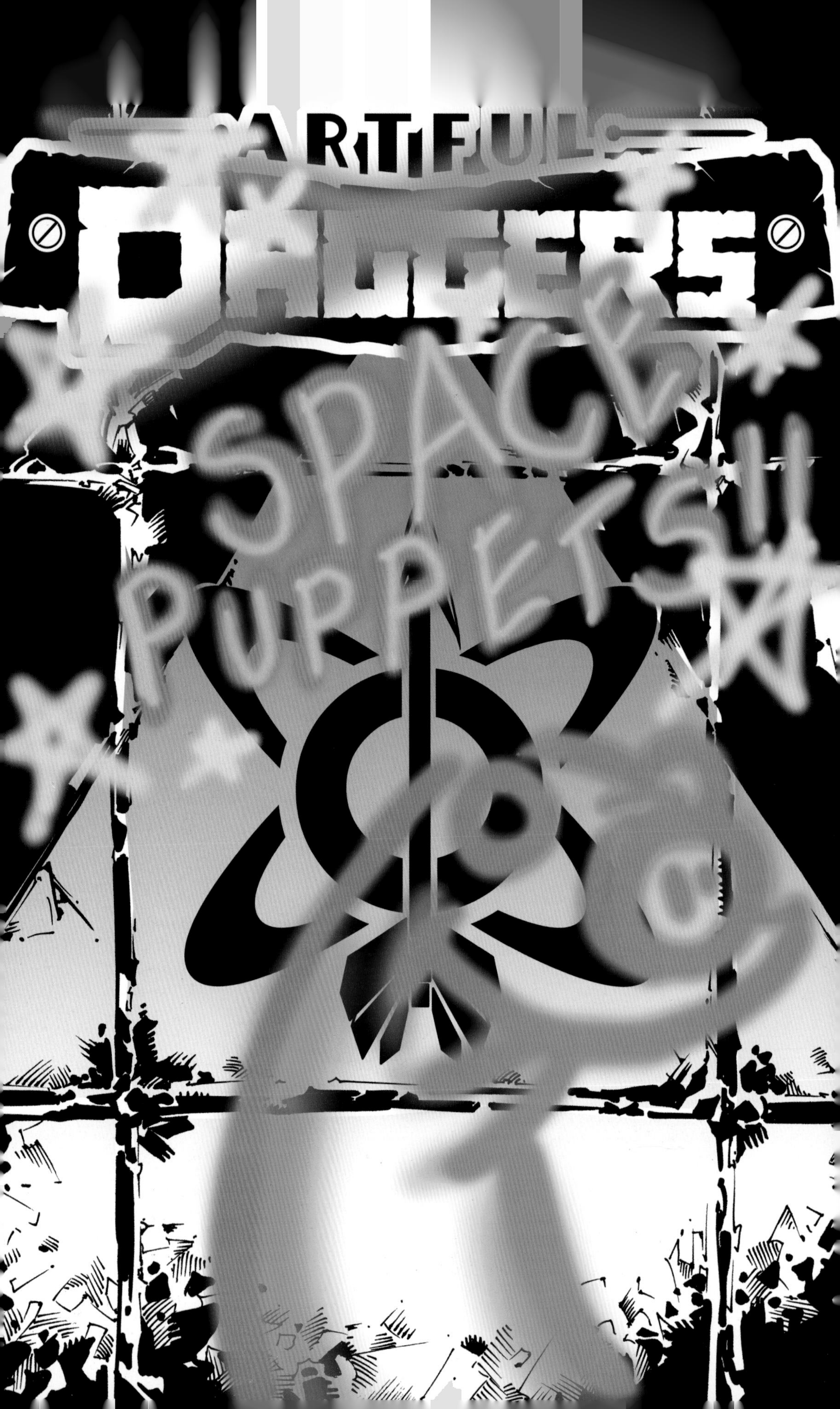
ARTFUL
SPACE
PUPPETS!!

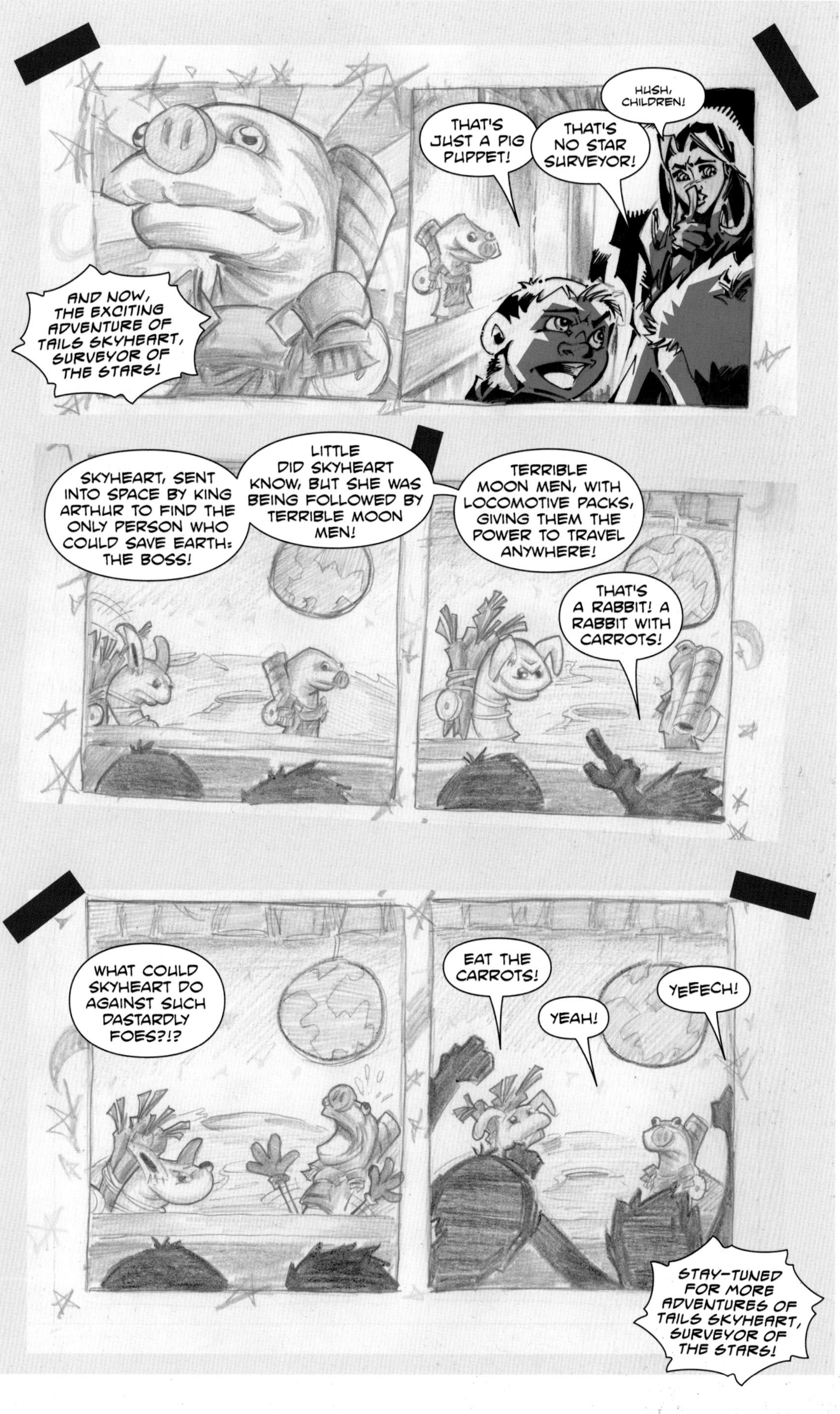
AND NOW, THE EXCITING ADVENTURE OF TAILS SKYHEART, SURVEYOR OF THE STARS!
THAT'S JUST A PIG PUPPET!
THAT'S NO STAR SURVEYOR!
HUSH, CHILDREN!
SKYHEART, SENT INTO SPACE BY KING ARTHUR TO FIND THE ONLY PERSON WHO COULD SAVE EARTH: THE BOSS!
LITTLE DID SKYHEART KNOW, BUT SHE WAS BEING FOLLOWED BY TERRIBLE MOON MEN!
TERRIBLE MOON MEN, WITH LOCOMOTIVE PACKS, GIVING THEM THE POWER TO TRAVEL ANYWHERE!
THAT'S A RABBIT! A RABBIT WITH CARROTS!
WHAT COULD SKYHEART DO AGAINST SUCH DASTARDLY FOES?!?
EAT THE CARROTS!
YEAH!
YEEECH!
STAY-TUNED FOR MORE ADVENTURES OF TAILS SKYHEART, SURVEYOR OF THE STARS!

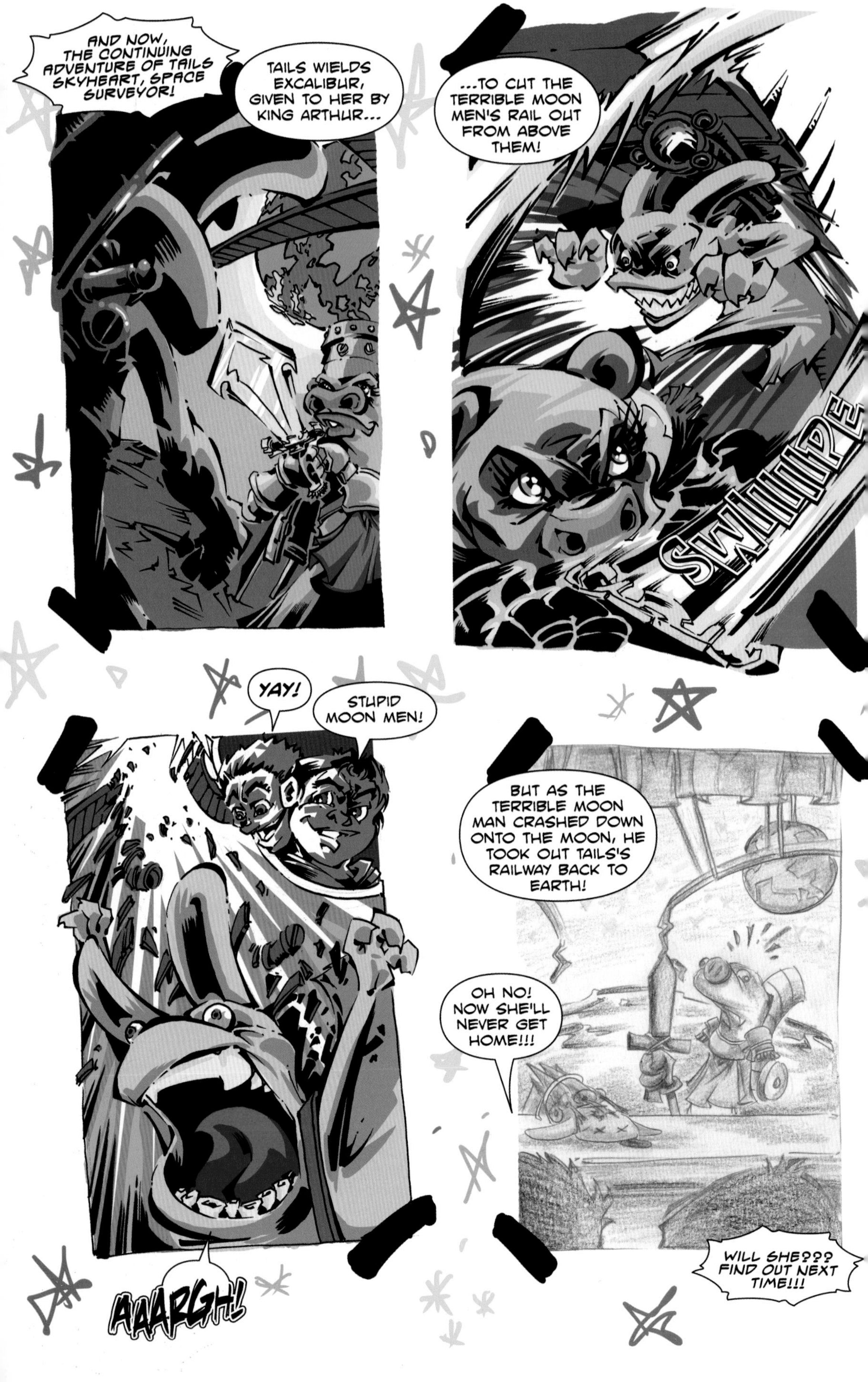

AND NOW, THE CONTINUING ADVENTURE OF TAILS SKYHEART, SPACE SURVEYOR!
TAILS WIELDS EXCALIBUR, GIVEN TO HER BY KING ARTHUR...
...TO CUT THE TERRIBLE MOON MEN'S RAIL OUT FROM ABOVE THEM!
SWIIIIPE
YAY!
STUPID MOON MEN!
AAARGH!
BUT AS THE TERRIBLE MOON MAN CRASHED DOWN ONTO THE MOON, HE TOOK OUT TAILS'S RAILWAY BACK TO EARTH!
OH NO! NOW SHE'LL NEVER GET HOME!!!
WILL SHE??? FIND OUT NEXT TIME!!!

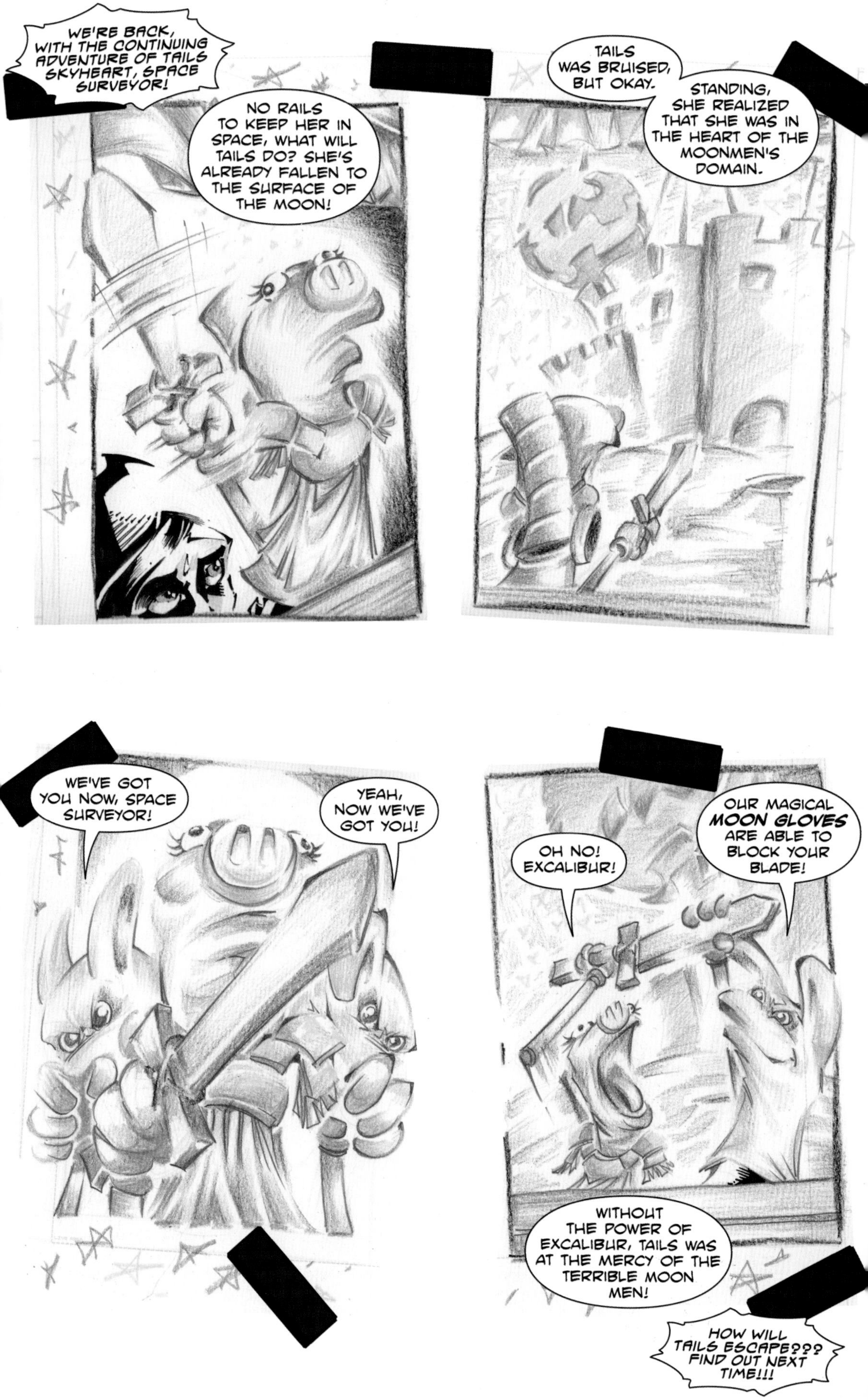
WE'RE BACK, WITH THE CONTINUING ADVENTURE OF TAILS SKYHEART, SPACE SURVEYOR!
NO RAILS TO KEEP HER IN SPACE, WHAT WILL TAILS DO? SHE'S ALREADY FALLEN TO THE SURFACE OF THE MOON!
TAILS WAS BRUISED, BUT OKAY.
STANDING, SHE REALIZED THAT SHE WAS IN THE HEART OF THE MOONMEN'S DOMAIN.
WE'VE GOT YOU NOW, SPACE SURVEYOR!
YEAH, NOW WE'VE GOT YOU!
OH NO! EXCALIBUR!
OUR MAGICAL **MOON GLOVES** ARE ABLE TO BLOCK YOUR BLADE!
WITHOUT THE POWER OF EXCALIBUR, TAILS WAS AT THE MERCY OF THE TERRIBLE MOON MEN!
HOW WILL TAILS ESCAPE??? FIND OUT NEXT TIME!!!

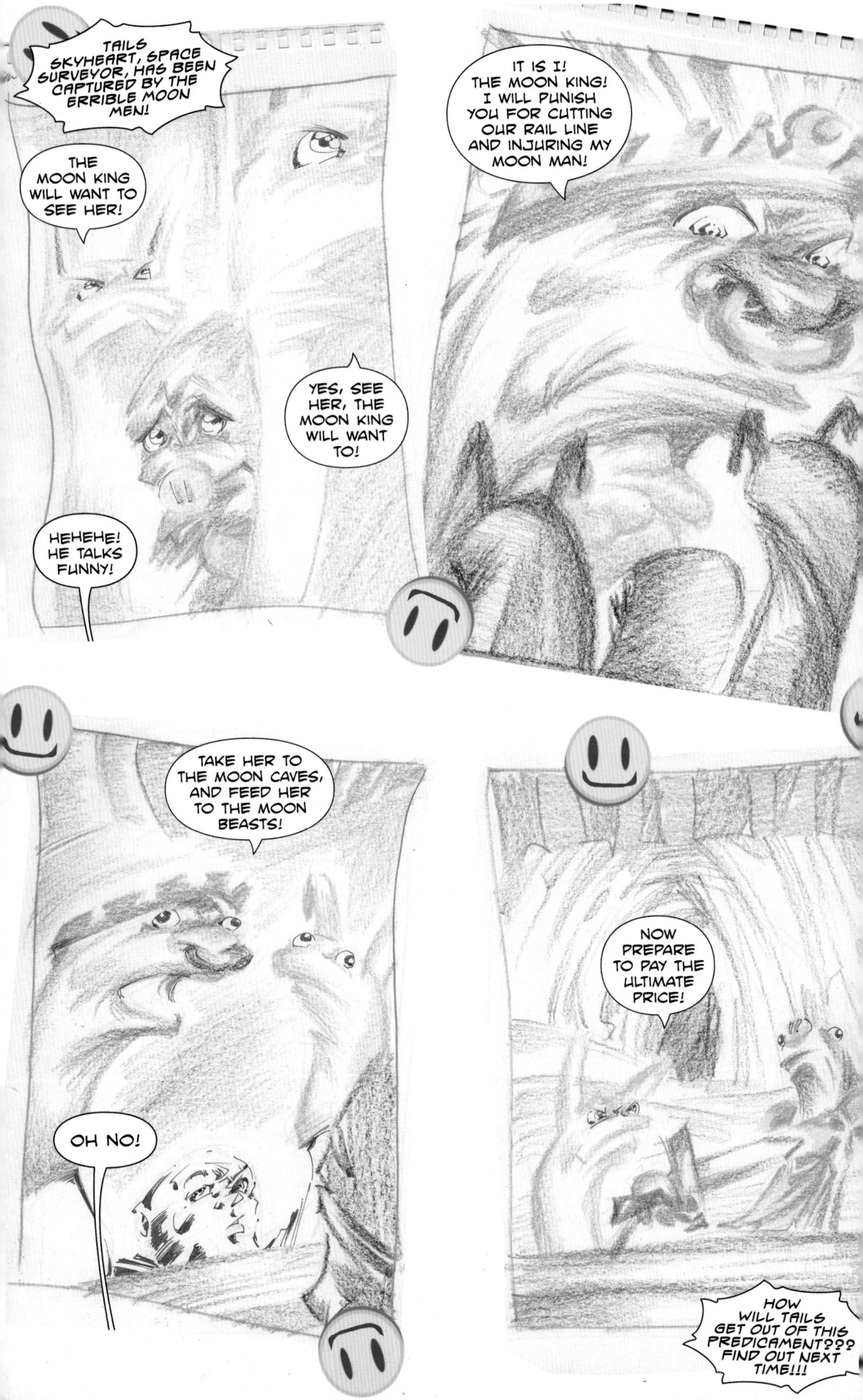
TAILS SKYHEART, SPACE SURVEYOR, HAS BEEN CAPTURED BY THE ERRIBLE MOON MEN!
THE MOON KING WILL WANT TO SEE HER!
YES, SEE HER, THE MOON KING WILL WANT TO!
HEHEHE! HE TALKS FUNNY!
IT IS I! THE MOON KING! I WILL PUNISH YOU FOR CUTTING OUR RAIL LINE AND INJURING MY MOON MAN!
TAKE HER TO THE MOON CAVES, AND FEED HER TO THE MOON BEASTS!
OH NO!
NOW PREPARE TO PAY THE ULTIMATE PRICE!
HOW WILL TAILS GET OUT OF THIS PREDICAMENT??? FIND OUT NEXT TIME!!!

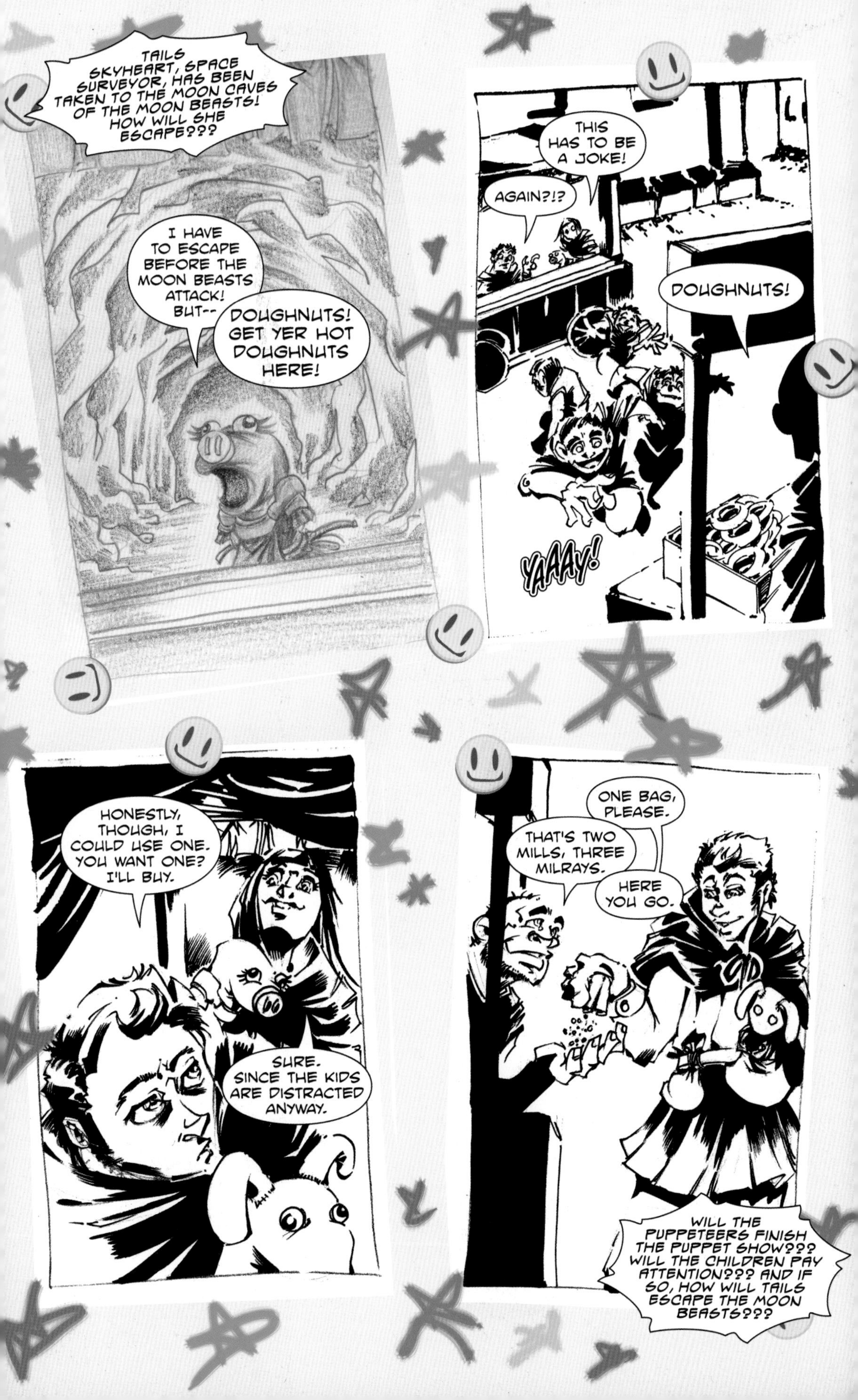
TAILS SKYHEART, SPACE SURVEYOR, HAS BEEN TAKEN TO THE MOON CAVES OF THE MOON BEASTS! HOW WILL SHE ESCAPE???
I HAVE TO ESCAPE BEFORE THE MOON BEASTS ATTACK! BUT--
DOUGHNUTS! GET YER HOT DOUGHNUTS HERE!
THIS HAS TO BE A JOKE!
AGAIN?!?
DOUGHNUTS!
YAAAY!
HONESTLY, THOUGH, I COULD USE ONE. YOU WANT ONE? I'LL BUY.
SURE. SINCE THE KIDS ARE DISTRACTED ANYWAY.
ONE BAG, PLEASE.
THAT'S TWO MILLS, THREE MILRAYS.
HERE YOU GO.
WILL THE PUPPETEERS FINISH THE PUPPET SHOW??? WILL THE CHILDREN PAY ATTENTION??? AND IF SO, HOW WILL TAILS ESCAPE THE MOON BEASTS???

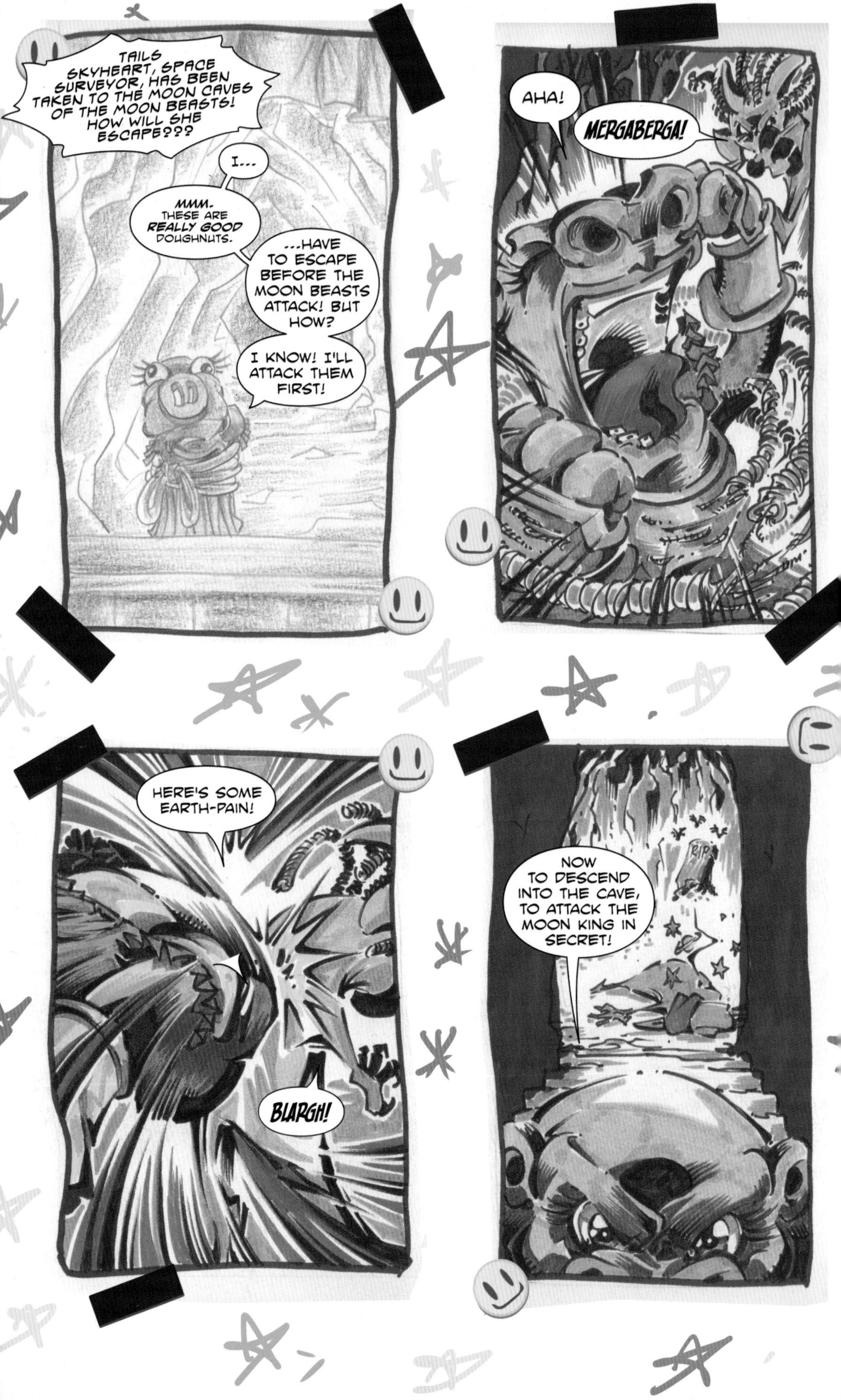
TAILS SKYHEART, SPACE SURVEYOR, HAS BEEN TAKEN TO THE MOON CAVES OF THE MOON BEASTS! HOW WILL SHE ESCAPE???
I...
MMM. THESE ARE REALLY GOOD DOUGHNUTS.
...HAVE TO ESCAPE BEFORE THE MOON BEASTS ATTACK! BUT HOW?
I KNOW! I'LL ATTACK THEM FIRST!
AHA!
MERGABERGA!
HERE'S SOME EARTH-PAIN!
BLARGH!
RIP
NOW TO DESCEND INTO THE CAVE, TO ATTACK THE MOON KING IN SECRET!

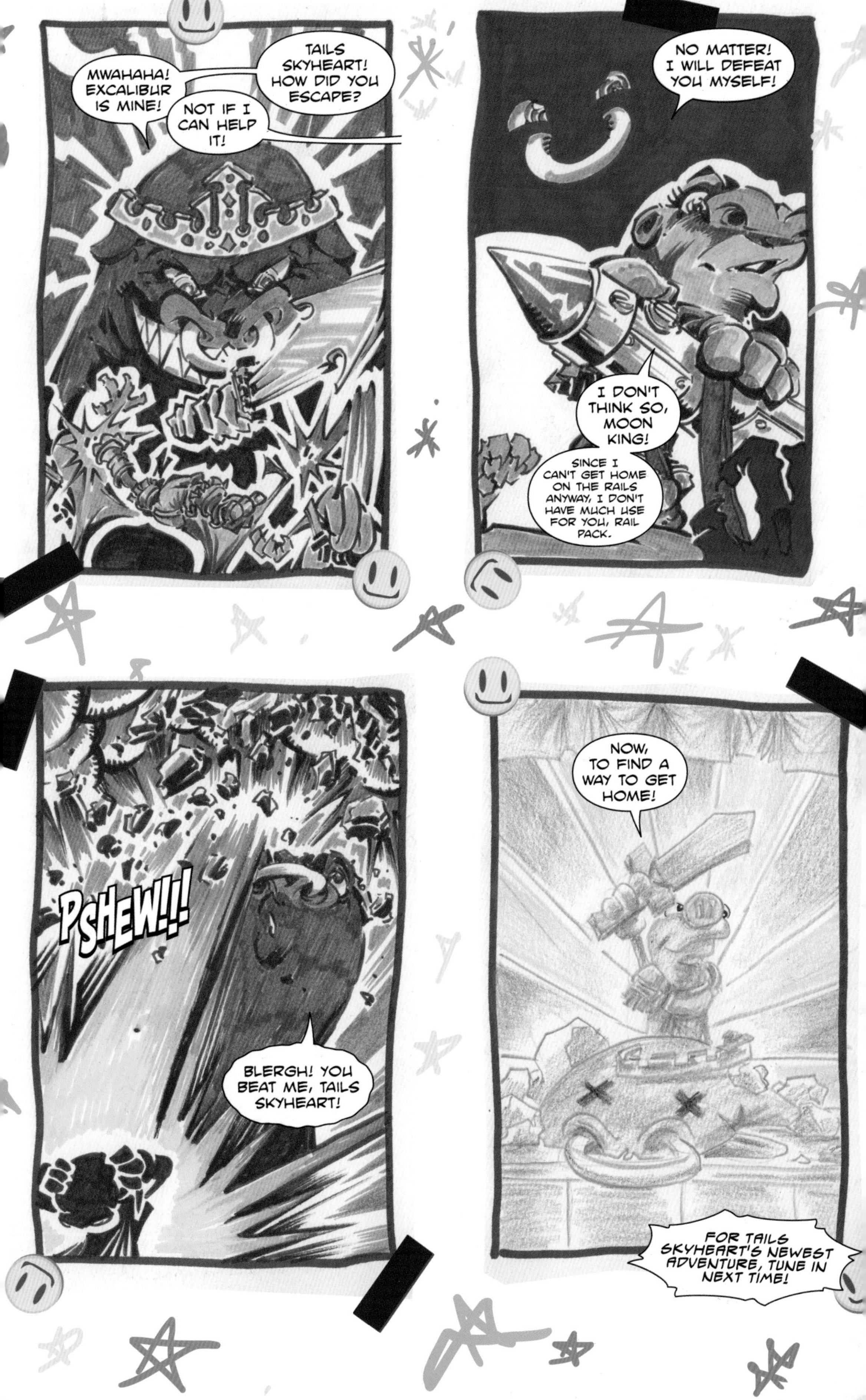
MWAHAHA! EXCALIBUR IS MINE!
TAILS SKYHEART! HOW DID YOU ESCAPE?
NOT IF I CAN HELP IT!
NO MATTER! I WILL DEFEAT YOU MYSELF!
I DON'T THINK SO, MOON KING!
SINCE I CAN'T GET HOME ON THE RAILS ANYWAY, I DON'T HAVE MUCH USE FOR YOU, RAIL PACK.
PSHEW!!!
BLERGH! YOU BEAT ME, TAILS SKYHEART!
NOW, TO FIND A WAY TO GET HOME!
FOR TAILS SKYHEART'S NEWEST ADVENTURE, TUNE IN NEXT TIME!

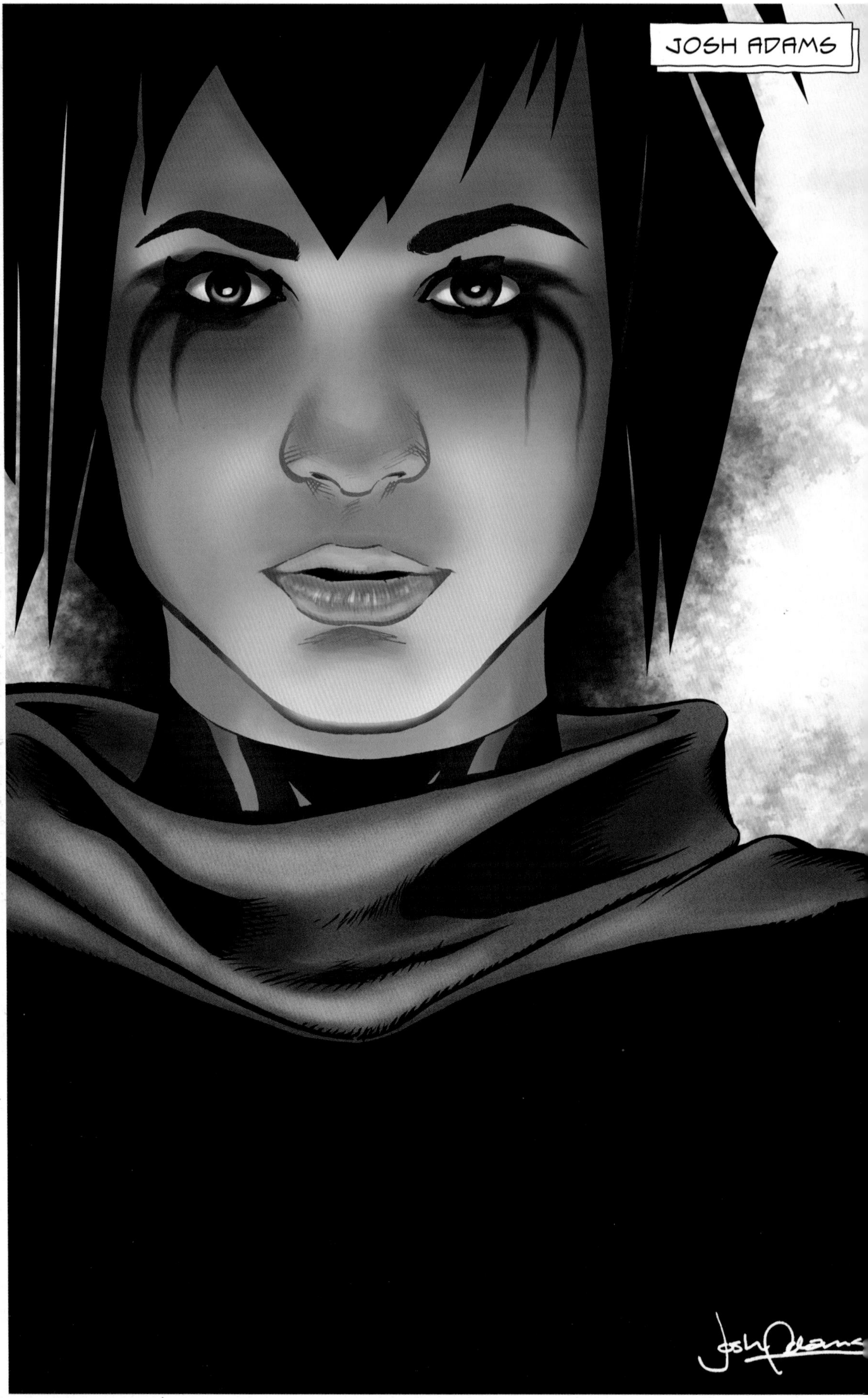
JOSH ADAMS
Josh Adams

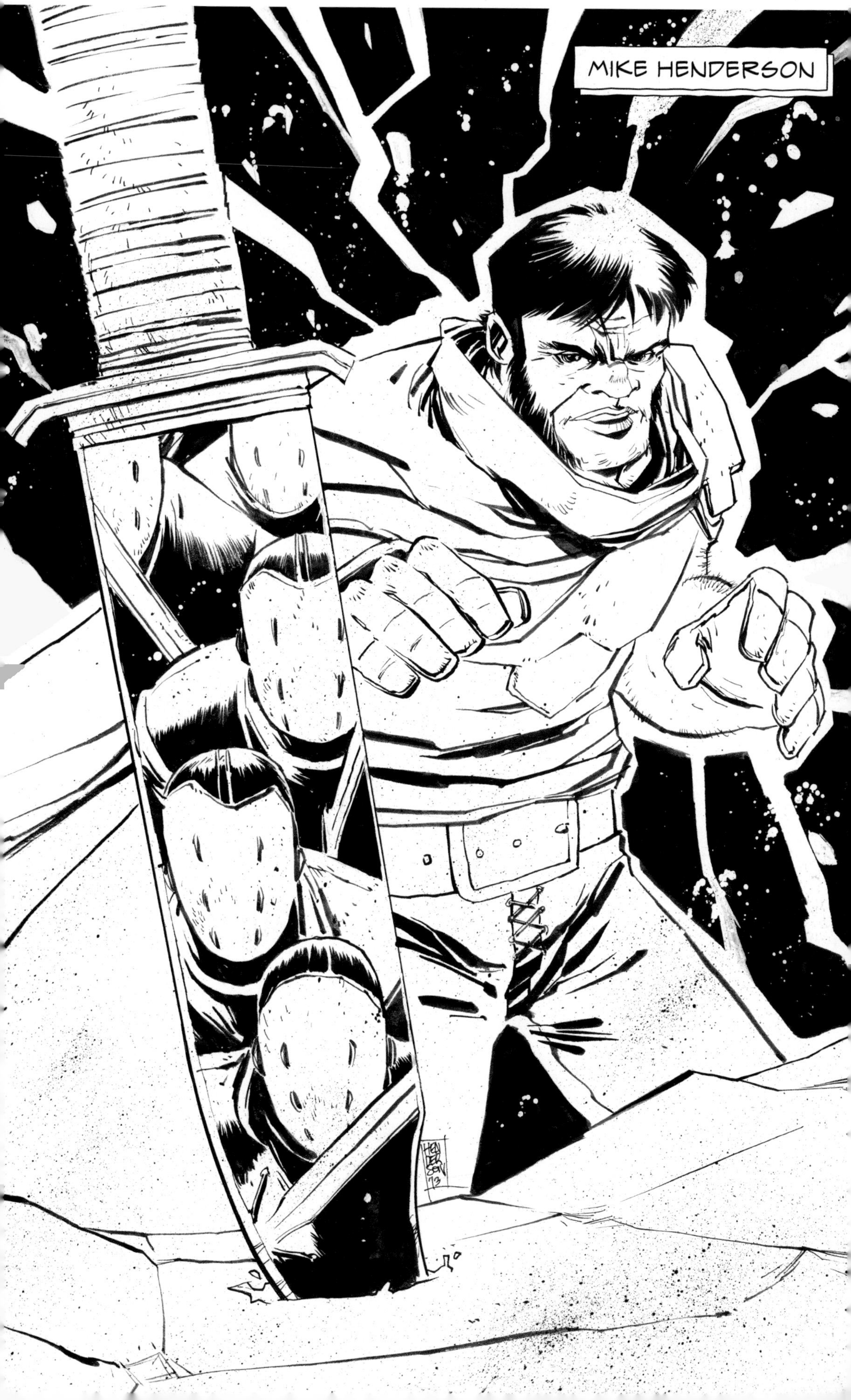
MIKE HENDERSON

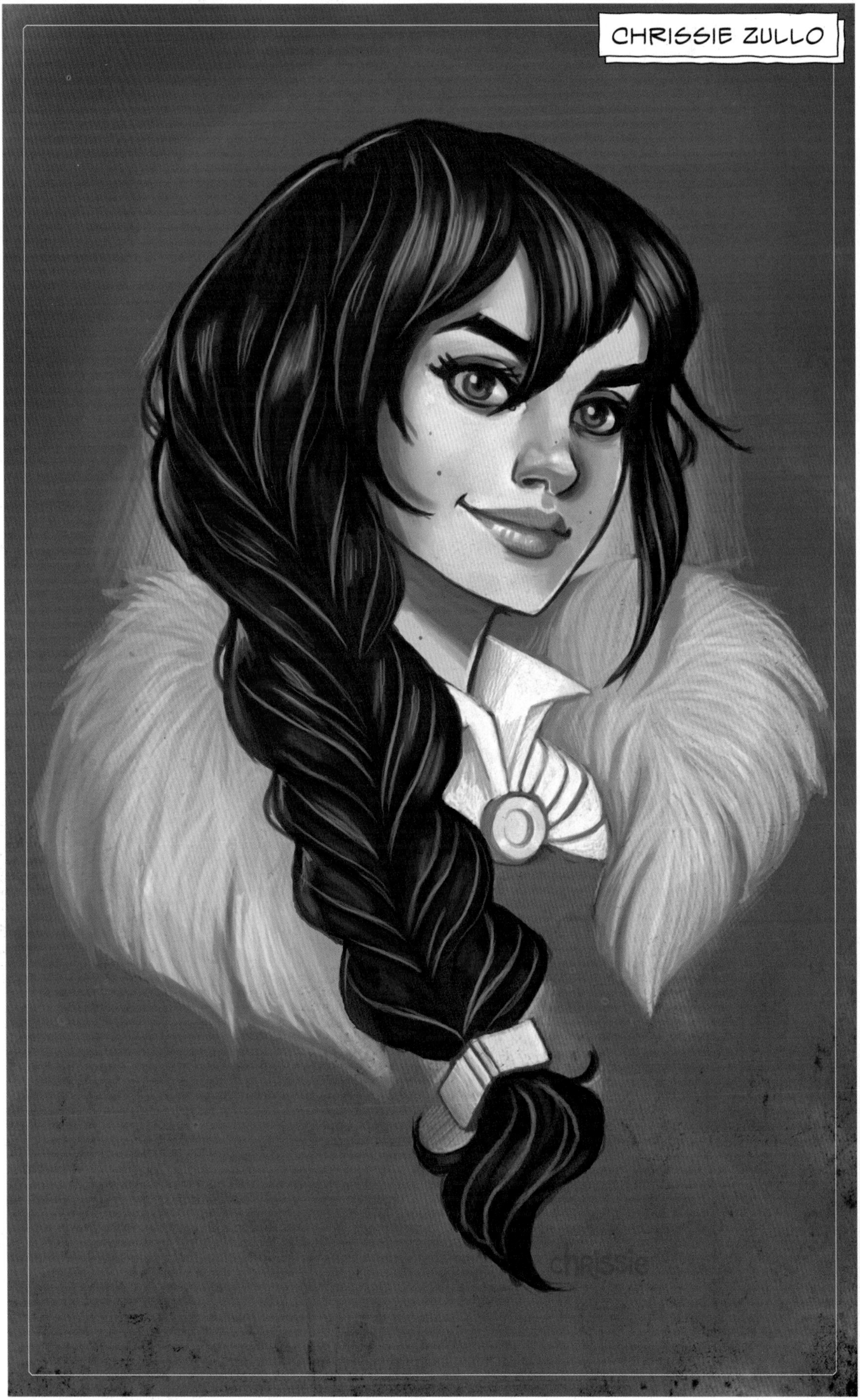

CHRISSIE ZULLO

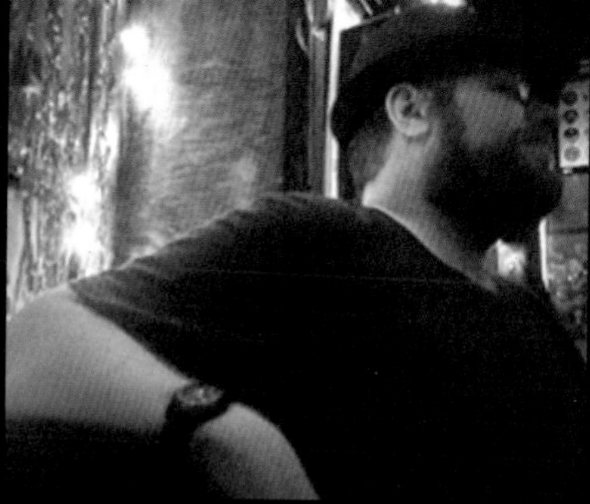

ADAM P. KNAVE is a Harvey and Eisner award winning editor and writer who has written a bunch of prose, as well as co-writing *AMELIA COLE* and *ACTION CATS* for Monkeybrain Comics and *NEVER ENDING* for Dark Horse. He edits Jamal Igle's *MOLLY DANGER* and other comics, all while living in Portland, OR. You can find out more at adampknave.com.

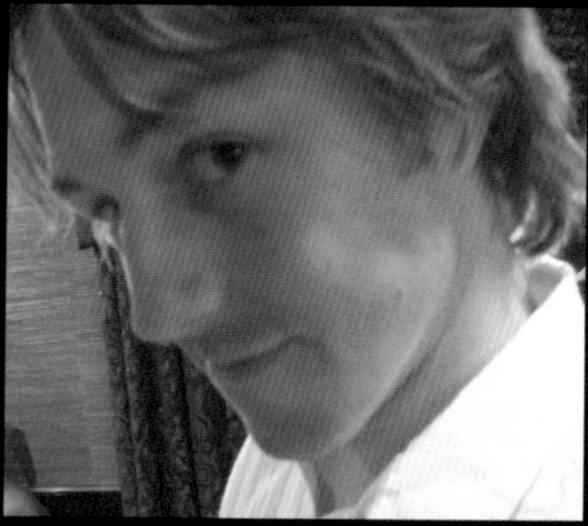

SEAN E. WILLIAMS has a background in theatre, film, and television, and now writes comics and prose from the wilds of Minnesota. His credits include *FAIREST* for Vertigo and *THE VAMPIRE DIARIES* for DC Comics. You can find him at seanewilliams.com.

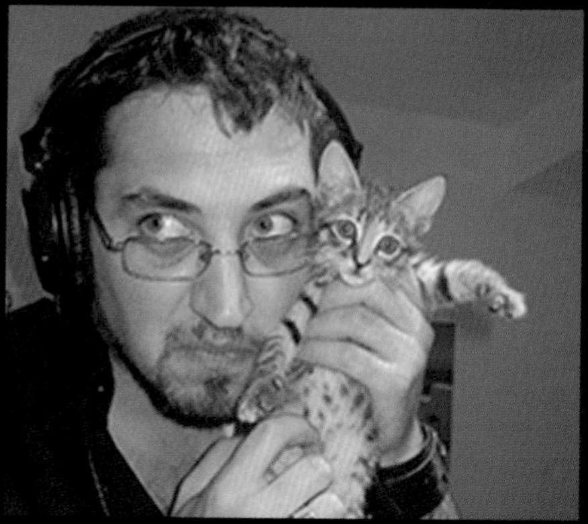

ANDREW LOSQ is a video game designer, animator, illustrator, and comic book artist. He lives in Granada, Spain with his wife Allison. *ARTFUL DAGGERS* is his first published comic book work. He enjoys production meetings over beers, philosophical arguments, and drawing until his fingers break off. His other current and upcoming projects include *ZEKE AND PANDORA: THE STOLEN KING* and *BORN TO THE FALL*.

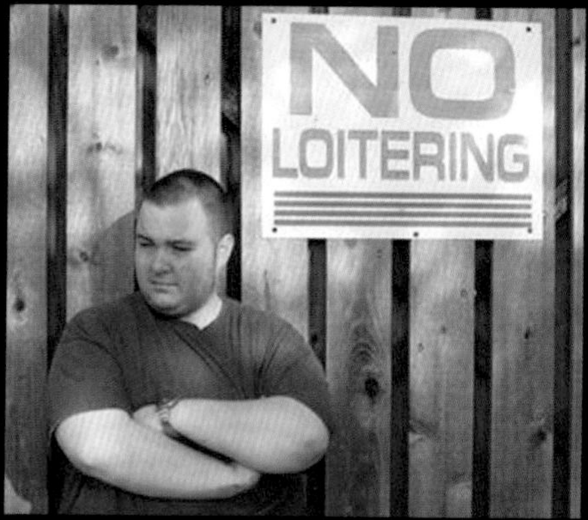
NO
LOITERING

FRANK CVETKOVIC is a comic book letterer, whose work has appeared in: *ARTFUL DAGGERS*, *BLACK WRAITH*, *DEPARTMENT O*, *HERO CODE*, Jamal Igle's *MOLLY DANGER*, and *NEVER ENDING*. He is also the writer of *PUNCH UP* and *MUTE*. He currently lives in Cleveland, OH, where the home teams never win and the rivers occasionally catch fire.

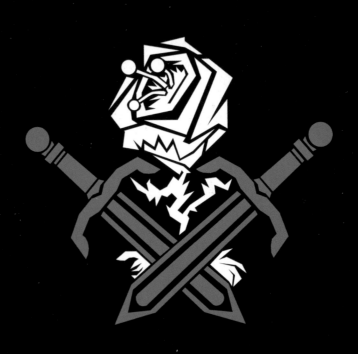